Hopkins of Dartmouth

Lester K. Henderson

HOPKINS OF DARTMOUTH

The story of Ernest Martin Hopkins
and his presidency of Dartmouth College

by Charles E. Widmayer

Published by Dartmouth College through
The University Press of New England
HANOVER · NEW HAMPSHIRE · 1977

The preparation of this book was coordinated
by Edward Connery Lathem
Dean of Libraries and Librarian of the College

Contents

Author's Note

IT HAS NOT BEEN the purpose of the author to write a biography of Ernest Martin Hopkins. Commissioned by the Trustees of Dartmouth College, this book is primarily an account of the Hopkins presidency. But the personal qualities of Mr. Hopkins are so large a factor in the story of those twenty-nine years that the biographical element must be given considerable attention. His life prior to assuming the Dartmouth presidency has been sketched, and also his activities after retirement, which makes it appropriate, perhaps, to call this volume a semi-biography. It is, in part, a remembering; and the author, who served in President Hopkins' office for five years, 1933–38, and had the privilege of a close working association with him during the final twelve years of his administration, has made no spurious effort to conceal his admiration and affection for this extraordinary man. The comprehensive story of the Hopkins years at Dartmouth has needed telling, both for those who have some remembrance of them and for those of younger age who are familiar with Dartmouth's Hopkins Center for the visual and performing arts, but who know very little about the man whose name it bears.

The factual material for the book has been assembled from a careful study of *The Dartmouth*, the *Dartmouth Alumni Magazine*, *The Bulletin*, trustee records, financial reports, office scrapbooks, all the Hopkins addresses and writings, and, of utmost importance, the voluminous correspondence that Mr. Hopkins left behind him. The reader will note that direct quotation has been freely used, in order that Mr. Hopkins might speak for himself in the statement and interpretation of his views about education and national affairs, in both of which fields he was an influential and respected figure.

The Hopkins story as told here would have been much less personal and authoritative, and much less anecdotal, had it not been for the great good fortune of having available the tape-recorded interviews with Mr. Hopkins that Edward Connery Lathem, Librarian of Dartmouth College, conducted over a period of several years. These candid and lively reminiscences have served to add human interest to many events of the Hopkins era, and to give to the story a dimension that could come only from Mr. Hopkins himself. To Mr. Lathem, to whom the Dartmouth Trustees entrusted general responsibility for bringing this book into being, the author is indebted for help in more ways than can be counted. Special thanks are due also to Mr. Hopkins' daughter, Ann Hopkins Spahr, who has encouraged the project and been more than generous in talking about her father, in providing family material, and in reading the manuscript before publication. A great many others were helpful with their recollections of Mr. Hopkins and his presidency; notably, among them, Harvey P. Hood, Lloyd K. Neidlinger, Warner Bentley, and the late Professor Stearns Morse. Papers loaned by Mrs. Russell R. Larmon were of great value.

Finally, warmest thanks are due the staff of the Dartmouth College Archives in Baker Library, where most of the research for this book was done over a period of two years. Cooperation as complete and cheerful as one could possibly have wished for was extended by Kenneth C. Cramer and Walter W. Wright and by their associates, Kristina Ashton, Catherine Hepburn, Erika Parmi, and Suzy Schwoerke.

C.E.W.

Hopkins of Dartmouth

A Break with Tradition

A N appropriate coat of arms for any newly elected college president could well be a gowned figure defiant upon a field of doubting Thomases. Certainly it is a rare president who takes office amidst universal agreement that the selection committee has made the right choice. In the case of Ernest Martin Hopkins, who was elected eleventh president of Dartmouth College on June 13, 1916, what he called "the spirit of agnosticism" was more rampant than is customary. In a radical departure from academic orthodoxy of that day, he was coming to the presidency not from the ministry, nor from the sacred groves of academe, but from the world of business. It was fitting that the very beginning of his presidency should be characterized by the non-conformity that was to be one of the distinctive qualities of his remarkably successful administration, extending over the next twenty-nine years.

With the one exception of John Wheelock, son and heir of Eleazar Wheelock, Dartmouth's founder, the presidents of Dartmouth College from 1769 to 1909 had all been ministers of the gospel. Mr. Hopkins' immediate predecessor, Dr. Ernest Fox Nichols, had broken the long string of preacher presidents, but he was a physicist of world renown and at the time of his election scholar presidents were coming into the ascendancy. Of Mr. Hopkins one member of the Dartmouth faculty sniffed, "Of course, he is not even an educator." The academic development of Dartmouth College over the next three decades proved this statement to be one of the least accurate evaluations ever to come from the scholarly mind.

The questioning of the choice of the Dartmouth trustees was restrained enough and not really widespread, but a small coterie of Dartmouth professors were outspoken in their belief that the death knell of Dartmouth academically had been sounded. Among the alumni of the College there were pockets of less erudite but more vehement opinion that the trustees

3

had been foolish, to say the least, to ignore Dartmouth tradition and to center their unanimous choice on a young man of 38 who had none of the clerical or scholarly credentials of the presidents under whom the alumni had been students.

As for the academic world at large, it was intrigued that Dartmouth, one of the historic New England colleges, should have gone off in such a novel presidential direction. But amidst the curiosity and the suspended judgment there was here and there a recognition that the election of a man with the experience and interests of Ernest Martin Hopkins had a special significance for all of higher education, symbolizing a closer drawing together of the college world and the world of affairs. This point was made in citations accompanying two honorary degrees conferred upon Mr. Hopkins almost immediately after his election. At Amherst College, where he was awarded the honorary Doctorate of Letters, he was cited as "proficient in the application of education to the work of great corporations." At Colby College, one week later, the citation for his LL.D. degree said: "His remarkable achievements in the field of applied economics are abundant prophecy of the better correlation between college training and practical life which President Hopkins will help all of us to understand and to achieve."

Editorial comment about the choice of a business man to hold one of the distinguished college presidencies of the country was printed from coast to coast. Here again, there were some who saw Dartmouth's action as a new and significant example of a closer relationship between business and higher education. Typical was the judgment of *The Outlook* in New York: "The selection of such a man illustrates not only the broadening of the American college, but also the broadening of the spirit of American business and industry. The barriers that used to be so firm between trade and science and the so-called professions are disappearing."

The editors of the *Philadelphia Bulletin* wrote: "There is a new and stimulating conception suggested here as to the mental equipment necessary for the modern college president. To use President Wilson's phrase, it is distinctly 'forward-looking' in its demand that a college president must be something more than a profound scholar, something else besides a collector of large endowments."

The *Seattle Times* said of Mr. Hopkins: "He is essentially a businessman and his administration may reveal to Dartmouth and other institutions of learning a way to render a better and broader and more effective service in their relations to the practical side of life. At any rate, his selection is a frank recognition not only of the fact that the administration of a college has become a business proposition, but of the fact also that the institutions of higher learning must get closer to the business, commercial, and industrial problems of man."

And closer to home, the *Boston Herald* declared: "Dartmouth is the first New England college to choose for its president a man whose experience and achievement have been primarily in the business world. . . . The consciousness that business is something very much greater than processes of trade is dawning. Its problems of production and distribution appear woven inextricably with those of human relations, national and international. The making of this consciousness socially operative will be perhaps the greatest task of the present century. America's share in it will impose on the college a task of leadership."

Mr. Hopkins must have found the significance ascribed to his business background a bit overdrawn, even though his personal experience and understanding of the industrial world gave him a certain singularity among college presidents. In the first press interview after his election he staunchly defended the old classical education, from which he himself had derived such benefit and personal satisfaction. The one thing that upset him was the expectation in some quarters that business efficiency would now be brought into the college world. "I never have been and never will be a so-called efficiency expert," he asserted.

The greater part of the editorial flurry, however, was based on the narrower ground of Dartmouth's departure from customary academic considerations in picking its new leader. While most of the comment was favorable, some of it reflected the skepticism expressed by those within the scholastic cloisters. "Seldom has the selection of a college president rested so much on trust as that of Ernest M. Hopkins to be Dartmouth's new leader," said the *Boston Transcript*. "Nearly all the 'book values' which customarily go to determine a choice of this kind are in his instance lacking. Mr. Hopkins is not a man widely known in the world of learning."

The *Lowell Courier-Citizen* told its readers: "The incoming president has his record all to make, unassisted by any antecedent probabilities, and very probably against a considerable degree of downright skepticism at the start. One recalls the case of President Eliot, although it is not by any means an exact parallel. Dr. Eliot started his memorable career as president of Harvard roundly opposed, and proved to be one of the greatest educators of his day. Candor compels full recognition of the fact that Mr. Hopkins will certainly undertake his task handicapped by much the same initital skepticism, to call it nothing more; but common fairness demands of Dartmouth men that they suspend hasty judgments and let the new president have a free chance to prove his capacities, as Dr. Eliot so conspicuously proved his."

The *Boston Journal* thought Dartmouth's trustees should "be congratulated on their determination to prove the courage of their convictions," and in the eyes of the *Journal of Education* "the trustees have given the academic world its greatest recent surprise. Not even the 1916–1917 *Who's Who* has heard of him. . . ."

Mr. Hopkins accepted all the comment, pro and con, with equanimity. The worst of it, after all, had been endured in the months just prior to public announcement of his election. The fact that he was the likely choice of the trustees had leaked out, setting off a critical barrage from certain members of the faculty and alumni body. Twenty-nine years later, when his administration ended, President Hopkins was to take special pains to forestall any such dispute about the trustees' choice of a new president. The announcements of his retirement and of the selection of his successor were made simultaneously. The way things were handled in 1945 would suggest that Mr. Hopkins was more disturbed by the 1916 events than he let on at the time. Any personal feeling, however, was definitely minor in comparison with his strong belief that certain things were the sole prerogative and business of the trustees. There were many times during his presidency when he took this firm, unequivocal stand about where the real authority of the College lay.

In his tape-recorded reminiscences some years after his 1945 retirement Mr. Hopkins said, "I never thought of myself as an educator. I was flattered when anyone called me one, but I never thought of myself as that. I always thought of myself as an administrator in an educational institution, and I think that's what I was." Many others would have added that he approached genius in his administrative skill and sagacity.

For the leadership of Dartmouth, Ernest Martin Hopkins could hardly have been better prepared. For eight years immediately after his graduation from Dartmouth in 1901 he was assistant and confidant of President William Jewett Tucker, and for one additional year, before leaving to embark upon a business career, he was chief assistant to President Ernest Fox Nichols, who succeeded Dr. Tucker. He returned in 1916 already possessed of an intimate knowledge of the College and of Hanover and its personalities.

Although he was not another of the preacher presidents who had headed the College for nearly all of its first 140 years, Mr. Hopkins was the son of a preacher and a deeply religious man. He was the eldest of the three sons of the Reverend Adoniram and Mary (Martin) Hopkins, and was born November 6, 1877 in Dunbarton, New Hampshire, where his father was Baptist minister. On both sides of the family his ancestors had been early settlers of New England. Solomon Hopkins, a Scotsman, came to Maine from Ireland about 1735. George Martin emigrated to Massachusetts from England about 1639, and seven years later married Susanna North, a martyr of the Salem witch persecutions. Other ancestors on his mother's side were John Perkins, who came to Massachusetts with Roger Williams in 1631, and John Boynton, who settled in Rowley, Massachusetts, in 1638.

Mr. Hopkins' father, Adoniram, a native of Maine, was graduated from Harvard (1874) and Newton Theological Institution. Beyond the ministry he had a lifelong interest in bettering public libraries and in modernizing and improving school systems. The idea that religion and education came close to seeking the same end was something President Hopkins derived from his father, along with an appreciation of the cultural advantage of being part of a minister's family. The first Hopkins pastorate had been in Dunbarton. The family moved several times, to Hopkinton and Franklin Falls and then to North Uxbridge, Massachusetts. One of young Hop's boyhood friends in Franklin Falls was George Moses, the future United States Senator, who saved him from drowning when he fell through the ice. Most of Mr. Hopkins' boyhood was spent in North Uxbridge, where at the age of twelve he began working during vacations in the nearby granite quarry, carrying tools. By the time he was ready for college he had risen from tool boy to yardman and timekeeper. The workday was long—eleven hours—and the pay was small.

The money that had been saved to send him to Phillips Academy, Andover, was needed by the family in the financial crisis of 1893, when ministers were at the head of the list of those not being paid. So young Hop went to Worcester Academy, where the principal promised him that all his expenses would be covered if he would serve as the academy's mail carrier. "The post office was two miles from the academy then," he recalled. "I'd pick up the mail at half past five in the morning and walk down two miles with it, and pick the mail up there and bring it back and distribute it to the boys' rooms. It wasn't always an enjoyable job, but it was a profitable one; and I think I owe a good deal to it, because from the point of view of exercise I had to take it." He had the job from 1893 until he was graduated three years later.

It was understood in the family that young Hop would be pretty much on his own financially when he went to college. His desire to enter Dartmouth had become more definite at Worcester, especially because his classmate and closest friend there, Charles A. Proctor, was going to pursue his college studies in Hanover. Hop's father was reconciled to Dartmouth, but as a Harvard man he wanted the satisfaction of knowing that his son could have gone to Harvard. To please his father, Hop took the preliminary examinations for Harvard at the end of his junior year at Worcester and passed them, with the result that "father at that time was willing to give up on it." In order to earn money for college, Mr. Hopkins delayed entering Dartmouth and taught for one year at the North Uxbridge Grammar School. He also coached the Uxbridge High School football team, on which his brother Louis was fullback. (Both of his brothers were to follow him to Dartmouth, Louis in the Class of 1908 and Robert in the Class of 1914.)

Ernest Martin Hopkins finally arrived in Hanover in the fall of 1897 and almost got into trouble at the very start when, in a foreshadowing of his presidential distaste for gifts with strings attached to them, he told Dean Emerson he couldn't accept a scholarship which required him to sign a statement that he would neither swear nor drink nor smoke. Another scholarship which did not require such an oath was found for him, but unfortunately it did not provide enough financial help and in the middle of freshman year he ran short of money and decided to drop out and return to his job at the granite quarry. "I was very despondent at that period," he recalled. "I felt I could never make up the work and there wasn't any use going back to college or anything."

His friend Charles Proctor was responsible for turning the situation around. Coming home from work one afternoon, Hop found young Proctor, then a Dartmouth sophomore, sitting on the porch, waiting for him. Proctor, who was living at home with his widowed mother in Hanover, told Hop that he had it all figured out: he could live with the Proctors at very low cost and get an eating club job, and could make up his academic work by carrying extra courses. That was the way things worked out after Hop returned to college in the fall of 1898. Later, when he was elected editor of *The Aegis*, the college yearbook, the job paid enough to allow him to give up waiting on table, which he heartily disliked, and additional earnings came from tutoring and writing editorials for *The Dartmouth* when the editor was in a jam, which was a rather constant state of affairs.

Of the successful effort to catch up with his class, Mr. Hopkins years later remarked: "I don't think they'd let me do it now, but I carried at least one extra course all the rest of my course; and there was one semester when they let me take two, in order to even up on things."

All during his undergraduate years Mr. Hopkins had inspiration from President Tucker, in addition to his own innate desire, to do his very best. He had a maturity and a record of campus achievement that made him one of the outstanding members of his class. After being editor of *The Aegis* in junior year he became editor of *The Dartmouth* as a senior. He was class president, student member of the Athletic Council, winner of the Lockwood Prize in English composition, and a member of Palaeopitus, which he helped to transform from a secret senior society to a democratic one that eventually became the top organization in student government.

In the spring of his senior year President Tucker called him in and invited him to take the job of office assistant, which the trustees had just authorized. "I don't think anybody was ever more surprised in his life

than I was," Mr. Hopkins recalled. "It wasn't at that moment any overwhelming love of Dartmouth College; it was the privilege of being in close
contact with Dr. Tucker that was the appealing thing." The reasons for
President Tucker's favorable opinion of young Hopkins are not hard to
surmise, but perhaps more than anything else it was the maturity of the
editorials in *The Dartmouth* that attracted his attention.

Mr. Hopkins' initial duties in the president's office were "pretty me-
nial," but before long Dr. Tucker had delegated to him most of the undergraduate problems that did not fall within the province of the dean's
office. He took the initiative in expanding student social life, and in addition to directing the College Club, the name given to a series of Saturday
night "smokers" with guest speakers, he arranged class and faculty recep-
tions and was in charge of the Dartmouth Assemblies, for which his own
dance cards, now preserved in the College archives, were always filled. In
January 1903 he gave a foretaste of his bold spirit by bringing to Hanover
the Ben Greet Shakespearean Players at a cost greater than the amount
usually spent for a whole year of student social programs. President
Tucker's hesitancy was dispelled when Professor "Clothespins" Richardson of the English Department backed up Mr. Hopkins and promised to
cover personally any loss if the ticket sale fell short of expectations. The
performance was a huge success and netted two thousand dollars. Upon
suggesting to Ben Greet that colleges and universities in this country
would be ideal places for his troupe to perform, Mr. Hopkins found himself accompanying the company to Chicago and acting as manager. Having
smoothed out some internal difficulties and having successfully landed the
troupe at the Hull House, he was invited to stay on as permanent manager,
but he did not find that opportunity particularly enticing. The Ben Greet
Players returned to Hanover in 1904 and 1905 and again, many years later,
after Mr. Hopkins had become president of the College. On that last visit,
Mr. Hopkins dropped by the dressing room, not expecting to be remembered, but no sooner had he entered the room than Ben Greet threw his
arms around him and greeted him as if he were his dearest friend.

In 1903 Dr. Tucker asked Mr. Hopkins to assume the additional duties
of graduate manager of athletics, a position which had been created two
years earlier. The first incumbent, Irving French, had brought some system to the scheduling of games, but the finances of the athletic program

were in dismal shape. Mr. Hopkins' first move was to seek a better deal from Harvard. Although the Dartmouth game had been drawing as large crowds as the Yale and Princeton games, Dartmouth was getting only $500 and not a percentage of the gate. The Hopkins proposal was that Dartmouth also be put on a percentage basis. "Well, what do you want?" the Harvard people asked him. "I don't care," replied Mr. Hopkins. "I just want to establish the principle of a percentage agreement. We'll talk about the amounts later." Harvard cautiously asked if ten percent would do. Mr. Hopkins countered with fifteen percent, and that is what was settled upon. This meant income of approximately $6,000 the first year, and in a single stroke the financial problem for Dartmouth athletics was largely solved.

Mr. Hopkins had the athletic job for two years, until in 1905 he was named the first Secretary of the College. This placed him in charge of all important academic occasions, including Commencement, and he soon became, as well, the central figure in planning and developing a stronger organization of the alumni. President Tucker was the initiating force in the effort to bring about a more unified structure of the alumni classes and clubs, which up to that time had been going their individual ways in a loose and ineffective fashion. He and Mr. Hopkins had discussed this weakness many times, and Dr. Tucker looked to his young associate to put a new system and a new program into effect. Following a call from President Tucker to all secretaries in December 1904, a meeting was held in Hanover in January 1905 and the Dartmouth Secretaries Association was formed. Mr. Hopkins became secretary of the new organization, in effect its executive head. One of the association's first moves was the creation of an alumni magazine, the *Dartmouth Bi-Monthly*. Mr. Hopkins was elected editor, and the first issue appeared in October 1905. Three years later the magazine became a monthly, the present *Dartmouth Alumni Magazine*, and Mr. Hopkins also edited this for two years.

As alumni magazine editor, he displayed an informed interest in higher education in general, as well as in the work of Dartmouth College. In an editorial about the new preceptorial system established at Princeton by Woodrow Wilson, he praised it as a reaction to the advance of German university methods in American education and expressed his low opinion of the "fetishism towards the Ph.D. degree." This brought denunciation from Professor Sidney B. Fay of Dartmouth, but the editor stuck to his guns, explaining that he was protesting against the spirit of fetishism and not against the degree itself. In an article he contributed to the February 1910 issue of *Educational Review*, he extended his thoughts about the function of the undergraduate liberal arts college and about the doubtful value and relevancy of Ph.D. training for college teaching.

"The possession of the degree," he wrote, "has the two great advantages of certifying to three years of advanced study and of indicating a capacity for close and accurate work and the consequent discipline. It has, for colleges, the disadvantages that it ignores breadth of knowledge while it seeks depth, it disregards the general in its search for the particular, it forms the habit of acquisition of knowledge without regard to its dissemination, and it makes for research rather than culture. The characteristics of the degree have great value in the proper place. The fountains of knowledge would be dry and inspiration would be nil, were it not for the men who have lived and worked imbued with the spirit of research; and it is from the results of their labors that we get much of the raw material from which culture is made. But the training which fits men for accomplishment of such sort inevitably tends to make them impatient of the work and methods necessary to college teaching."

One wonders what personal experiences lay behind Mr. Hopkins' strong feeling that too much importance was given to the Ph.D. as a criterion for employment as a college teacher. It was a view he never relinquished and that at times led some to think of him as anti-intellectual. But as he stressed, he did not denigrate the degree, only what seemed to him to be the foolish idea that the Ph.D. was essential to being a respected faculty member in an undergraduate college, or that it had anything to do with being a good teacher. Whatever the personal basis for this view might have been, it is certain that his irreverence toward the doctoral degree was bolstered by William James, whose writings he knew thoroughly. He was familiar with "The Ph.D. Octopus" which James had written for the *Harvard Monthly* of March 1903 to express his disgust with the whole Ph.D. system and his belief that it was subverting American higher education. Mr. Hopkins was to quote James more frequently than anyone else in his presidential addresses. He mentioned him in his very first Convocation address in September 1916 and again in his inaugural address two weeks later.

With his editing and writing, involving a concern for the purpose of the undergraduate college, plus general administrative duties and his work at the center of the alumni program, Mr. Hopkins was building up a body of experience that, later on, was bound to be impressive to Dartmouth's trustees when they set about the task of picking a new president. The scope of his responsibilities was enlarged in 1907 when President Tucker's health broke and doctors told him that he could no longer carry the heavy burden of the presidency. Dr. Tucker informed the trustees of his intention to resign in May of 1907. Professor Francis Brown of Union Theological Seminary, a Dartmouth graduate of 1870, was the board's unanimous choice for president, but when he declined, Dr. Tucker was asked to continue in office on a partial basis until a successor could be chosen. One of the conditions of President Tucker's acquiescence was that he continue to have the assistance of young Hopkins. Professor John King Lord was named acting president, but much of the day-to-day operation of the president's office became Mr. Hopkins' responsibility. In carrying out his tasks during this interval the young secretary of the College occasionally encountered the resentment of faculty members who thought he was usurping powers. "I had my delegation from both the president and the trustees," he later explained, "but on the other hand I couldn't stand on the campus and state that. But that was the point when I began to really have major responsibilities." One of the things he did in place of Dr. Tucker was to travel on the alumni circuit and speak about the College.

The resignation of President Tucker finally took effect on July 1, 1909. Since personal relationship with the outgoing president was almost entirely his reason for remaining with the College, Mr. Hopkins expressed the desire to resign also and to establish himself in some other field. Dr. Tucker persuaded him, however, that it would be only fair to President-elect Nichols to stay on for at least one more year and help smooth the transition to the new administration. Mr. Hopkins' nine-year tour of duty as presidential assistant finally ended on August 15, 1910. Six months later he also deprived President Nichols of his private secretary. He and Celia Stone, who had been secretary to Presidents Tucker and Nichols, were married February 2, 1911, at the home of Dr. Tucker.

Mr. Hopkins ruefully reminisced that Miss Stone hadn't looked upon his coming into the president's office with any overt pleasure. But a determined effort on his part to break down that barrier was crowned with success. "As a matter of fact, I gave a lot of thought to that particular project," he recalled. "I think that I'd had a good deal of experience skating helped me a good deal on that, because she loved to skate and I loved to skate. In those days almost invariably the river would freeze over before it was covered with snow, and it was wonderful skating down there.

"That was where the first intimacy of contact began—in going skating—and then canoeing. There was a great deal of canoeing on the river in those days. It happened our tastes ran along pretty parallel on things of that sort. There was the skating and the canoeing, and we both loved horses. She had a horse and I had a horse, and we did a great deal of riding. Eventually it kind of blurred out the office competition."

Throughout his life Mr. Hopkins often said that President Tucker was the greatest man he had ever known and that the chance to be so closely associated with him had been the greatest privilege of his life. Tucker was an extraordinary man, striking in appearance and forceful in personality, possessed of an almost tangible nobility. The students who attended Dartmouth under him held him in reverential awe and never forgot him. Many said that his spiritual influence, exerted chiefly through his chapel talks, remained with them through all the years after college. Along with these qualities, Dr. Tucker had a keen intelligence and a flair for bold action that was scarcely to be expected from one who was an ordained minister and who had come to the Dartmouth presidency from a professorship at the Andover Theological Seminary. As an example of this boldness, he solved in a most imaginative way the problem of how Dartmouth could, without having the needed funds, build badly needed dormitories. He persuaded the trustees that dormitories could be built with endowment money and then carried on the College books as investments—an action roundly denounced by the General Education Board, which called it illegal and financially reprehensible. Mr. Hopkins, when he became president of the General Education Board many years later, took special delight in being shown a booklet in which the Board recommended to others the Dartmouth plan of using endowment money to build student residence halls.

At Andover, Dr. Tucker was a proponent of "progressive orthodoxy" and was one of the small group of professors who founded the *Andover Review* and fought for a new and enlarged role for the church in modern society. He not only taught homiletics but introduced a course in social economics. He was one of the five liberal theologians who figured in the long, drawn-out Andover heresy trial, 1884–1892, which finally ended in the Massachusetts Supreme Court, with the defendants vindicated. To the conservative clergy of New England he remained a dangerous man, and Mr. Hopkins reminisced that when in his junior year at Worcester Academy he disclosed his intention of going to Dartmouth instead of Harvard, the Congregational minister in his home town of North Uxbridge came to the Hopkins house to pray that he might be dissuaded from attending the college over which Dr. Tucker presided. When Mr. Hopkins' father finally went along with the wishes of his son, another minister in town never spoke to Adoniram Hopkins again. Although young Hop could not have been aware of it then, he and Dr. Tucker were to prove to be kindred spirits, and the eight years they spent together in the president's office served to develop in Mr. Hopkins those attitudes and personal qualities which made him, after President Tucker, perhaps the most beloved leader in Dartmouth's history.

There was a natural affinity between the Tucker and Hopkins administrations. In a real sense, the administration of President Hopkins was a carrying forward and a bringing to fruition of policies begun and goals set during the Tucker years. In response to Professor John Moffat Mecklin's inquiry about some of the formative influences in the years before he became president, Mr. Hopkins in 1943 wrote: "I can say very sincerely and without the slightest trace of affectation that I haven't done anything except build upon foundations which were laid deep enough and solid enough during the administration of Dr. Tucker. Whatever merit there may be in Dartmouth today goes back to the work he did under infinitely greater difficulties and calling for greater expenditure of thought and effort than has been required at any time since."

True enough, but this evaluation by President Hopkins near the close of his own administration passed over the numerous advances that were distinctly his own. It can fairly be said that he took Dr. Tucker's vision and inspiration and institutionalized them, and in the process he met his own problems with good judgment and liberalism and with a boldness that often exceeded that of his presidential mentor. It was one of those fortunate confluences of life that brought the two men together and that permitted one of them, in full accord, to carry forward the work of the other.

When Mr. Hopkins left Hanover in the summer of 1910 it was to take a position with Western Electric, a subsidiary of American Telephone and Telegraph Company. He had become acquainted with a number of Dartmouth men who held executive positions with the telephone company and in thinking about a business career this was the firm he wanted most of all to join. Henry B. Thayer, Dartmouth 1879, was president of Western Electric at the time. Mr. Hopkins was assigned to Chicago and, with the title of director of education and training, was given the job of recruiting college men for the company. Following his suggestion that men be sought in every region, he first went to the Pacific Coast. From the University of Washington he traveled into California and then tacked north and south across the country, obtaining in his progression a first-hand acquaintance with many institutions of higher learning. In selecting some three or four hundred men, he divided them about evenly between technically trained and liberal arts men. Theodore N. Vail, president of AT&T, became interested in Mr. Hopkins' intuitive skill in picking men and in his ideas about the sort of educational background that trainees for the company should have. Mr. Hopkins in turn developed a great admiration for Mr. Vail, who was an industrial statesman far ahead of his time. In his reminiscences, he was to say that Dr. Tucker, Mr. Vail, and Newton D. Baker, under whom he served as Assistant to the Secretary of War in World War I, were the three greatest men he had known in his life.

After more than a year with Western Electric, Mr. Hopkins was summoned by Mr. Vail who said he had been informed that Edward Filene wanted Mr. Hopkins to come to Boston to take on the job of assembling a work force for the new and bigger Filene store that was then being built. It was an article of faith among telephone staff people that once you left the company there was no chance of being taken back. Mr. Hopkins told Mr. Vail that he didn't want to lose his place with AT&T, even though the Filene offer would more than double his salary. Mr. Vail urged him, however, to take the Filene job; he advised him, in fact, to try several kinds of personnel jobs in the next four or five years, in order to acquire broad experience in what was then a relatively new field. The understanding was that Mr. Hopkins would then return to the telephone company in an enlarged role.

On January 1, 1912, Mr. Hopkins became educational and employment manager of William Filene's Sons, Inc. The management wanted to make a change in the type of help it was hiring, and it considered the store expansion an opportune time to do so, since the work force was being increased from 800 to nearly 3,000 persons. It was a tremendous job, not only to hire the right people but to train them in time for the grand opening in September 1912. Mr. Hopkins was like the conductor of a gigantic, untried orchestra. But when the doors were thrown open on inaugural day, the brand-new help performed extremely well. Mr. Hopkins' success in getting people to give their best rested on his genuine concern for workers as individuals and on his natural ability to make friends. A little over a month after the opening of the new store he was elected president of the Filene Cooperative Association, the employees' organization, receiving 2,321 of the 2,582 votes cast.

With his main task for Filene's completed and with Mr. Vail's advice in mind, Mr. Hopkins in January of 1913 moved on to Willard, Sears and Company of Boston to be supervisor of personnel. This provided a different sort of challenge. Beginning as wool merchants, the company had acquired sheep ranches and mills for the manufacture of coats, and also had added the American Felt Comaany, the Eastern Leather Company, and the United Printing Machinery Company. Mr. Hopkins had overall supervision of personnel, and although he remained with the company for a year and a half, he increasingly disagreed with its policies and operations, some of which he considered of doubtful legality, and particularly he opposed the 54-hour week for workers in the mills. When he received an offer from the Curtis Publishing Company in Philadelphia, he gladly accepted it and took up his work with them on October 1, 1914. As manager of the employment department he had responsibility for the four divisions of employment, instruction, welfare, and health.

The Philadelphia period was one in which Mr. Hopkins began to acquire national stature in the personnel field and to visit business schools as lecturer on industrial personnel management. Lectures were given at the Wharton School of the University of Pennsylvania, Harvard Business School, and Dartmouth's Tuck School. He was a founder in Philadelphia of the Employment Managers Association, the first of its kind. This came about in conjunction with the Taylor Society, a scientific management movement just getting started. Mr. Hopkins was on the executive committee of the National Association of Corporation Schools and on the board of managers of the National Society for the Promotion of Industrial Education. Through the latter he became a friend of Charles Steinmetz, the research genius of General Electric. Discussions about human relations in industry led also to friendships with John Wanamaker in Philadelphia and with both Cyrus Curtis and Edward Bok of Curtis Publishing. Mr. Hopkins recalled that only a dozen or so men in the whole country were then engaged in personnel management in any significant way.

An address by Mr. Hopkins at the annual meeting of the Society to Promote the Science of Management was published in the January 1915 issue of *Industrial Engineering*. "The function of the workman is to produce—and to do this efficiently he must be scientifically selected for his job, and his health and welfare must be carefully conserved," he wrote. In another article, in the *Ladies Home Journal* of March 1915, he enunciated what was at the heart of his philosophy of dealing with others: "You must know people in a unit of one." A man or woman, from whatever walk of life, was in his eyes a fellow human being. Bossing others was alien to his nature, and people had the feeling they were working with him, not under him.

In his book, *Human Values Where People Work* (Harper, 1960), Thomas G. Spates, former vice president of General Foods and Professor of Personnel Administration at Yale, picked Mr. Hopkins as one of his pioneering heroes among men who put human and spiritual values at least on a par with other values at the places where people work. He cited him as one of those concerned with the dignity and self-respect of workers as individuals. Professor Spates particularly called attention to a management philosophy Mr. Hopkins expressed in a May 1920 address before the

Taylor Society in Rochester, New York. Work had become distasteful and uninteresting to many people, Mr. Hopkins said, and since they looked upon it as merely a way of acquiring the means for self-expression outside of working hours, the demand for shorter hours and more pay was bound to be incessant. The answer, he contended, was "to inject back into industry something of the opportunity for self-expression, the development of one's personality, so that man shall understand his responsibility in the economic world and shall have some joy in meeting it."

Late in 1915, four years after he left Western Electric, Mr. Hopkins was told that Mr. Vail thought it was time for him to come home. The message was relayed by the president of the New England Telephone Company, to whom he became assistant in January 1916. The move brought him back to Boston, where he had been located in two of his previous jobs. The return to the telephone company was a happy event for him, and he knew that he could now settle down to his life's work, with the prospect of rapid executive advancement.

Although Mr. Hopkins considered his years spent at Dartmouth as student and as presidential assistant to be a completed chapter in his life, he still had close ties with the College through his all-important role in founding the Dartmouth Alumni Council and serving as its first president. The work he had done in founding the Dartmouth Secretaries Association in 1905 had always been, in his mind and in President Tucker's, the first step in a series of alumni organizational moves that would lead to something like the Alumni Council. There was urgent need to find a better way for trustees to be elected by the alumni. The plan to make five of the twelve trustees direct representatives of the alumni had been adopted in 1891. One so-called alumni trustee was to be elected each year from five nominees put forward by the General Alumni Association, and this, as Mr. Hopkins saw it, was a great way for the College to make one friend and four enemies every year. One important function of the Alumni Council, when it came into being, would be to serve as the agency for determining alumni representation on the board of trustees.

In his final year as secretary of the College, Mr. Hopkins had brought before the Secretaries Association the question of creating a new alumni organization which would be smaller and more effective than the General

Association and would serve as its executive arm. He was the key member of a committee named to bring in such a proposal, and at its March 1911 meeting the Secretaries Association approved the idea of an Alumni Council. The following year, while Mr. Hopkins was with Filene's, an Alumni Council constitution was drawn up and then was given general alumni approval by mail ballot. Each of five alumni districts throughout the country was to have three elected members. A total membership of twenty-five also included three men elected by the Secretaries Association, four ex-officio members, and three members-at-large to be chosen by the Council itself (the Secretaries Association did this at the start and elected Mr. Hopkins a member-at-large). Officially in being as of July 1, 1913, the Dartmouth Alumni Council met for the first time on November 7, 1913, in Philadelphia, with all but four of its twenty-five members present. Mr. Hopkins, who had headed the committee to arrange the program, was elected the Council's first president, and he was reelected the following year.

The Alumni Council assumed responsibility for the annual Alumni Fund in 1914, and the next year, by vote of the General Alumni Association, it also took over responsibility for the nomination of alumni trustees. Thus, ten years after the first step, the Tucker-Hopkins objective was achieved. For the first year of the new arrangement, the Alumni Council adopted the procedure of presenting three trustee nominees to the alumni for voting. Thereafter it offered a single name as the nominee of the Council, but provided that other nominees could be put forward by alumni petition. That system is still in effect today.

The Dartmouth board of trustees, welcoming the new Alumni Council, declared itself ready to entertain any questions the Council might want to direct to it. Without much delay, the Council at its June 1915 meeting voted that Council President Hopkins should appoint a committee of three, with himself as chairman, to prepare and present to the trustees a request for information about their policies concerning:

1) The financial and educational relationship between Dartmouth College and the State of New Hampshire.

2) The extent to which it is advisable to grant scholarships in excess of the income from funds given specifically for that purpose.

3) The expression of a definite educational intention on the part of the College authorities.

This action by the Council and Mr. Hopkins' involvement in it were of historic importance. More than any other factor, the ensuing definition of Dartmouth's purposes and aims by a joint committee of trustees and Council members, in which Mr. Hopkins played the dominant role, focussed the attention of the trustees on him as a man qualified to be the next president of Dartmouth College. President Nichols, whose real loves were scientific research and teaching, had become increasingly disenchanted with administrative work and had informed the trustees that he wished to relinquish the presidency.

Mr. Hopkins was asked to write the summary report of the discussions of the joint study committee. His forceful participation as Alumni Council representative had been matched on the trustee side by Frank Sherwin Streeter, Dartmouth 1874. Recognized as the leading member of the New Hampshire bar, Mr. Streeter had been Judge Advocate General on the staff of Governor Charles Busiel and for the rest of his life was known as General Streeter. He not only was a gifted corporation lawyer, having railroads, Western Union, and the Amoskeag Corporation among his clients, but he was a Republican power in the state and had served on the party's national committee. A man of large physical proportions, with stern and craggy features, he intimidated many, but where Dartmouth College was concerned he was filled with deep sentiment and devotion. Elected to the board of trustees in 1892, the year before President Tucker took office, he proved to be Dr. Tucker's strong right arm in progressive planning for the College and in getting the board's backing for actions that conservative trustees considered much too daring. Mr. Hopkins recalled that sometimes a board meeting was adjourned while General Streeter went to work and rounded up the necessary votes. He also remembered one occasion when legally minded members of the board were hesitant to do something that was not precisely authorized, and General Streeter pounded the table and said, "God damn it, I'd rather go to jail for doing something than to stay free for doing nothing."

The Tucker-Streeter team was very effective, and although the two men were far apart in their personalities, one gentle and spiritual, the other gruff and profane, they admired each other greatly. General Streeter's feeling for Dr. Tucker was little short of adoration. During the last eight years of the Tucker administration, General Streeter had, of course, come to know Mr. Hopkins intimately, and their working relationship was especially close during Dr. Tucker's illness. He saw in Mr. Hopkins a man closely akin to Dr. Tucker in ideas and spirit.

One Sunday morning early in 1916, Mr. Hopkins had a telephone call from General Streeter who was in the Elliott Hospital in Boston for an eye operation. "I want to see you," General Streeter said; and when Mr. Hopkins replied that he would drive in after breakfast, Mr. Streeter said he wanted him to come right away. In his tape-recorded reminiscences Mr. Hopkins gives a vivid account of how, without breakfast or stopping to shave, he set out on that icy morning and skidded into Boston from Newton, where he had taken up residence upon joining the New England Telephone Company.

"I had no idea, no faintest idea what he wanted to see me about," Mr. Hopkins recalled. "I went in, and he said, 'Sit down, sit down.' His head was all bandaged up. So I sat down, and he reached out and put his hand on mine, and he says, 'Nichols has resigned.'

"I expressed my surprise. He says, 'Well, you know why I sent for you, don't you?' I says, 'No, I haven't the faintest idea.' He says, 'You're going up there.'

"Well, there were several things to take into consideration. I mean, I knew the local situation pretty well, and I wasn't sure of my welcome. I knew what the outside public would think in regard to it. And, also, there was the very self-centered fact that I was getting about three times as much in income as the presidency paid, and I was on my way to about what I had been aiming at in the AT&T.

"So, I just tried to slow the thing down, and he got very impatient in regard to it. 'Well,' he says, 'fool around; you've probably got to fool around two or three months. That's natural, I guess. But you're going up there.' "

General Streeter was chairman of the trustee committee named to recommend to the full board the man to succeed President Nichols. His guess that there would be two or three months of "fooling around" fell short of the period of time that actually was devoted to the give and take of the matter. After much soul-searching Mr. Hopkins had pretty well decided that he ought not to take the job, for a variety of reasons; and Mrs. Hopkins, who knew Hanover as well as he did, was less than enthusiastic about being the president's wife in a town where she had grown up. At that point, however, Dr. Tucker entered the picture for the first time and through General Streeter sent word that he would like Mr. Hopkins to come and see him.

Dr. Tucker was very understanding of Mr. Hopkins' reservations, but said, "I just want to state one thing to you. You're the last Dartmouth man on the list . . . and if you don't come, the presidency is going to a non-Dartmouth man. Do you think that would be good?" Mr. Hopkins had to admit it wouldn't be good; and that, he recalled, was the turning point in his decision to accept.

Both Dr. Tucker and Mr. Hopkins were aware that the College had been losing the momentum built up during the Tucker administration. *The Dartmouth*, editorializing about the search for a new president, had called for "a great human leader" embodying the ideals of the historic college. Not only did Mr. Hopkins want to see the work of Dr. Tucker carried forward, because he believed in it with all his heart, but he had an equally intense feeling that Dartmouth should not be taken down the university road. And so the decision to stay with his business career was reversed, in the conviction that he could render a service of vital importance to Dartmouth at that particular point in its history.

The decisive interview with Dr. Tucker produced another statement by the president-emeritus that was startling to Mr. Hopkins. "I think the strangest thing ever said to me came from a man from whom I'd least expect it," Mr. Hopkins recalled, "and that was in the talk with Dr. Tucker. I don't remember just how I phrased the question, but I really wanted to know what he thought I had that qualified me for the position. And he says, 'You're a gambler. Dartmouth's at the stage where it needs gambling.' "

It was a perceptive judgment by Dr. Tucker. No doubt the recollection of it was a stimulus to President Hopkins when it became necessary to take gambling chances in the succeeding years of his administration. One wonders, also, if this adjuration from Dr. Tucker was not in Mr. Hopkins' mind when he spoke at the inauguration of his brother, Louis B. Hopkins, as president of Wabash College in December 1926. "An institution tends to be stationary when it ought to be galvanized," he declared. "It tends to hold back when it should go ahead. It tends to be cautious when it should be bold. . . . The college which is overcautious in its method or overfearful of making a mistake in its policy withers intellectually and dies spiritually even more promptly than the college which is guilty of mistaken boldness suffers grievous harm."

In his introduction to *This Our Purpose*, the collection of his addresses, articles, and other writings which was published by the College in 1950, Mr. Hopkins wrote: "The hesitance with which I considered the honor of the invitation of the Trustees to accept election as Dartmouth's president was very genuine. It was based in part on a genuine humility in regard to my qualifications for the position and in part on the fact that I had found the problems of business life intensely interesting, its associations pleasant, and its remuneration ample. When however I learned that among names of those being considered for the position mine was the last among those graduated from Dartmouth, I accepted. This decision was based on the belief that Dartmouth in common with a limited few other independent colleges of like kind had a unique and indispensable function in the rapidly broadening field of higher education. This might, it seemed to me, easily be lost sight of under administrative leadership not conditioned by influences and a philosophy such as had prevailed and proved dynamic at Dartmouth. If democracy was to survive, somewhere in the educational system there ought to be institutions primarily solicitous for the education of an intelligent citizenry. Like thousands of other Dartmouth men I had found in the cultural environment, in the close-knit fellowship of human associations, and in the place loyalty induced in a small northern New England village a mental stimulus and an emotional content which I was reluctant to see subjected to the possible hazard of suddenly imposed and radical change. The hazard existed, it seemed to me, of a shift of emphasis away from the conditions and objectives of undergraduate life in a traditional college wherein men had found available a general education and had been trained with some effectiveness for assuming the responsibilities of citizenship. My original reservations in regard to my ability to conform to the conventional picture of a college presidency gradually evolved into a question of whether I could render to Dartmouth College the particular service needful to perpetuation of the specific qualities which had distinguished her through a century and a half. In what is perhaps an excess of frankness, I believed I could more certainly than could any other whose name remained on the list of eligibles."

Only the trustees and a few of his closest Dartmouth friends in Boston, along with Mrs. Hopkins, knew at what sacrifice Mr. Hopkins was accepting the Dartmouth presidency. He had to forgo the AT&T career that meant so much to him (shortly before the matter of the presidency was settled he had been told he was being transferred to national headquarters), and the financial sacrifice was large—a drop in salary from $18,000 to $7,000. The sniping at his election by certain of the faculty and alumni therefore angered his closest friends, but Mr. Hopkins had forecast it and was philosophical about it. Perhaps, in his intuitive way, he also knew that most of the critics would come over to his side, as indeed they did in a very short time.

No more striking example of Mr. Hopkins' uncommon ability to win confidence and support can be found than in the story of what happened with a faculty group calling themselves "The Agnostics." Among the select membership were Professors Louis Dow, Prescott Orde Skinner, W. K. Stewart, Sidney B. Fay, Ernest R. Greene, George Ray Wicker, John M. Poor, W. H. Sheldon, and John Wesley Young. When it became known that Mr. Hopkins was likely to be the next president of the College, they were among the first to register dismay over his lack of academic credentials. Before he died Dr. Tucker gave Mr. Hopkins the letter of protest they had written, and as he passed it over he said he was sure Mr. Hopkins would be amused by it. The amusement rested in the fact that it was not long after he had taken office that President Hopkins was invited to join "The Agnostics" and to meet with them on alternate Saturday nights to discuss literature, philosophy, religion, politics, or any other subject that was agitating thinking men at the time.

Inauguration

PRESIDENT Hopkins assumed his duties in Hanover on August 1, 1916. The inaugural ceremony formally marking his taking office was delayed for two months, until October 6 when college would be in session. Since the President's House on North College Street was being refurbished for its new occupants, Mr. Hopkins rented a cottage at nearby Lake Sunapee and was a commuter to Hanover for the first few weeks. His resumption of Hanover life took place not only quietly but easily; in late September he wrote to Trustee Henry B. Thayer that he was having no trouble in getting acclimated again and that he was finding the faculty, students, and alumni considerate and helpful.

Prior to the October inauguration, an occasion at which the new president could meet with the entire College was provided by the Convocation exercises on September 21. In his address to the students on opening day, President Hopkins began by saying that too many men were in college without knowing why they were there. There was, he said, a "too prevalent blindness in the undergraduate bodies of American colleges to the fact that they are in a special way beneficiaries of the law of *noblesse oblige*. You are the men to whom special privilege of the finest sort is being offered. It is logical that from you, therefore, an especial sense of responsibility should be expected, as it will be."

With a bit of his business experience showing through, he added, "You can no more afford to lose time, to avoid disciplinary influences, or to allow yourself to fall into shiftless habits in college, than you would be allowed to do these at the work bench or the office desk." And a bit of his ingrained irreverence toward the academic establishment surfaced in the statement, "We should not fall into the error of thinking of education as a product restricted to institutions. The college offers the easiest and quickest way for a man to secure an education, but it does not offer the only way.

Education is simply a name for intellectual development, and many a man
who has never entered a college building is better educated than many a
college graduate."

In speaking of "the heritage that is ours in this historic college," he
sounded a note that was to recur many times in future addresses: ". . . may
we realize to the full the advantages of our environment, that our lives may
be lives of needful service." Education, at least a Dartmouth education,
was never, in his view, an end in itself; it was always seen as having its
greatest worth when devoted to serving others.

President Hopkins had the good fortune to be only thirty-eight and in
vigorous good health when he faced up to Inauguration Day. It was an
all-day affair, beginning with morning prayers in the chapel and ending
with a Dartmouth Night celebration that evening. In the course of the
proceedings, Mr. Hopkins gave addresses morning, noon, and night, and
responded countless times to charges and felicitations.

The main inaugural ceremony, in Webster Hall on the morning of
October 6, was preceded by an academic procession in which twenty other
college presidents and delegates from forty-five institutions took part.
Outdoors, the glorious October day was all that anyone could have wished
for; indoors, the atmosphere in Webster Hall, as later described by Mr.
Hopkins, was "stiff-necked" at the start. The academic world was not
honoring one of its own, and the general feeling for the occasion was polite
but cautious. However, the Governor of New Hampshire unwittingly
came to the rescue. The Honorable Rolland H. Spaulding was scheduled
to give the first of a series of salutations after President Hopkins had been
formally inducted and presented with the College Charter and the Wentworth Bowl. He knew President Hopkins well enough to ask him, "What
the hell is a salutation?" after he had been invited by the inauguration
committee to give one. Mr. Hopkins suggested he not let it bother him and
that he get his secretary, a Dartmouth man, to write it for him. The
Governor hurried to the inauguration from an appointment in Washington, and upon arrival he saw the text of his salutation for the first time. In
reading it, he began: "Mr. President, Alumni of Dartmouth College,
Ladies and Gentlemen: This happy occasion, an important *millstone* in
Dartmouth's progress . . ." The audience tried not to laugh but couldn't

help itself, as the Governor went right on. Later he asked President Hopkins what the laughter had been all about, and was told that he had given the most helpful speech of the morning when he labeled the induction of Dartmouth's new president a millstone rather than a milestone in Dartmouth history. After the Governor's mistake, those present recalled, the atmosphere unfroze and the audience became much more responsive.

President Hopkins took great delight in recalling this inauguration incident and used it against himself many times as his administration went along. "Hop was a great one for putting himself down," one of his closest Hanover friends said of him, "and he liked to do it jokingly with stories such as the Governor's slip." Some years later President Hopkins was able to add a sequel to the inauguration story. His very good faculty friend, Leon Burr Richardson, met him one morning in the local bookstore, where townspeople went to pick up their newspapers, and out of curiosity, he asked Mr. Hopkins what part of the paper he usually looked at first. "I always turn to the sports pages first, and then I read Little Orphan Annie," the president told him. "My God," Professor Richardson exclaimed, "the Governor was right!"

Governor Spaulding's slip of the tongue seems to be the one thing that everyone remembers about the Hopkins inauguration. Far more worthy of being remembered was the impressive inaugural address President Hopkins delivered on "The College of the Future." No copy of the report he had written some months before for the joint Trustee-Alumni Council committee can now be located, but it is more than likely that some of the points made in that report were developed in the inaugural address. His concept of Dartmouth's role in a world on the threshold of a new era was favorably received. The address was a reassurance to those who did not know what to expect of the College's new leader, and it went a long way toward bringing all but a few diehard critics to his side. *The Dartmouth* said, "Support which has hitherto been pledged to President Hopkins because of his past achievements and because of faith in the judgment of the men who selected him may now be reiterated on the more satisfying basis of his expressed hopes and plans for the remarkably successful future of the College."

President Hopkins opened his address with the assertion, "College is a means to an end . . . the end is constructive idealism interpreted in terms of service." The importance of the historic college in a world changed by war and new social forces, he said, would depend on a searching examination of itself and on the acceptance of "great obligation and great opportunity alike," including those projects that William James had called "the moral equivalent of war."

In his salutation before President Hopkins spoke, Chancellor Charles A. Richmond of Union University had somewhat gratuitously said, "I hope you will not be too efficient. Bear in mind that a college president is not merely a business man, and a college is not to be thought of as a business proposition." It was with greater force, therefore, that President Hopkins was able to tell the assemblage that he deplored the growing tendency to think of education as worth while only when it was utilitarian. He defended the cultural college and expressed his strong belief in the importance of the classics. "It is of the utmost importance," he said, "that our higher education should not become materialistic through too narrow a regard for practical efficiency. . . . I am emphasizing certain convictions about the older humanities, not from any lack of confidence and belief in the sciences, but simply because the sciences will not be subject to attack in the newer movements in education as will be the humanities."

The inaugural address went on to call for a "high-minded consecration to the needs of the state," but warned that the colleges must be "sensitive to the new note which is beginning to sound in our national affairs, as parochialism becomes less and less a characteristic, and as we come to recognize our inevitable responsibility among the nations of the earth." Where colleges in the past had prepared men largely for the professions, he said, and had set them apart in the communities in which they lived, the new requirement was that individualism give way to cooperation and group action for the good of society. This was particularly so because the majority of college men were going not into the professions but into newer careers in business and industry. The pernicious effects of unalloyed individualism, he added, needed to be recognized both in college teaching and in relations between the college and undergraduate body.

"In a large way the college exists for the individual student," President Hopkins admitted, "but it does not exist so truly for the individual student as for the generation of college men, and it does not exist for either as definitely as for the social group which is the state. It is an easy and a pleasant thing to say to an undergraduate member of the college what properly interpreted is true—that the institution is established and maintained for his benefit. If, however, application of this statement is interpreted to mean that the college lives to meet his personal convenience or to enhance his personal success, as apart from the needs of society and his ability to contribute to them, wrong is done the man, and the college trust has been maladministered."

The remainder of the inaugural address was devoted to two points—the responsibility of the college to develop character as well as intelligence, and the need for a broader alumni interest and participation in the educational work of the college. Concerning the development of character, President Hopkins said:

The introduction of university methods into college teaching, the influence of professionalized scholarship in the chairs of instruction, and the marked disinclination of men of the present generation to consult together concerning the deeper phases of life have, all together, so altered the once existing relationship between teacher and student that the old-time formative influence of the college faculty on student character has too greatly disappeared. . . . Forms of expression change from generation to generation, and manifestations of spiritual instinct differ widely from those of a century and a half ago. But the initial obligation rests upon us to make the college influential in the development of those traits vital to well-proportioned goodness.

Scholarship as a product of the college is incomplete except as it be established on the foundation of character which is not only passively good, but which is of moral fiber definite enough to influence those with whom it is brought into contact. By as much as evil directed by intelligence is more dangerous than brainless badness, by so much is the college open to the danger of doing the country an ill turn if it ignores its responsibility to safeguard and develop character as it undertakes to stimulate mentality.

The portion of the Hopkins inaugural address devoted to the desirable relationship between a college and its alumni has since been recognized as a landmark definition. The American Alumni Council, a few years ago, declared that what Mr. Hopkins had urged with regard to continuing intellectual ties between college and alumni was the fountainhead of the movement known today as continuing education. What President Hopkins said on that inaugural morning is worth quoting at some length:

The demands which will be made upon the college in the years immediately before us will be insistent and heavy. The knowledge of this compels us to strive with unwonted effort to realize all our resources, and to have all our assets quick assets. There will be few such possibilities of added vigor to the college as in the development of what has come to be known as the alumni movement until, in far greater measure, the solicitude and the intelligence of the alumni—more truly even than their financial means—are directed to furthering the true interests of the college.

Such strength as the American college lacks it lacks, in the main, because of the too great confinement of interest among its men to the college of their undergraduate days. Many a man, through lack of opportunity for anything else, draws all the inspiration for his enthusiasm for his college from his memories of life when an undergraduate, and feeds his loyalty solely upon sentimental reverence for the past. The misfortune of interest thus confined falls alike upon the individual and upon the college. In general, the alumni of our American colleges have little knowledge of educational movements or college responsibilities on which to base any interest that they may be disposed to give to the evolution of college thought. It is needless impoverishment for a man to be the recipient of the bounty of his college for the brief season of his membership and thereafter to miss being a participator in its affairs as a going concern.

The ability of Dartmouth to continue to justify its existence in a large way will be greatly increased or seriously curtailed by the degree of willingness of the alumni to seek knowledge of what the function of this College should be, and how its function should be accomplished. Any college which could have the really intelligent interest and cooperation of a large part of its alumni body in working out its destiny to major usefulness would become of such striking serviceableness as to be beyond comparison. I am a great believer in the desirability of organized effort to get every individual alumnus enrolled as a financial contributor, but I believe in this most largely because of my conviction that, as a people, we are so constituted that where a man gives his money he there gives his interest.

There has been no phase of college activity which has been of such personal interest to me as has been the alumni movement; there has been none in which I have believed greater possibilities of good to exist. I am convinced, however, that this movement will fail of major usefulness unless it bases itself, and is based by the college, upon intelligent understanding of the problems which education must face. . . . Knowledge of conditions in the time of a man's own undergraduate course will not be sufficient. He must know the problems of today, and foresee the general characteristics of those of the future, and his efforts at all times must be rigidly to hold the college to its highest ideals. . . .

The tendency of college men to seek careers outside the professions, the tendencies of the professions themselves to become so highly specialized as to necessitate the complete engrossment of thought of the men who follow them, and the ever increasing demand of the age on all, requiring constantly greater intensity of effort and more exclusive utilization of time in men who wish to do their respective shares of the world's work, impose a duty upon the college which formerly belonged to it in no such degree, if at all. Contacts with what we broadly classify as the arts and sciences are less and less possible for men of affairs. In many a graduate the interest in or enthusiasm for these which the college arouses is, therefore, altogether likely to languish, or even die, for lack of sustenance.

If the College, then, has conviction that its influence is worth seeking at the expense of four vital years in the formative period of life, is it not logically compelled to search for some method of giving access to this influence to its graduates in their subsequent years! The growing practice of retiring men from active work at ages from sixty-five to seventy, and the not infrequent tragedy of the man who has no resources for interesting himself outside the routine of which he has been relieved, make it seem that the College has no less an opportunity to be of service to its men in their old age than in their youth, if only it can establish the procedure by which it can periodically throughout their lives give them opportunity to replenish their intellectual reserves. It is possible that something in the way of courses of lectures by certain recognized leaders of the world's thought, made available for alumni and friends of the College during a brief period immediately following the Commencement season, would be a step in this direction. Or it may be that some other device would more completely realize the possibilities. It at least seems clear that the formal educational contacts between the College and its graduates should not stop at the end of four years, never in any form to be renewed.

The general reaction to the formal events of Inauguration Day was expressed by Dean Frederick S. Jones of Yale, when he spoke at the luncheon following the morning ceremonies. "I only want to say," he stated, "with an apology and with the hope that I may not be misunderstood, that some of us go away from this meeting with a certain degree of satisfaction. We go away with a feeling of contentment, because we came with a certain measure of misapprehension or of doubt. We had heard of President-elect Hopkins; we knew something of his career. We wondered, frankly, what he was going to lay down as the law for the future policy of Dartmouth College, and we felt that it was quite possible, sir, that you might take an attitude that could not but have its effect on the other colleges of New England and the United States. So, frankly, some of us came here with something more than curiosity. I will say that we came here with some doubt, and we go home contented, feeling very certain that the note in your presidential address this morning rang true."

Another speaker at the luncheon, Luther B. Little, Dartmouth 1882, who was later to be a trustee, said, "Some day, someone standing hereabouts will congratulate the College, the alumni, the trustees, the student body, and generations of students yet to come, on this day's work." The elation among President Hopkins' backers was such that General Streeter, who had a sort of father-son relationship with the new president, felt impelled to admonish him that he should not "get the bighead, become arrogant, and fail in consideration to others." Events of the ensuing years proved that never was such a warning less needed.

President Hopkins spoke at the luncheon and then had a respite of a few hours before he returned to Webster Hall, to preside at Dartmouth Night. There he declared that if the inaugural events went on much longer he would have to ask the audience to lend him not their ears but their throats. To those who heard him speak over succeeding years, it is interesting that at that Dartmouth Night he used the quotation from Stevenson's essay "The Lantern Bearers"—"those who miss the joy miss all"—that became so closely identified with him. These words reappeared in the farewell remarks he made when he turned the presidency over to John Sloan Dickey twenty-nine years later.

In his Dartmouth Night introduction of James Parmelee Richardson, Dartmouth 1899, an intimate friend and a leader of Dartmouth alumni affairs in Boston, President Hopkins made the first public announcement that Mr. Richardson was to be named Joel Parker Professor of Law and Political Science at the College. This was a bombshell to the members of the Department of Political Science, whose approval of the appointment had not been sought. In fact, the appointment remained to be ratified at the meeting of the trustees the next morning, although there was no question about an affirmative vote. What ensued was a hot skirmish between the new president and some portion of the faculty, made up not only of department members but also of others who got into the fight on the general principle that the faculty had been by-passed and deprived of its established rights.

Looking back on the episode many years later, President Hopkins characterized the appointment as "one of my free and easy actions," something he indulged in from time to time, not often but without any hesitancy when he felt that the good of the College required such exercise of his presidential authority. President Tucker had the same propensity to act boldly, but he was inclined to secure trustee sanction first; Mr. Hopkins was more willing to act on his own responsibility, especially where he knew, as he said, that although the authority wasn't spelled out anywhere, it wasn't forbidden either.

Mr. Richardson had twice previously been invited to join the Dartmouth faculty, but had declined in favor of continuing his Boston law practice. With the retirement, in June 1916, of James F. Colby as Joel Parker Professor of Law and Political Science that chair became vacant, and President Hopkins found Mr. Richardson receptive to the idea of filling it. When it became known that Governor McCall intended to appoint Mr. Richardson a Justice of the Massachusetts Superior Court, President Hopkins moved quickly and made the Dartmouth proffer definite. Not only that, he decided to name Mr. Richardson chairman of the department, in an effort to make a dent in the existing system whereby the head of a department served virtually for life and wielded enormous power over department personnel and courses. Word of Mr. Richardson's impending professorship having leaked out prior to trustee action, President Hopkins decided he would announce it as an accomplished fact when he introduced him as a Dartmouth Night speaker.

Professor Frank A. Updyke thought he deserved the department chairmanship, if not the Parker chair, on the strength of his seniority, and he, not so much from personal aggrievement as from the prodding of faculty colleagues, became the central figure in the protest lodged with the president. Mr. Hopkins referred to the consolidated faculty opposition as "The

Union." He knew that what was involved was not only some residue of the feeling against his election but also a test of the power of the faculty over the new president. On that clear-cut issue he was ready to take up the challenge.

President Hopkins met with the faculty dissidents and expressed himself as willing to listen to their complaints, while not in any way conceding that he had acted beyond his authority. He took the occasion to explain why he considered it vitally important to make an appointment such as Professor Richardson's from time to time. His position was: 1) the College does not exist primarily, or even to an overwhelming extent, for meeting the requirements of the universities from above; 2) the College's emphasis should in the main be on teaching ability more than research ability, although the latter has its importance; 3) interest in students is as vital as interest in subjects in an undergraduate college faculty; 4) the trend toward departmental rather than institutional loyalty has no place at Dartmouth; and 5) great general truths need to be transmitted through teachers whose personalities make these truths vital. He also stated that he was in favor of having rotating chairmanships instead of heads of departments whose terms were unlimited.

In a letter to his Boston friend, Morton C. Tuttle, regarding the faculty's indignation, he wrote: "I am perfectly willing to say to anybody that every now and then we are going to salt in a man of the old-time faculty type when a good position becomes available."

The Dartmouth chapter of the American Association of University Professors, which had interested itself in the case, met on October 26 and named a committee to confer with the trustees about a greater faculty voice in all faculty appointments in the future. These discussions, to which President Hopkins gave his backing, extended over some months and led finally to trustee approval, in June 1917, of a Faculty Committee Advisory to the President, empowered to consult with the president on all faculty appointments, promotions, and refusals to reappoint, above the grade of instructor. In the cases of instructors, the consultation was to be with the department chairmen. At the same time, the trustees reaffirmed the principles of academic freedom and of tenure for professors and associate professors, and agreed to the safeguards of due notice and written statements of cause when faculty appointments were terminated. The advisory committee was to consist of five members, chosen by the president from eight nominees of the faculty, plus the dean. This committee, with one additional member, is still in force today.

The trustees also approved a Faculty Committee on Conference with the Trustees, consisting of three members from each group, to discuss matters of common interest. This committee existed for some years, but was eventually supplanted by other specific forms of trustee-faculty consultation.

Professor Richardson assumed his professorship and the chairmanship of the Department of Law and Political Science in the fall of 1917. He proved to be an outstanding teacher, as well as a notable member of the Hanover community, and his course in constitutional law became a "must" for students planning on legal careers. One assistant professor resigned in protest, but that was the only casualty from "the free and easy action" President Hopkins later admitted he probably should not have taken. The positive result was the creation of the Committee Advisory to the President, which has had an important and effective place in the College's administration ever since.

Duly inaugurated and with the faculty mollified, Mr. Hopkins settled down to the job of being president. When he first took office he had thought of making Martin Hopkins his official name, because he disliked Ernest and the shorter version would be easier to sign. But then he remembered Woodrow Wilson, who was known as Tom Wilson when he was at Princeton and who began using his middle name when he went into politics. During the Tucker period Mr. Hopkins had found Wilson arrogant and opinionated, and decidedly not his favorite college president, so he thought better of following his example on nomenclature. Ernest was mitigated by Martin, however, and the full name Ernest Martin Hopkins was almost always accorded him during his presidency. The simpler Martin Hopkins might have led some people to confuse him even more than they already did with Mark Hopkins, the educator who sat on one end of a log.

The Early Years

DARTMOUTH COLLEGE when Mr. Hopkins took over the presidency was still essentially a New England college, although its parochialism had begun to diminish under Dr. Tucker and Dr. Nichols. Three-fifths of the undergraduate enrollment of 1,442 came from the New England states, with Massachusetts and New Hampshire having the largest representations. Most of the remaining two-fifths came from New York, Illinois, New Jersey, Ohio, and Pennsylvania. Admission was by a combination of examination and certification by an approved school. For subjects not certified the student could take College Boards in June or Dartmouth's own examinations in September.

Dartmouth in 1916 granted the A.B. and B.S. degrees and offered a curriculum that was standard for the time. Hebrew had been dropped since Mr. Hopkins' undergraduate days, but seven new departments had been added: Biblical history, archaeology, fine arts, music, comparative literature, psychology, and physiology. Twenty-seven departments were grouped under three divisional headings: Languages and Literature, Mathematics and the Physical and Natural Sciences, and History, Social Sciences and Philosophy.

The undergraduate college faculty numbered ninety-nine men, one-third of them Dartmouth graduates. Among the tenured professors were a number of outstanding teachers: Charles Darwin Adams and Harry E. Burton in the classics; Fred P. Emery and Curtis Hidden Page in English; William K. Stewart in comparative literature; Louis Dow and Prescott Orde Skinner in French; Ashley K. Hardy in German; Herbert Darling Foster and Frank Maloy Anderson in history; Frank H. Dixon and George Ray Wicker in economics; George Dana Lord in archaeology; Charles N. Haskins, John Wesley Young, and John M. Poor in mathematics and astronomy; and Edwin J. Bartlett, Gordon Ferrie Hull, William Patten,

James W. Goldthwait, Charles E. Bolser, and John H. Gerould in the sciences. At the assistant professor level were names to become well known to generations of Dartmouth men: Richardson, Chivers, Proctor, Lingley, Griggs, Childs, Lambuth, Meservey, and Wright among them. Faculty salaries were low, even for that day. Professors averaged $3,000, associate professors $2,450, assistant professors $1,830, and instructors $1,160.

The administrative staff was small, consisting of seventeen officers and ten staff assistants. Under President Hopkins it never did attain great size. Six years later, in 1922, the administration had grown to twenty-two officers and twenty-five assistants, not counting staff personnel for the library and the academic departments. By 1930 there were thirty-five administrative officers, and in President Hopkins' final year, 1944–45, the number had increased to forty-five. Most of the growth over three decades was related to new deans for the faculty and freshmen, four additions to the business staff, new health and personnel services for students, an enlarged library administration, and new social programs for students.

The board of trustees with which President Hopkins began his administration was unchanged from that which had elected him, except for his replacing President Nichols. The trustees who had served for some years were General Streeter, Judge William M. Chase, Benjamin Ames Kimball (known as Uncle Ben to his colleagues on the board), Francis Brown, Lewis Parkhurst, and Albert O. Brown. Board members who had served for only a short time were Dr. John M. Gile, Henry B. Thayer, Henry L. Moore, Edward K. Hall, and Governor Rolland H. Spaulding, ex officio. Seven of the twelve trustees were residents of New Hampshire, as required, and all but Governor Spaulding were Dartmouth graduates.

The big problems facing the president and trustees in the fall of 1916 were the kind that only money could solve. But money was in woefully short supply. Dartmouth's endowment of $4.2 million was not producing much income, tuition at $140 a year was low, and the fledgling Alumni Fund, which raised $10,170 in 1916, was not yet providing the financial help that was to come in later years. Faculty compensation was perhaps the most urgent problem at the start of the Hopkins administration, and not far behind were a number of plant needs, including chemistry and biology buildings, a new library, at least one new dormitory, an enlarged heating plant, and an improved athletic field. The possibility of America's involvement in the war in Europe made all these needs more difficult of solution, and it was not until after the war, in fact, that the College began to move forward on both salaries and plant development. Meanwhile, President Hopkins proposed to the trustees that they authorize temporary bonuses for the entire teaching staff, and these payments were made in December of 1916. A second bonus was distributed in January of 1918 and a third in the academic year 1918–19. Timely help came from Edward Tuck, Class of 1862, Dartmouth's greatest benefactor, who in June 1917 added $180,000 to the Amos Tuck Endowment Fund for instructional purposes.

Another problem to which President Hopkins gave high priority at the outset of his administration was one that involved him more personally. Under President Nichols, who was glad to be relieved of administrative detail, two of the top officers of the College had established autonomous fiefdoms and were virtually co-equal with the president. Both would have been receptive to a call from the trustees to be the College's new president. Craven Laycock as Dean of the College was fully in charge of academic affairs. Homer Eaton Keyes had been named Business Director to remedy President Nichols' small aptitude in financial matters, with authorization to report directly to the trustees. By Mr. Hopkins' standards this was an untenable administrative arrangement, quite aside from his own personal instinct for executive authority, and he set about establishing a new chain of command which made all administrative officers responsible to the president and only the president responsible to the board of trustees. The response of the two officers chiefly concerned was less than cooperative.

President Hopkins recalled that during his first six months on the job Dean Laycock stayed clear of him and rarely spoke to him. That could not go on, he decided, so one night he surprised the dean by appearing on his doorstep and asking to come in for a talk. The gist of the conversation was that there could be only one chief executive in the College administration, and Mr. Hopkins was determined that he as president was going to be it. He invited Dean Laycock's help and cooperation on that basis; otherwise there would have to be a new dean. "I really think it was a relief to him," President Hopkins said in later years. "The spirit of working together was established then and there." The two men not only collaborated harmoniously but they developed a deep friendship and an affection for each other. It was Dean Laycock who urged Mr. Hopkins to go down to Springfield, Massachusetts, and face a group of alumni who were diehard dissidents. His advice was good and the trouble spot was eliminated.

President Hopkins' problem with Business Director Keyes was more difficult and took longer to solve. "Homer felt that he had jurisdiction over salary scales and everything else where any money was spent," President Hopkins recalled, "and I told him no, I wasn't having any of it." The contest of wills lasted for nearly five years, until Keyes finally resigned in 1921. "That broke up a lifelong friendship and I was sorry about it, but it was one of those unpleasant things you have to do, that's all." The crux of the disagreement between the two men was President Hopkins' view that there could be no such thing as separating the business policy and educational development of the College. "For the educational welfare of the College some things that make good business sense simply cannot be done, and the president has to step in and decide the matter," Mr. Hopkins wrote to Morton Tuttle in reviewing that period. He was willing to move ahead on some projects even though the funds were not definitely in hand. In 1919, Keyes tried to get the trustees to oppose the Hopkins idea that the appropriation for instruction would have to be increased from $250,000 to $750,000 within ten years. He called it impossible—but the instruction budget actually reached $900,000 in less than a decade.

The physical facilities of the College had been the concern of the business director and when Keyes resigned in 1921 that responsibility was handed over to the treasurer. Halsey C. Edgerton, 1906, became treasurer of the College in the same year Mr. Hopkins assumed the presidency. For all twenty-nine years of the Hopkins administration he was to be a tower of strength as manager of Dartmouth's finances. His Yankee prudence took the College safely through two world wars and the Great Depression, as well as through other times of tight resources, and he and Mr. Hopkins worked together closely and harmoniously to build up the financial strength and stability that the College carried into the modern era.

In recalling the goals he had in mind when he first took office, President Hopkins mentioned not only increased faculty salaries, new plant, and administrative reorganization; he spoke also of the need to develop among the students a greater respect for scholastic achievement. That particular goal applied to the alumni body as well, for he believed that the educational purposes of the College could never be accorded first place in under-graduate thinking until the alumni had the same attitude and made their influence felt. Dartmouth at the time of Mr. Hopkins' inauguration was in the midst of its so-called "sweat shirt era," when the rugged, he-man life was esteemed and campus notables were athletes and other extracurricular leaders. The aim of bringing intellectual achievement up to at least an equal footing was reflected in the earliest addresses President Hopkins made before students and alumni, and in this effort he received the whole-hearted support of a pleased faculty.

During his first year, President Hopkins raised the question of using the college plant all year by instituting a system of four quarters instead of two semesters with a long summer vacation. He first made the proposal to the Class Secretaries Association in March of 1917 and later that month presented it to the trustees for their consideration. The desperate need for more funds was one reason for the idea, and another influence was the remembrance from business days of the way in which college men in industry often sagged in effort during holiday periods and the summer. The trustees without any commitment referred the proposal to the Faculty Committee on Instruction, which rendered a favorable report and then won a vote of approval by the general faculty. President Hopkins, in writ-ing to an alumnus, said he did not believe in waiting until someone else tried something before Dartmouth adopted it. "Whatever Dartmouth does I wish her to do on the basis of her own thinking," he stated, "and I never yet knew anybody to acquire leadership by waiting to be a follower." While the four-quarter system would have been innovative among Eastern private colleges, it was already in operation at the University of Chicago, and Mr. Hopkins arranged a visit to study their plan, learning that there could be a gain of about 20 percent in annual income.

Opposition to the four-quarter plan developed among the alumni, and was spearheaded by the Dartmouth Alumni Council. Then when it be-came known that President Hopkins himself was having second thoughts about the possible weakening effect on class organization and on badly needed alumni support, the Council's opposition became emphatic. The alumni view proved to be decisive and the faculty recommendation that year-round operation be adopted was allowed to languish. President Hopkins later said that the Alumni Council had saved him from making a mistake, but there were some who believed a mistake had been made, in backing off and losing for Dartmouth the opportunity to demonstrate educational leadership among the undergraduate colleges.

The year 1916–17 was, in truth, no more propitious for instituting a fundamental change in the College's educational program than it was for making a start on all the specific goals President Hopkins had set for the initial period of his administration. The clouds of war hung over the land, and the uncertainties were greater for an all-male college than for other institutions. There were even some, convinced that the United States could not avoid involvement in the war, who suggested that the College think about coeducation, at least as a temporary way of staving off financial disaster. Mr. Hopkins himself was an outspoken advocate of all-out preparedness for war, and he spoke at New Hampshire patriotic rallies in Littleton, Manchester, and Laconia. At Laconia on April 5, 1917, the day before Congress declared war on Germany, he called for universal military service, denounced German aggression as subversive of all the ideals of this country, and berated selfish individualism as a drag on the nation's spirit of unity and cooperation.

Dartmouth undergraduates, who had given only minimal support to a voluntary military training program at the College in the spring of 1916 and who had not rushed to President Hopkins' side in the debate over U.S. preparedness, underwent a complete change in spirit once war was declared. The College now moved quickly to meet the general student wish for military training, and when the War Department stated that it had neither equipment nor officers to send to the colleges, the trustees hired Captain Porter Chase of the First Corps of Cadets at Boston to direct the College's own training program. He arrived in Hanover eight days after the declaration of war and soon had twelve companies, totaling 1,095 men, drilling daily. In return for twelve hours of drill a week students were permitted to drop one course. Extracurricular activities, including athletics, were cancelled and student life consisted only of classes and drill. President Hopkins did not take the War Department's response as the final answer on securing equipment, and with the help of Senator Hollis of New Hampshire he succeeded in getting real guns sent to replace the wooden ones being used by Dartmouth trainees. The Dartmouth training unit shrank in size as students left college for active service, and by late May some 550 men had withdrawn.

That same month, Captain Chase was joined on campus by Captain Louis Keene of the Canadian Expeditionary Forces, who had returned from overseas with combat wounds. Captain Keene instructed the students in digging trenches, which honeycombed the athletic field, and also in bayonet practice and rifle drill. He ultimately took charge of the Dartmouth training unit when Captain Chase was called to active duty. Although Dartmouth was unsuccessful in having an officer training unit located at the College, it was assigned a Military Stores School at the Tuck School of Business Administration. There in six six-week sessions, extending until May 1918, five hundred men were trained for duties with the Ordnance Division of the War Department. In America's second year of war, a Training Detachment of the U.S. Army was based at Dartmouth under the command of Captain Max Patterson. These were drafted men who were instructed by Thayer School's engineering faculty in telephone work, radio, motor repair, carpentry, and cement construction. Over five hundred men were trained in two sessions and plans were being made to double the unit's size, when the influenza epidemic in September 1918 cancelled them.

College opened in the fall of 1917 with 1,020 men enrolled, including 412 freshmen. Military training was continued under Captain Keene and all freshmen were required to take six hours of such training a week. The residence sections of fraternity houses were closed, in order to take up some of the slack in dormitory income. In his Convocation address, President Hopkins spoke of the need for unusual effort and assured the students that being in college to prepare for the burdens of the postwar world was as important as being in the battle lines. In a public speech he came out for higher war taxes and backed the idea of conscripting all war profits and all labor for work where needed. Shortly after, he announced that by eliminating long recesses Dartmouth would shorten the college year to end in late May.

President Hopkins was determined to maintain Dartmouth's regular academic program, with no reduction of faculty, believing that military training on the campus should supplement rather than replace academic courses. Although it was a great temptation to admit as many freshmen as possible, he set a policy of not lowering entrance requirements. This meant financial hardship for the College, but after the war it allowed an easy resumption of the regular academic program, where other institutions had the problem of students enrolled without full qualifications. The deficit for the year 1917–18 was budgeted at $110,000, but careful management and stringent economies held it to $50,000. This was covered by the Alumni Fund, which met the challenge by going far beyond any previous effort and raising $66,000.

Late in January of 1918, President Hopkins was asked to come to Washington to serve as Director of the Bureau of Industrial Relations on the staff of Quartermaster General George W. Goethals, of Panama Canal fame. He was offered a commission as lieutenant colonel, but he did not wish to be tied down for the duration of the war. (His choice of civilian status was not regretted when General Goethals berated his subordinates for unbuttoned uniforms and other forms of military dereliction.) Mr. Hopkins took up his duties on February 1 and had a desk in General Goethal's office, although he traveled a great deal to Army warehouses and to places where labor disputes had to be settled. He dealt with Samuel Gompers, John L. Lewis, and other labor leaders, and in general saw to it that industry and labor worked together without friction to produce the needed war supplies.

President Hopkins delegated specified authority for running the College to Dr. John M. Gile, a trustee residing in Hanover, and to Dean Craven Laycock and Business Director Homer Eaton Keyes. Twice a month he returned to Hanover for three-day periods, usually over weekends, and managed to maintain general direction of College affairs. Between trips he kept up a steady correspondence with his Hanover staff. On May 5 he sent a wire from Washington to *The Dartmouth*, urging men under draft age to remain in college. The draft, he pointed out, was recruiting all the men who could possibly be provided with training and equipment. "In the large," he wired, "there is no need so imperative as that we should not sacrifice the training of minds for the tremendous efforts which the country must make after the war."

Goethals had a friendly relationship with Mr. Hopkins (Dartmouth gave the general an honorary degree after the war), but he was a prickly character and did not get along with everyone. He took the job of Quartermaster General with the understanding that it would not involve him in any direct dealings with President Wilson, and he was not sure that he wanted much personal contact either with Secretary of War Newton D. Baker, under whom he served. Consequently, Mr. Hopkins more and more acted as the liaison man between the Secretary and the Office of the Quartermaster General. This led to Mr. Hopkins' being named, on May 20, 1918, to the post of Assistant to the Secretary of War, in charge of industrial relations for all the Army Corps—Quartermaster, Ordnance, Signal, Aviation, and Construction. His was the job of seeing that the steady flow of war supplies was not impeded by labor disputes or, if disputes did occur, that they were settled as quickly as possible. At the same time, he became chairman of the Cantonment Adjustment Commission, which settled disputes in construction work for the Army, and also War Department representative on the National Adjustment Commission of the Shipping Board. In a postwar tribute, Secretary Baker praised Mr. Hopkins' competent handling of his duties and said that industrial relations were one thing the Secretary of War never had to worry about.

Mr. Hopkins' office in the old State, War and Navy Building was next door to that of Franklin D. Roosevelt, who as Assistant Secretary of the Navy was roughly his counterpart on the Navy side of the war effort. They played some golf together and developed a warm friendship that lasted for many years, until 1936, in fact, when Mr. Hopkins wrote an *Atlantic Monthly* article expressing his distrust of the New Deal. While it lasted the relationship was so close that President-elect Roosevelt in 1932 sent emissaries to Mr. Hopkins to see if he would accept appointment as either Secretary of War or Secretary of the Interior in his first Cabinet.

Stanley King, later president of Amherst College, was also in Mr. Baker's office with Mr. Hopkins. Other good Washington friends were Felix Frankfurter, an intimate from Boston days, and Walter Lippmann, both of whom served on the War Labor Policies Board. One person in Washington with whom his acquaintanceship did not become more congenial was Woodrow Wilson. Secretary Baker sent Mr. Hopkins to the White House one day with a private message that was to be placed only in the hands of the President, but Wilson refused to receive him. Mr. Hopkins was certain that he had been snubbed because he had publicly supported Charles Evans Hughes for President in the 1916 election.

The closest personal ties during the Washington period were with Newton D. Baker. He and Mr. Hopkins had an ideal working relationship and enjoyed each other's company outside the office. Both were interested in national and international issues, as well as higher education, and it was their custom to walk home together at night, after a long day's work, and to discuss every sort of postwar question. Mr. Hopkins had unbounded admiration for the character and abilities of his wartime boss, and he often said that he was the finest extemporaneous speaker he had ever heard. One example he remembered had to do with a speech delivered in Boston. Mr. Baker was being roundly denounced in that area because he had not given in to the agitation for sending General Leonard Wood, the local hero, overseas (General Pershing, the U.S. commander in chief, had said he would resign if the Secretary did). Mr. Baker expected to encounter the worst when he kept his date to speak at the Boston meeting, but he brightened up one day with the thought of having company and said to Mr. Hopkins, "I have a great idea, you are going with me." As recounted by Mr. Hopkins, they arrived at the meeting and received a cool welcome. But Mr. Baker, without a prepared text, launched into his address and before long had his audience on their feet cheering. Years later, when Mr. Baker came to Hanover to give the principal address at the dedication of Dartmouth's new Baker Library (not named for him), he told President Hopkins he was afraid his prepared address was not going to hit the right note. At the urging of Mr. Hopkins he discarded it in favor of speaking extemporaneously. "And it was a magnificent address, just perfect for the occasion," Mr. Hopkins recalled.

After President Hopkins had been in Washington for six months, some alumni criticism developed over his absence from the College. Lewis Parkhurst took this more seriously than did his fellow members of the board of trustees and raised the question of whether Mr. Hopkins ought not to return. Mr. Hopkins, knowing that he had the larger matters of administration well in hand and that it was only the daily minutiae of the office that he was leaving to others, could live with alumni criticism, but trustee questioning of his being in Washington struck a raw nerve. He blew up in a letter to General Streeter. The trustees should decide, he wrote, whether they wanted a president or a chief clerk. If the latter, he could return to the business world where lucrative opportunities were open to him. A board overly restrictive with regard to the president's activities, he added, would lose for Dartmouth any chance of leadership. "Men guiding academic institutions," he said, "have shut themselves off from the affairs of the world too much and have devoted themselves too much to details of administration. What academic institutions in the main need is more contact between their administrators and the outside world, and more vision of what the world expects from academic institutions."

General Streeter, once again taking a paternal attitude, replied, "You ought to be spanked if you think I needed such a letter." He added he could figure out for whom the letter was really intended and that he would see that copies were sent to all the trustees. He closed with the admonition, "Keep your shirt on and don't get het up," and signed himself "your practical friend."

As things turned out, the question of Mr. Hopkins' absence from Hanover need not have arisen. He was back in the fall of 1918, retaining only nominal connection with the War Department and available for emergency service on industrial disputes. Undergraduate enrollment was by now down to 750 men, more than half of them freshmen, and only sixty-eight seniors were in college. But the College was making no grab for large numbers and was still holding to the policy of not lowering its entrance requirements. The situation would have been worse for all colleges that fall had the government not established the Students' Army Training Corps. The Dartmouth SATC was activated on October 1, 1918, under the command of Captain Patterson, later promoted to major, who was already in Hanover in charge of the Army Training Detachment. Class A of SATC consisted of 612 men over eighteen, who were enlisted in the armed forces and subject to a strict military regimen, which began at 6:15 a.m. and ended with lights out at 10:15 p.m. Also enrolled were 109 students under eighteen, who were subject to military rules but who were not enlisted men and therefore received no service pay. To these 721 Dartmouth undergraduates was added a Class B group of 450 enlisted men, who were sent to Hanover for vocational training.

The college year was divided into four twelve-week quarters, and age rather than college class became the basis for student classification. Athletics were kept to a minimum, fraternities were closed, and the campus atmosphere was strictly military, and looked it with students uniformed, equipped, and armed. To supplement the regular curriculum and to meet a War Department requirement, the College gave a special SATC course for all Class A trainees, entitled "Issues of War and Peace" and taught by faculty members drawn from ten departments.

The Students' Army Training Corps had a short life. With the end of the war on November 11, 1918, its reason for being also ended and the Dartmouth unit was demobilized in mid-December. However, the quarter system was maintained through June 1919, and the first of the men who had left for military service returned for the winter term beginning in January. Undergraduate enrollment increased to 953 and some of the fifty-one faculty members who had engaged in war activities also resumed their academic work in Hanover. By vote of the faculty and trustees, varying amounts of academic credit for military service were granted to students returning to their undergraduate courses. Continuation of the quarter system after the armistice gave Dartmouth a second chance to adopt it as the regular academic schedule, but both students and alumni were against it and President Hopkins did not revive his original advocacy of the idea. At the time of the demobilization of the SATC, Dartmouth also had the chance to establish an Army ROTC unit on campus, but President Hopkins turned it down. He did not give the Army very high marks on its dealings with the colleges during the war, and it was partly for that reason that in World War II he turned to the Navy in his efforts to get a training unit at the College.

Dartmouth came through the war period without the deficit it had been willing to incur in order to maintain its educational and admission standards. In the year 1918–19 the payment from the government for SATC and other military programs amounted to $179,480, including $75,000 for educational costs. The deficit at the end of the year was only $19,000, and this again was covered by the Alumni Fund.

The year 1918–19 marked a turning point in the financial fortunes of the College. Word was received that Dartmouth was one of several colleges designated to get a large bequest from Mrs. Russell Sage, eventually amounting to $800,000, which the trustees decided to use for endowment of faculty salaries. Mr. Tuck added $220,000 to the Tuck endowment for instructional purposes, and from Alice Hamilton Smith of Durham, New Hampshire, came an unrestricted legacy of $128,000. The total of more than $1.2 million in gifts and bequests was the biggest for any year in Dartmouth's history. Of the Russell Sage money, Dartmouth did not actually receive the first $500,000 until the next year and the balance until 1921–22, but it was an expectation against which the College could safely borrow. "Uncle Ben" Kimball, who was president of the Concord and Montreal Railroad, raised some needed money through the Manchester banks, and President Hopkins recalled with amusement that Dartmouth Row was mortgaged so some security could appear on their books.

The instructional budget for 1919–20 was increased to $329,000, compared with $227,000 and $204,000 for the two war years. This was made possible, in part, by a tuition rise from $140 to $200 for freshmen, an increase which became applicable to all students in 1920–21. Further progress in faculty compensation was made for the year 1920–21, when the instructional budget went up to $434,000. The Dartmouth Alumni Council in June 1919 had submitted a report urging a $5,000 minimum salary for full professors and increased pay proportionately for other ranks. One year later, President Hopkins was able to tell the Council that ten full professors would be at that figure and that efforts would continue to bring the whole faculty up to the recommended levels.

Not only better compensation but an improved student-faculty ratio was an objective. In the postwar years the 18:1 ratio that existed when President Hopkins took office was gradually improved to 13:1 by the fall of 1921. Thirty-five new teachers, some of them filling the vacancies created by wartime departures, joined the staff in the fall of 1919, and more additions in the next two years brought the faculty up to a total of over 160, compared with the ninety-nine at the start of the Hopkins administration. With her appointment as Instructor in the Russian Language for 1918–19, Mrs. Norman Hapgood became the first woman to be a regular member of the Dartmouth faculty.

Upon settling down to his presidential job after wartime service in Washington, Mr. Hopkins was able to devote himself to the College's most urgent plant needs as well as to salary matters. In March of 1919 the trustees named an advisory committee on physical development, consisting of President Hopkins, Mr. Kimball, and Mr. Parkhurst. Trustee action followed soon after. Work was begun in the fall of 1919 on a new dormitory, which was completed the next year and named for Elijah Topliff, 1852, who earlier had left the College $240,000, which was used for land and plant improvements. Before the Alumni Council in October of 1919 President Hopkins spoke of the deplorable condition of the athletic field and suggested that a new one ought to be an alumni project. In December plans were announced for a Memorial Field honoring the 112 Dartmouth men who gave their lives in World War I. An alumni drive launched in 1920 eventually raised $225,000 which, with funds added by the Dartmouth College Athletic Council, assured realization of the undertaking. Construction began in the summer of 1921 and the new stadium was dedicated in the fall of 1923.

The trustees also voted to proceed with a new chemistry building, although the funds for the $460,000 structure were not in hand. It was dedicated October 29, 1921, and named in memory of Benjamin H. Steele, 1857, whose brother Sanford H. Steele, 1870, left $249,000 to the College for that purpose. The balance of the total cost for building and equipment was carried as a debt for seven years, until a legacy from Thomas P. Salter of Portsmouth, New Hampshire, enabled the trustees to pay it off.

Friendships with Mr. Hopkins and confidence in his leadership were large factors in the gifts and bequests that began to flow to Dartmouth in the postwar years. One such bequest was the $100,000 left to Dartmouth by Theodore N. Vail, the president of AT&T, in 1920. Another was the $300,000 bequest made the same year by Benjamin Ames Kimball, who had often discussed with Mr. Hopkins the importance of administrative skill and the desirability of such training in the college curriculum. Of similar character was the gift of $138,000 made by Rolland H. Spaulding— he of the "millstone incident" when governor—to build a swimming pool, which was ready in December 1920 as a welcome addition to Dartmouth's athletic and physical education facilities. In that same college year, College Hall was remodeled; nine holes were added to the golf course, thanks to additional funds from Henry H. Hilton, 1890, who had financed the original nine; and work was begun on enlarging and improving the heating plant. The following year saw the completion of a faculty apartment house, a start on eight new faculty houses, and the purchase and remodeling of the old Commercial Hotel at the corner of College and Lebanon Streets for use as a dormitory, named South Hall. More dormitory space was created with the construction of Russell Sage Hall, begun in the fall of 1922 and occupied one year later.

While notable progress was being made with regard to faculty and physical plant, President Hopkins also had it very much in mind to take the lead in strengthening and transforming the relationship of the alumni to the College. In his reminiscences years later, he said, "I spent the hardest work for the first three or four years on getting the alumni organized." He might have added educated as well as organized. While he had great faith in the alumni and in what they would ultimately mean to the advancement of the College, he knew that alumni interest in the College on the basis of nostalgia and athletics would have to be replaced by a more serious interest in Dartmouth as an educational institution and by an understanding support of its historic role as an undergraduate liberal arts college. Doubts about the future of the traditional college of liberal arts had been voiced at the close of the war, and this in itself was enough to send President Hopkins on the offensive about the worth and unique contributions of colleges such as Dartmouth. This theme was one he never abandoned, and as he hammered away at it and developed it, beginning with his postwar addresses, he gradually came to be the country's foremost spokesman for the liberal college.

To Charles H. Donahue, 1899, one of his closest Boston friends, he wrote in October 1917: "The value of the alumni to the College is almost wholly a matter of whether they can be made to make their interest and solicitude intelligent or not." And to Edwin Webster Sanborn, 1878, he wrote shortly thereafter that if he had the choice of an endowment of many millions and an alumni body keenly interested in higher education, he would unhesitatingly choose the latter, because such support in the long run would be a "living endowment" of limitless possibilities.

In his first year as president, Mr. Hopkins made a swing of eight alumni clubs in January 1917, going as far west as Minneapolis. His talks dealt with his desire that Dartmouth become a truly national college producing men of brains and character and health, an independent cultural college free to serve as the terminal point of formal education for most of its men (as it was for 75 percent at that time) and not as a way station catering to the requirements of the universities.

It was not until after the war that he was able to return to the alumni circuit in any planned and serious way. The first postwar tour, in 1918–19, was notable for the purely educational level on which he addressed alumni. The seriousness of the wartime effort must be carried over into the peacetime work of the College, he told them. He defined Dartmouth's educational purpose, spelled out the difference between liberal education and vocational training, and repeated his belief that the ultimate end of education is service to society. The responsibility of the College, he went on, was to meet the world's need for men of intellectual strength, because the problems of the next generation were going to be world problems. As for the alumni's part in all this, the need, he stated, was for more than financial help, essential as that was; it was for understanding and support of Dartmouth's educational program, for concern with its intellectual quality. Appreciation of the work of the faculty would be helpful, he said, and the alumni's moral influence on the students in support of intellectual standards would result in toning up the whole of undergraduate life.

President Hopkins purposely took this message of high seriousness to the alumni in those early years, and it was the level on which he continued to talk to them thereafter. A battle was joined with those whose College interest he considered superficial. That he won the battle hands down was attested by the way the alumni in time listened to him with respect, supported him enthusiastically, even affectionately, and broadened and deepened their interest in all aspects of the College's work, educational as well as social, athletic, and financial. One of Mr. Hopkins' presidential colleagues once asked him what he talked about when he visited the alumni. "Education," Mr. Hopkins replied. "Good Lord, how do you get away with that?" the colleague asked him.

President Hopkins was assiduous in visiting Dartmouth alumni centers from coast to coast. He let himself in for very strenuous itineraries, and in most cities he was willing to fill speaking engagements besides those with the alumni, believing that these extra appearances were beneficial to the College.

His schedule for 1919–20 was especially heavy and is a good example of the effort Mr. Hopkins put into bringing both alumni and non-alumni groups into touch with Dartmouth. In November he addressed a Manchester conference on New Hampshire's industrial and political goals. In January he addressed the New Hampshire Constitutional Convention in Concord, the National Association of Boot and Shoe Manufacturers in New York, and the Commercial Club in Keene, New Hampshire, as well as alumni clubs in Hartford, Manchester, and Boston. February's schedule included the Winooski Valley Teachers Association in Montpelier and the Dartmouth Club of Springfield, Massachusetts. In March and April, with Trustee Lewis Parkhurst, he embarked on an extended tour to Missouri, Texas, California, Oregon, Washington, Montana, Colorado, and Illinois, a trip which had as one of its objectives the stimulation of more student applicants from the West. Beyond the scheduled alumni dinners in each city, President Hopkins spoke in St. Louis to the Chamber of Commerce and the staff of the Commonwealth Plant; in Palo Alto to an assembly at Stanford University; in San Francisco to a Commercial Club luncheon; in Portland at a chapel service of Reed College and at a Civic League luncheon; in Tacoma to two high school assemblies and a Commercial Club luncheon. During two days in Seattle he delivered an address on "The New Obligations of Higher Education" at the University of Washington and spoke to the College Club, the Women's University Club, and three high school assemblies. On he went, speaking in Spokane to the Advertising Club, in Butte to the Montana School of Mines and a high school assembly, in Denver to the Civic and Commercial Association, in Omaha at a YMCA supper, a Chamber of Commerce luncheon, and a gathering of prospective students. After a month's respite in Hanover, Mr. Hopkins in early May addressed the alumni and two high school assemblies in Atlanta, and then went to Rochester, New York, to give the principal address at a joint conference of the Taylor Society, the National Organization for Promotion of Scientific Management, and the Rochester Chamber of Commerce. All this added up to forty-five speaking appearances, in addition to what was expected of him in Hanover.

The visit to Tacoma produced one of the most amusing of the Hopkins anecdotes. Among the College's investment income was the rent from a Tacoma house that had been given by an alumnus in the ministry. The house was of modest value, yet it produced a remarkably high income; so President Hopkins and Mr. Parkhurst, out of curiosity, decided while in the city to take a look at it. Late one morning they arrived at the house and knocked on the door in order to make themselves known to the occupants. The large black woman who finally came to the door waited for no words from the callers. "You boys gonna hafta come back after three," she said. "The girls had a hard night." The College divested itself of ownership without much delay. Mr. Parkhurst was shocked that money should be coming to Dartmouth from such a source, but Mr. Hopkins relished the humor of the situation, and it became a story he delighted to tell, although he was careful to pick the right audience.

Greater alumni interest in the educational work of the College, the goal toward which President Hopkins was driving, did not come about quickly or easily. The poor record of the Dartmouth football team in the fall of 1921 brought to the surface the priority that athletic success still had in many alumni minds. There was grumbling about the football coach, of course, but also about the overemphasis on scholastic standards which, it was claimed, was scaring good athletes away from Dartmouth. This dissatisfaction was especially prevalent in the Springfield and Chicago areas, the two alumni centers where criticism of the election of Mr. Hopkins as president had been strongest. Ironically, the man whose academic credentials had been questioned was now under attack for being too serious about Dartmouth's scholastic standards. One irate alumnus claimed that the College was becoming "a bunch of Phi Beta Kappa sissies with no red corpuscles in their bodies" and wondered how a successful football team could be produced from "a student body made up of perfect ladies."

President Hopkins' reaction to such grumbling was another display of the firmness with which he stuck to his views when he believed the welfare of the College was at stake. In a letter to his close friend, Natt W. Emerson, 1900, he did not hide his disgust with "the carper against scholastic standards." But the strongest statement of his position was made in his letter to an alumnus in Chicago, who had written that Dartmouth

College would be little known if it were not for its athletic prowess and that athletes from the West would be discouraged from applying for admission if the administration kept on overweighting the academic side. President Hopkins replied that he not only disagreed with this statement but that he was indignant on behalf of the College. "Nothing could so quickly kill the College or so promptly suppress the interest in it which the public has as the carrying out of a policy by which academic standards should be altered or eased for the sake of the athlete," he wrote. "I would never lift a finger to help a man into Dartmouth solely because of his athletic ability, and the athletic teams would be far better off if none such were ever sent here." On this point, he added, "there is absolutely no compromise." Going on, he expressed the College's genuine interest in intercollegiate athletics and its willingness to help any athlete desiring a college education and qualified for it, "but we are interested in them," he wrote, "on the basis of our teams being made up of Dartmouth men incidentally in athletics rather than on the basis of athletes incidentally in Dartmouth College. . . . As I view the interest of the College, the greatest need of the present time is for a common understanding among the alumni and the administration in regard to what the College is all about. . . . So long as I am directing things at Dartmouth, I shall argue that the first requisite for the College is to make good in its primary job—that of being an educational institution—and I shall further argue as a corollary of this, that in the long run the better it is in this capacity the better it will be all around."

The last two months of 1921 might well have been the low point in President Hopkins' lifelong belief in the value of alumni to Dartmouth's strength and progress. He had worked hard for five years to raise the sights of the alumni about the true nature and purpose of the College, and one poor football season had disclosed how much more remained to be done. In his depression, he wrote to Mr. Parkhurst, "If our Dartmouth alumni would come back to Hanover and spend some of the time here in talking about the value of intellectual attainments and expressing some commensurate interest in the faculty that they do in the football coaches, and if they would get over being drunk before they get to the boundaries of Hanover and would keep sober until they leave, their presence in Hanover would become a help to the interests of the College which they, as well as we, wish to conserve." The clouds eventually lifted, but not until three alumni—Larry Bankart, Jess Hawley, and Clark Tobin—had been named to a football advisory board; Joe Gilman had made a swing of alumni clubs to discuss Athletic Council policy; and Hawley had been chosen to replace Jackson Cannell as head football coach, beginning with the 1923 season. Dartmouth went on to the national football championship in 1925, and if President Hopkins had been of the "I told you so" kind, he could have called the attention of the Springfield and Chicago groups to the impressive number of top-ranking scholars on the team.

The multiplicity of outside activities in which President Hopkins engaged in the early years of his administration was thought by some to be an overspending of his energies, but he was convinced that it was essential for him as administrative head of the College to keep in touch with outside interests. He shouldered the extra burden because he believed that his activity in the right places would give a boost to Dartmouth's public image. This strenuous program, more purposeful than it must have seemed to some, was carried on for about five years. Then in 1922 he decided the College was now less in need of that kind of promotion, and he began to decline outside invitations and memberships. The excess of applicants for admission by then had, indeed, led to stories in the national press that Dartmouth was the most popular college in the country.

Mr. Hopkins' concern for industrial relations did not cease with his election to the Dartmouth presidency, and for a few years thereafter he continued to serve as a consultant and to take part in industry and government conferences. In the summer of 1917 he made a month-long study of employment methods for the Winchester Arms Company in Connecticut, and that fall he became a member of the Committee on Industrial Relations of the U. S. Chamber of Commerce. In February 1919, Newton D. Baker named him public representative and chairman of the Emergency Construction Wage Commission, a wartime agency which was revived to settle a dispute involving the building trades and construction of Quartermaster Corps terminals in seven major ports. Two years later, Governor Brown of New Hampshire named him chairman of a commission to make a study of employers' liability and workmen's compensation and to report its findings to the state legislature with recommendations for changes in the state laws.

President Hopkins' interest in New Hampshire affairs was very real, and through his willingness to speak to civic and industrial groups, both large and small, and to serve on various state commissions, he became widely known and respected and was often quoted in the state press. In the fall of 1922 the *Granite Monthly* conducted a poll to determine the five leading persons in the life and thought of New Hampshire. President Hopkins was first by a wide margin. One editorial at the time characterized him as "courageous, patriotic, one of the greatest college presidents." Another said, "No other citizen approaches him in intellectual grasp of the greatest questions of the day."

One of Mr. Hopkins' greatest services to the state was his work with the Committee on Revision of the New Hampshire School System, to which Governor Bartlett appointed him in December 1918. With General Streeter, who was chairman, he helped formulate the school system that is in effect today. The committee recommended a State Board of Education, which would appoint a Commissioner of Education, and it also proposed equal and universal educational opportunity, a standardized school year, minimum course requirements for all students, certification of teachers, and safeguards for student health. Mr. Hopkins wrote the report's opening section depicting the general educational situation in the state, and he was primarily responsible for the recommendation that no member of the State Board be a professional educator. The committee's report was enacted into law by the state legislature in March 1919, and General Streeter was named the first Board chairman.

The State of New Hampshire had for some years been making modest financial grants to Dartmouth College. The amount was $10,000 in the first year of the Hopkins administration and $15,000 in each of the next four years. Mr. Hopkins persuaded the trustees that the College would be better off without any financial dependence upon the state, and after the 1920–21 grant no further request was made and the support ended. The legislature itself provided a decisive reason for ending the financial relationship when it got up a petition calling for the dismissal of Professor George Ray Wicker, whose liberal teaching of economics had included the

citing of Trustee Benjamin Ames Kimball of Concord as a horrible example of a conservative capitalist. It was Mr. Kimball himself who moved
during a board meeting that the trustees ignore the petition, on the grounds
that the legislature had no business telling any Dartmouth professor what
or how to teach.

If Dartmouth got its last $15,000 from New Hampshire in 1920–21, it
more than made up for the lost annual income at about the same time,
thanks to an earlier gift from the state. The College contracted to have the
Brown Company of Berlin, New Hampshire, cut and buy the soft wood in
the Second College Grant, a 27,000-acre tract of northern forest land con-
veyed to the College by the state legislature in 1807. Gross receipts from
the contract amounted to $1.50-million and produced income of $50,000
annually over the forty-year period before the next cutting. By an act of
the New Hampshire legislature in 1919, the College had been authorized
to use for general purposes that part of the annual income not needed for
scholarships for New Hampshire boys, for which purpose the gift had
originally been made.

Judge William M. Chase, who was a trustee from 1890 to 1917, had
tried to persuade the board to accept an offer of $250,000 for the Second
College Grant, arguing that it was inappropriate and possibly illegal for
the College to be in the lumber business. President Hopkins and most
members of the board did not agree, seeing a handsome financial potential
in lumbering the Grant. They entrusted to Dr. John M. Gile the negotia-
tions with the Brown Company, which resulted in a financial realization
far in excess of what the board had anticipated. Timber alone produced
six times the sum for which Judge Chase had wanted to sell the whole
Grant. In recalling this episode and the cautious, legalistic thinking of
some board members, Mr. Hopkins once quipped, "All my troubles in life
have been with lawyers."

The fact that President Hopkins' way of doing things was usually the
very opposite of legalistic certainly contributed to the rapidity with which
he and the faculty found themselves working together in harmony and
mutual respect. His inclination, when he was approached by faculty members with ideas they wanted to carry out, was not to throw up roadblocks
but to tell them to go ahead and he would somehow find whatever money

might be needed. Beyond that, he had made clear the high priority he gave to better faculty salaries, and he was keeping even with the faculty, if not ahead of it, in trying to raise the scholastic standards of the College. Most important of all was the complete freedom he guaranteed to the faculty to teach as they pleased. John Moffatt Mecklin, who was offered the position of Professor of Sociology in 1920, described in his book *My Quest for Freedom* how he had come to Hanover to discuss the job. "I met President Hopkins," he wrote, "and he captured me for Dartmouth. Here was a college president of a type I had often heard about but had never known in the flesh. Cordial, courteous, tolerant, he discussed with me the proposed position. He gave me complete freedom to teach what I had long wished to teach." The Mecklin appointment was one that was managed largely by President Hopkins himself—not quite the "free and easy action" of the Richardson case in 1916, but an action for which he was willing to take personal responsibility because he was sure it would bring to Dartmouth another great teacher. Besides, Professor Mecklin was the sort of man to whom he was glad to offer haven. Mecklin had been forced to resign from the Lafayette faculty when he deviated from Presbyterian orthodoxy, and then at the University of Pittsburgh his freedom and academic security were uncertain because he was an outspoken critic of the steel industry.

In 1918 President Hopkins had encouraged the faculty to undertake a study of the curriculum. One year later the Committee on Instruction brought in its report which was approved by the faculty as a whole and then by the trustees. The A.B. and B.S. degrees were retained, the Latin requirement was revised but still kept as a basic part of undergraduate study, and the system of majors and minors was dropped in favor of majors only for juniors and seniors. The big innovation consisted of two new courses required of all freshmen. One was a one-semester course in "Problems of Citizenship," taught cooperatively by faculty from the departments of history, economics, political science, and sociology. The other was a one-semester course in "Evolution," taught by the science departments. The new educational program went into effect in the fall of 1920. At the same time, the College inaugurated the requirement that all freshmen and sophomores, to qualify for the degree, must engage regularly in some form of recreational athletics, and elective sports were offered in addition to the calisthenics that had previously constituted physical education.

The year 1919 saw formal adoption of President Hopkins' idea of having rotating chairmen rather than permanent heads for the faculty departments. Chairmen were appointed by the president for two-year terms, and the principle of rotation was implicit in the new system. At the same time, the twenty-five departments were reorganized into seven divisions, each division to have a chairman elected by its members for one year. Faculty suffrage was broadened by giving voting rights to all except instructors in their first year of service.

When Dartmouth observed its Sesquicentennial in October 1919, President Hopkins used the occasion to state his belief that the faculty held the place of first importance in the life of the College. His assignment was to give a brief credo of Dartmouth College in the postwar world, and in this address he said, "I hold it true beyond the possibility of cavil that the criterion of the strength of a college is essentially the strength of its faculty. If the faculty is strong, the college is strong; if the faculty is weak, the college is weak. Plant, material equipment, financial resources, administrative methods, trustee organization, alumni enthusiasm and loyalty, are but accessory to the getting and holding of strength at this point, none of them insignificant in importance but all of them subordinate. To the extent that any of these is a contributing factor to increased strength in the instruction corps, to that extent it is of major importance. All else is of less consequence."

Also notable in his Sesquicentennial address was a sort of declaration of independence for the College. "The whole spirit of the foundation of Dartmouth College," he said, "even when interpreted through the context of modern conditions, is a challenge to develop original thought and to do intelligent pioneer work; to ignore convention if it becomes restrictive and to avoid standardization if it becomes entangling." Adding that he wanted Dartmouth to do nothing simply for the sake of being different, he nevertheless claimed for the College a responsibility "separate and apart from that which in general appertains to the American college," and he concluded, "I simply pause in this open forum to beg the indulgence of our guests if for a moment we more than suggest a conviction that our task is one distinguished by uniqueness. With such premises, therefore, our conclusion is bound to result that, be our problem what it may, we purpose to seek its solution first in the light of our own experience and of our own reasoning, and only secondly in the light of a comparative study of what has been deemed wise elsewhere."

The four-day observance of the Sesquicentennial consisted of Dartmouth Night on Friday, held in a huge tent on the campus; a football game, won against Penn State, on Saturday; religious services on Sunday; and Anniversary Day, with an academic procession, on Monday. Principal speakers, in addition to President Hopkins, were Justice Wendell P. Stafford of the Supreme Court of the District of Columbia and President Marion L. Burton of the University of Minnesota. Among the participants in educational conferences were Irving Babbitt, Felix Frankfurter, Alexander Meiklejohn, and William Allan Neilson.

At two points in his address President Hopkins referred to "selective processes of admission." That phrase and the credo of independence he enunciated indicate that he was giving thought at the time to the necessity of devising Dartmouth's own system for choosing the men to be admitted to the College. The first pressure of more applicants than the College could accommodate had been experienced that very fall. The unexpectedly large enrollment of 1,732 men was greater than for any prewar year, and the freshman class of 667 was the largest for any college in the East, with one hundred other applicants turned away.

In the early 1900's there were basically two schools of thought about the best way of admitting men and women to college. Both were predicated on a specified minimum of secondary-school preparation, particularly in English, mathematics, Latin, and history, with a modern language and a science substituted for Latin in the case of B.S. candidates. Backed by the prestige of Harvard, Yale, and Princeton, one school of thought held that the adequacy of preparation could be determined only by examinations, and College Board tests were virtually the sole basis for accepting or rejecting applicants. The other school of thought, to which Dartmouth adhered, believed that if an approved school certified satisfactory work by an applicant, that was adequate evidence of his preparation in those subjects for which certification was allowed. Dartmouth, for example, required twelve and one-half units of preparatory work—four years of Latin, three of English, two and one-half of mathematics, two of modern foreign languages, and one of history. Eight units could be covered by certification, the rest by examinations. If eight units could not be certified, then the applicant was required to take examinations in all five subjects. It was possible to be admitted with conditions; for example, if the applicant did not have the full four units of Latin, he was required to take more than the one year of college Latin prescribed for all A.B. candidates. Under this system at Dartmouth, any man could enter if he met the unit requirements and could prove that he had a dormitory or off-campus room in which to live. Priority of application determined the assignment of rooms and therefore was of major importance, but President Hopkins did a lot of the admissions work himself in the earliest years, and he always had a few rooms tucked away so that last-minute applicants with special qualifications could be accommodated. Today, it seems strange to read copies of letters and telegrams in which the president of the College was informing a boy about the room he could have.

In 1917–18, Dartmouth made certificate admission less rigid for men of high rank in approved schools, and four years later the system was further simplified by granting admission without conditions to any man who stood consistently in the top quarter of his secondary-school class and offered three units of English and two and one-half of mathematics. President Hopkins, in announcing this step, said, "College admission is now so mechanical and formal as to exclude in many cases men with capacity for superior intellectual accomplishment." Making it possible for more Western boys to come to Dartmouth was one reason for adopting a less specific set of requirements. On his trip to the Pacific Coast the previous year, Mr. Hopkins had found that many schools were technically unable to meet, or had no desire to meet, the entrance requirements of Eastern colleges. Oregon schools, for instance, taught their students Oregon history in preference to classical history, and in many Western schools Latin and Greek were not considered indispensable, as they were in the East. With its less rigid plan, Dartmouth said in effect that it would assume responsibility for the content and quantity of the candidate's preparatory work if the school would guarantee its quality.

The trend in admission policy at Dartmouth and other colleges served only to harden the attitude of those who favored the examination system. Academic standards were being jettisoned, they claimed, and all of American higher education would suffer if admission requirements were eased. President Hopkins' answer was that passing examinations was no real test of an applicant's ability to do college work. Examinations could be passed by means of cramming, and moreover, the necessity of preparing students for examinations was limiting the freedom of the secondary schools and forcing them to shape their educational programs to the prescriptions of the colleges.

Meanwhile, the postwar increase in the number of college applicants continued at Dartmouth at a rate higher than for any other private college in the East. The application list for the Class of 1924 had to be closed early, in April 1920; and the next year the list was closed even earlier, in February, when it reached 1,600 more than the planned size of the freshman class. A survey of forty institutions in 1921 disclosed that thirteen had turned away applicants. Dartmouth led the list with 1,600, followed by Princeton with 1,500, and Pennsylvania with 750. Harvard had to refuse 229 applicants, and Yale none. The College was still operating on the certificate-examination system, and with a surplus of candidates for admission, it became obvious that priority of application could no longer be accorded such importance and that a new and better way of choosing the entering class had to be found.

The Dartmouth trustees first discussed a new admissions system in April of 1921. At their next meeting in October they formally approved the Selective Process for Admission and set a limit of 2,000 on total undergraduate enrollment. The thinking of President Hopkins dominated the new plan, which received wide coverage in the press as a radical innovation and also stirred up a storm of discussion at both the college and secondary-school levels. Although devised with the help of the Faculty Committee on Admissions, the Selective Process was adopted by direct action of the trustees. President Hopkins resisted faculty control of admissions, feeling that this was an area of trustee responsibility, and fearing, perhaps, that those features of the new plan which supplemented the purely scholastic might be watered down under faculty control.

The essence of the Selective Process for Admission was defined in President Hopkins' statement, "The College unreservedly holds that definite evidence of intellectual capacity is indispensable, but it believes that, after such evidence is established, positive qualities of character, wide range of interests, and capable performance in school activities should operate as determining factors in selection." The plan gave preference to New Hampshire men and sons of alumni, and it sought to achieve broad geographical representation in the student body by giving preference, among men of equal scholastic ability, to applicants from west of the Mississippi River and south of the Mason-Dixon line. It also aimed at a student body drawn from many different schools and from varied economic levels. The original inclusion of the professions and vocations of parents as a factor in selection was generally disliked and it soon disappeared.

Not only was the central philosophy of Dartmouth's Selective Process of Admission unique, the procedure for obtaining information about applicants was equally innovative. Three forms were to be filed concerning each candidate for admission: one by himself, detailing his school activities and other interests; one by the principal or headmaster of his school, providing a personal rating; and one by an alumnus, also giving a personal rating after an interview with the applicant. These forms, together with the boy's scholastic record, provided the basis for a decision by the director of admissions, a position newly created by the trustees and filled by E. Gordon Bill, dean of freshmen.

The Selective Process came in for its full share of attack, especially from those advocating the examination system of admission. It was called an undermining of the scholastic foundations on which college admissions had always rested and, by some, a clever subterfuge to get more athletes into Dartmouth. The secondary schools, on the other hand, were generally pleased with the plan. It placed trust in them, it accorded them a new and more determinative role in the college admissions process, and it broadened the base on which selection was made, giving to the "well-rounded" boy with solid but not brilliant scholastic achievement a chance he had not had before.

In defending the Selective Process and expounding its principles, President Hopkins emphasized that Dartmouth was going its own individual way in order to get the diversified student body it wanted. If one of the functions of the College is to breed citizenship, he said, then contact with a broader spectrum of citizens is needed: "An undergraduate gets a considerable part of his education from association with his fellows, and the more broadly representative your undergraduate body, why the better your educational process." If education is to be put to social use, he said, then the character of the applicant is an essential factor in selection. What the man is himself needs to be taken into consideration along with what he knows.

Although devised for the fuller realization of Dartmouth's own educational purpose, the Selective Process had profound effect upon all other colleges and universities. Princeton in 1922 adopted a selective process based on scholarship and character, with ratings from school principals added to test scores. Within five years most Eastern colleges had followed Dartmouth's lead to some degree. President Lowell of Harvard even came to Hanover to see what the Selective Process was all about. At that time Mr. Lowell could see no sense in it as long as Dartmouth could get a sufficient number of students from New England. Some years later, when the Hopkins family had established a summer home on Mt. Desert Island in Maine, Mr. Hopkins took President Hadley of Washington University in St. Louis to meet President-Emeritus Eliot of Harvard, who summered nearby. When President Hadley remarked that he intended to reform his admissions program along the line of Dartmouth's, Mr. Eliot burst out, "I pray you, don't adopt the Dartmouth system. This young man has done more to demoralize educational standards than any man in the history of American education." As they came away, Hadley jokingly said to Mr. Hopkins, "Did you say that President Eliot was a *friend* of yours?"

Brains and character and health comprised the educational trinity for President Hopkins. The first two were heavily weighted in the Selective Process; the third was a lesser factor, but it received attention in other pioneer ways in the early years of the Hopkins administration. The importance of health was learned by Mr. Hopkins in his years of personnel work before becoming president, and the idea that health was both bodily and mental was acquired from the War Department in World War I.

Dartmouth in the fall of 1919 not only adopted its new physical education requirements for the two lower classes; it also made it compulsory for freshmen to eat in Commons, so there would be dietary supervision of the meals eaten by students the first year away from home. In June 1921, Dr. William R. P. Emerson, 1892, was brought to Hanover to make a study of freshman health, and that fall he joined the staff as specialist in nutrition and physical fitness. First steps toward a full-time program in mental hygiene were taken that same fall when Dr. Charles P. Bancroft, a Concord psychiatrist, began coming to Hanover for two days every two weeks to meet with students referred to him by faculty members or deans. With the help of Dr. Arthur H. Ruggles, 1902, the College then established a regular psychiatric counseling service, said to be the first full-time program of its kind in any college. The year 1921 saw counseling developments in other areas as well. The first dean of freshmen was appointed in June and, with the help of a Freshman Council, was given responsibility for the special oversight and guidance needed by first-year men. In October, the College inaugurated a vocational counseling program, with Professor Richard W. Husband advising seniors and juniors and Professor Gardner C. Basset doing the same for sophomores and freshmen.

Up until January 1921 President Hopkins had been steadily on the job for the College or for the War Department in Washington. His self-imposed work load was tremendous, and although he was in his early forties and had great vitality, the trustees urged him to take an extended vacation, lest he wear himself out. His leadership of the College was firmly established and widely praised, and his friends were as one in wanting it to continue unabated in the years ahead. Accordingly, with Mrs. Hopkins and daughter Ann, who was then three years old, he went to Asheville, North Carolina, for a two-months stay. Ann, unfortunately, became ill and was hospitalized for much of that period, but the trip did provide Mr. Hopkins with a lengthy respite from the cares of his office.

A fellow guest at the Grove Park Inn in Asheville was Calvin Coolidge, who had been elected Vice President on the Harding-Coolidge ticket in November and was vacationing before taking office in March. He and Mr. Hopkins revived an acquaintanceship from Boston days, when Coolidge was lieutenant governor of Massachusetts and Mr. Hopkins was with the telephone company. Spotting Mr. Hopkins upon arrival at the inn, Coolidge shook off reporters who descended upon him by saying, "Excuse me, gentlemen, but I am late for an appointment with that man." The two New Englanders took daily walks together, and far from being "Silent Cal" on those occasions the Vice President-elect was a very talkative man, particularly and repeatedly on the subject of Senator Henry Cabot Lodge's having blocked, as he believed, his securing of the Republican Presidential nomination at the party's convention in Chicago the previous June. In addition to walking with Mr. Coolidge by day, Mr. Hopkins had the pleasure after supper of dancing with Mrs. Coolidge, her spouse being a confirmed non-dancer. It was, however, a pleasure of brief duration each evening, for Mr. Coolidge, who believed in retiring early, would after the passage of but a short time suddenly march out on the dance floor, take his wife by the hand, and say, "Grace, time to hitch up and head home." Thereupon Mrs. Coolidge would look at Mr. Hopkins, smile resignedly, and depart without protest or hesitation. An equally memorable happening was that Mr. Hopkins' golf game flourished in North Carolina and he went all the way to the finals in the Asheville Country Club's handicap tournament.

After Calvin Coolidge became President of the United States, Mr. Hopkins visited him at the White House several times. On one occasion, Coolidge summoned him to a private meeting and said he wanted his opinion of an idea he was mulling over, that of adding a Secretary of Education to the Cabinet. Mr. Hopkins replied that he didn't like the idea at all, mainly because he was afraid it would lead to government interference with private education. Mr. Coolidge listened impassively to all his guest had to say. Then, as the session concluded, he said simply, "Well, you've just talked yourself out of a job." Mr. Hopkins was never sure how seriously Coolidge meant that comment, but it was his first Cabinet "offer."

President Hopkins returned from his North Carolina vacation in March 1921, just in time to encounter a minor alumni outburst over his having been featured in a full-page newspaper advertisement promoting *Red Book* magazine. He had written a testimonial as a favor to his friend, Editor Karl Harriman, and some alumni thought it was undignified—a criticism that lost some of its impact when Booth Tarkington and President

Angell of Yale subsequently appeared in the same advertising series. Mr. Hopkins took the carping in stride, but not without a rejoinder: "I do have an overpowering inclination about once in so often to do something to indicate to some of our alumni that a man does not bind himself body and soul to drab neutrality on all subjects even if he does accept a college presidency."

Drab neutrality was never a Hopkins characteristic, and the alumni had had previous opportunities to learn that. Following World War I he had been an active and public supporter of the League of Nations, and he had been in the press again with a denunciation of the New York legislature for expelling five Socialist members, and then with a denunciation of the raids that Attorney General A. Mitchell Palmer was conducting against "alien radicals." He called the raids a "witch hunt motivated by hysterical fears," and declared that the arbitrary deportation of immigrants suspected of being Bolsheviks was a mockery of American justice. Throw Bolshevism open to public scrutiny, he advised, and then there would be nothing to fear. American labor would never succumb to it, because working men were too educated for that to happen and because unionization was a safeguard against radicalism. "Abhorrent as some aspects of radicalism might be," he told the New Hampshire Constitutional Convention in January 1920, "they are still not so hateful that the United States can afford to adopt the methods of the Czar and tear men away from their families on the word of some immigration sub-official." And in a letter to Newton D. Baker he wrote, "I do not believe that we are called upon . . . to absorb such indigestible material as is represented by the genuine ultra Red. The method, however, by which it was undertaken to correct this evil was, to my mind, subversive of all for which Government stands and if allowed to pass unrebuked was available for the suppression of anything any time to which a governing group might have antagonism."

This public position led, in turn, to denunciation of Mr. Hopkins himself. He was called "a parlor Bolshevik" by the conservatives, some alumni among them, but there was an offsetting chorus of approval from liberals in the country. Some months later, when a trustee expressed concern about the danger of Bolshevism, Mr. Hopkins jokingly told him, "If the Reds are going to take everything anyway, it might be a good policy to blow all we have before they can touch it."

In May of 1919 President Hopkins jumped into another public controversy when he gave his support to Professors Charles H. Judd and Leon C. Marshall of the University of Chicago, who were under attack from the Education Committee of the National Industrial Conference Board because in the civics lessons they prepared for use in public schools they gave equal attention to labor's side in their treatment of the question of labor versus management.

In May 1921 President Hopkins was in the news once more when he answered Thomas A. Edison, who had criticized higher education because college students had done poorly on a factual questionnaire Edison had distributed. The ability to think, not to know trivial facts, is the aim of education, Mr. Hopkins said. Any business picking a man on the basis of a test such as Edison's would be making a mistake, he told a reporter from the *New York World*.

Some months later, President Hopkins found himself being quoted in the press again, although he hadn't intended to be. As a part of the premillenialist movement, the Committee of Nine of the Northern Baptist Convention had written to him urging that he weed out heretical members of the faculty who did not teach the Bible as literal truth. A copy of Mr. Hopkins' stinging reply was given to an interested Dartmouth minister, who proceeded, without clearance, to read it at a church meeting in Concord. A newspaper reporter was present, which resulted in a request from the Associated Press and others that the exchange of letters be released. President Hopkins finally provided the desired text so that newspaper accounts would at least be accurate. He rejected the position of the Baptist extremists in very strong terms, saying, "The minute that education becomes something besides a sincere and open-minded search for truth, it has become a pernicious and demoralizing influence rather than an aid to society and an improver of civilization." He branded the committee's thinking as archaic and in general let go with all guns. An editorial in *The New York Times* agreed with him, but declared that the Hopkins broadside "seems rather more formidable than the target requires."

One further demonstration that "drab neutrality" was not Mr. Hopkins' style came in the spring of 1922, when college presidents were surveyed on the question of Prohibition. Of the 158 presidents canvassed, 136 said they were in favor of it, but President Hopkins was not one of them. Although he had approved of Prohibition in 1918, he now had his doubts. Widespread violation of the Volstead Act was encouraging disrespect for all law, he feared. In a May 1922 letter to Wilder D. Quint, he wrote, ". . . as long as my friends among the captains of industry, the judges, and the men of professional repute and wealth have their cellars stocked with booze, I object to legislation and conditions which deny even beer to the laboring man—and to the academic official." His change of opinion was brought about, in part, by the difficulty of controlling the liquor problem in the colleges, Dartmouth among them. College campuses had become fertile ground for bootlegging, with student ingenuity finding many ways to beat the law, and at Dartmouth in June 1920 a shocking tragedy had occurred when a senior, Henry Maroney, was shot and killed by another student, Robert Meads, in a quarrel over a bottle of liquor. It was a grim period for Dartmouth and a trying one for President Hopkins, who was personally blamed by Meads' father in statements so libelous that they finally required a public answer. A policy of holding nothing back from the press was ordered by Mr. Hopkins, and although the publicity was intense, it was of short duration and the incident slipped into history.

A happy event for President Hopkins, after he had returned from his southern vacation, was the inauguration of the Dartmouth Alumni Lectures on the Guernsey Center Moore Foundation immediately after Commencement in June 1921. As a memorial to his son, Henry L. Moore, 1877, a former trustee, gave an endowment for the lectures, which put into effect an idea Mr. Hopkins had presented in his inaugural address. The first lecture series for the alumni extended over eight days following Commencement, with daily lectures by Roscoe Pound, dean of the Harvard Law School, and by Ralph Adams Cram, architect and commentator on social problems. The second set of lectures, in 1922, was given by Professor William Lyon Phelps of Yale and Professor Charles A. Beard of Columbia. Later, the Guernsey Center Moore Lectures were scheduled during the college year and thus lost their original alumni character.

The years 1921 and 1922 saw a number of developments relating to undergraduates. The sophomore Green Key Society was founded in May 1921 and was patterned after the University of Washington's Knights of the Hook, who had been student hosts to the Dartmouth football team the previous fall. Green Key, subsequently changed to a junior society, has ever since extended personal hospitality to athletic teams and others visiting the College. The Dartmouth Outing Club's chain of cabins was enlarged in 1921–22, and by that year the intercollegiate athletic program had grown to the point where Dartmouth teams were competing in twenty-one sports, compared with only nine sports the year before Mr. Hopkins became president. Something that President Hopkins had long wanted to do was to remove the restriction against student use of the College's athletic facilities on Sunday, but he knew that most of the trustees had strong feelings about the Sabbath. He made his case, however, in the spring of 1922, pointing out the great need for more recreational opportunities for students on the weekends. The trustees agreed to open things up for the afternoon only, and without outside publicity. Mr. Hopkins had expected John King Lord to oppose his idea, but it was Professor Lord who was strongly for it and who even suggested that maybe the College should think of scheduling athletic contests on Sunday.

President Hopkins did not conduct the daily chapel service as regularly as Dr. Tucker had, but he often was the speaker. He had a deeply religious nature, and because of his family background he was well versed in the Bible, from which he usually drew his chapel themes. He made a special effort to meet with student groups when invited, and the gatherings he enjoyed most were the informal ones at D.O.C. cabins. In May 1922 he instituted a series of senior class meetings at which he spoke on the problems, policies, and aims of the administration. When he gave a year-end summary of undergraduate life in 1922, he expressed his pleasure over a greater appreciation of scholastic achievement, greater group responsibility for the quality of student life, and the more active role Palaeopitus was taking in the governance of student affairs.

In the summer of 1922 President Hopkins made his first trip abroad, to visit Edward Tuck. One year earlier Mr. Parkhurst had suggested that he make such a trip, but Mr. Hopkins was reluctant to go for fear that his visit would be interpreted as a fishing expedition for more money. "I should like to meet him on the plain basis of a Dartmouth alumnus who has done a lot for the College to whom it would be a pleasure to bring a most intimate account of what the College is doing," he said. In 1922, however, there arose an issue on which the trustees wanted Mr. Tuck's opinion, and it provided a reason, other than the general one stated by the president, for making the trip to Paris. Dartmouth's investment assets were mainly in bonds, which were safe but which had a low rate of return and no chance of appreciating in value. Mr. Hopkins wanted to realize more income and to provide for growth in market value by shifting a larger part of the College's portfolio into common stocks. The board was extremely hesitant about it and wondered, "What would Mr. Tuck say?"

During the first four years of the Hopkins administration Mr. Tuck had made his gifts and had communicated with the College through Trustee Benjamin Ames Kimball, a close friend who visited him regularly in France. He corresponded with President Hopkins from time to time, and then after Mr. Kimball's death in 1920 he began dealing directly with the president, making a meeting between the two desirable. To cover the cost of President Hopkins' coming to see him he sent a check for $2,000, as he had done for Dr. Tucker and Dr. Nichols. Up to 1922 Mr. Tuck had given Dartmouth $1.6-million for endowment and another $200,000 for plant. He and Dr. Tucker had roomed together in college, and in 1899, six years after Dr. Tucker became president, Mr. Tuck unexpectedly and entirely on his own sent $300,000 to the College to endow better pay for the president and faculty. That was the beginning of a long series of benefactions that totaled $4.7-million before his death in 1938. Dartmouth's Amos Tuck School of Business Administration, the first graduate school of business in the country, was founded by Edward Tuck in memory of his father, a graduate in the Class of 1835 and a trustee from 1857 to 1866. His gifts for many years were made to the Amos Tuck Endowment Fund, until in October 1922 he suggested that its name be changed to the Edward Tuck Endowment Fund, since his father had an appropriate memorial in the business school.

A native of Exeter, New Hampshire, Mr. Tuck entered the consular service in Paris the year after he finished college. He soon moved into banking, with the house of Munroe and Company, and although he became the head of the firm's New York branch, he divided his time evenly between New York and Paris. Upon retirement from banking in 1881, he made Paris his permanent home. Mr. Tuck was an astute investor, and the growth in the value of his own holdings of bank and railroad stocks made him a very wealthy man. He was financial adviser on American investments for many notables and government officials of France. His charitable acts and his gifts to the French nation were on a grand scale, and he was by common accord the leading foreign citizen of France, which revered both Mr. Tuck and his wife and bestowed upon them its highest honors. The Tuck home in Paris and their Chateau de Vert-Mont in the Commune of Reuil-Malmaison were gathering places for the leading personages of France, as well as for the foremost citizens of this country when they visited France.

Mr. Hopkins sailed for Europe on the *Rotterdam* on July 22, 1922, and was in France and England for six weeks. He first went to visit the Tucks and was their guest at Malmaison. Mr. Hopkins recalled that for a couple of days he and Mr. Tuck did not feel at ease with each other. For one thing, Mr. Hopkins did not exactly fulfill Mr. Tuck's preconception of a college president, and then there was between them quite a difference in age, Mr. Tuck being within one month of eighty and Mr. Hopkins being forty-five. But they soon found that they had much in common and the strongest bond of all was their common concern for the future of Dartmouth College. Out of this first get-together was to develop an intimate and congenial relationship. In the words of Dartmouth's historian, Leon Burr Richardson, ". . . a tie of the strongest personal affection soon united them—Mr. Tuck, his immediate family largely gone, regarding the head of the College almost as a son and the institution itself as his own responsibility, without, however, in the slightest way interfering in its management."

Mr. Hopkins during his first visit with Mr. Tuck in 1922 laid before him the question of stocks versus bonds in the management of the College's investment assets. Mr. Tuck's answer was emphatic: "You tell the trustees of Dartmouth College I never owned a damn bond in my life, and I never expect to." But more than the shared view about the virtue of stocks, a shared propensity for enjoying life made the two men companionable. They had fun together. Mr. Hopkins recalled one evening in Paris when he and Mr. Tuck were supposed to go to the opera. Upon ascertaining that Mr. Hopkins had no more desire to go the the opera than he had, Mr. Tuck proposed the Folies Bergere instead and then sent the chauffeur to pick up an opera program they could leave conspicuously on a table upon their return home that night. As they were going down the aisle to their front seats at the Folies, some Dartmouth men in the balcony spotted them and immediately rendered a cheer for Prexy Hopkins. Mr. Tuck enjoyed President Hopkins' discomfiture, but his turn was to come. The cast of the revue was aware that the famous Mr. Tuck was in the audience, and as one scantily clad demoiselle swung out over the orchestra seats on a wire, she ticked him with her foot and exclaimed, "Eddie, where have you been keeping yourself? I've missed you!"

Mr. Tuck had a sparkle in his eye and a lively sense of humor. Two amusing incidents that happened during Hopkins visits had to do with dogs. The Tucks always kept dogs and at Malmaison they maintained a small burial ground for them. A widow from a nearby estate had been allowed to bury a favorite pet there too, and one day she arrived with flowers to place on its grave. As soon as he heard about this, Mr. Tuck ordered the Rolls Royce brought around and then he gathered up a large bouquet of roses. "Where on earth are you going?" Mrs. Tuck asked him. "I'm driving to the cemetery to put these on Jack's grave," he replied. Jack was the widow's departed husband. The other anecdote had a Paris locale. Mr. Tuck each night before retiring took his poodles for a walk on the Champs Élysees. One night one of the poodles ran away and could not be found, but Mr. Tuck was not too concerned because he was confident of finding it the next morning. After breakfast he went out looking and was lucky enough to encounter a gendarme who told him he knew who had his dog—a *fille de joie* who resided not too far away. Mr. Tuck went to where she lived, found the poodle being well looked after, and as an expression of his appreciation left fifty francs on the mantel. When he reported all this to Mrs. Tuck and Mr. Hopkins at lunch, Mrs. Tuck's main concern was for the girl. "Ed, are you sure fifty francs was enough?" she asked him. With a straight face, he answered, "Well, it's all I ever used to leave."

After the 1922 visit, President Hopkins went to see Mr. Tuck every two or three years. As an indication of his regard for Dartmouth's president, Mr. Tuck insisted that he should have an appropriate residence in Hanover, and he made gifts aggregating $132,000 to build and furnish the President's House, which was ready in 1925 and is still in use today. He stopped his gifts to Exeter Academy because he felt a visit there by President Hopkins had not been accorded suitable importance. In 1925 he added $725,000 to the Edward Tuck Endowment Fund, which followed an addition of $200,000 made in 1923 and other gifts of lesser amounts. When the annual income from his endowment fund did not come up to what he thought it should, he several times made up the difference out of his own pocket.

President Hopkins' European trip was concluded with several weeks in Great Britain. He made a special point of visiting a number of English universities, and while at Oxford University he was able to spend some time with the poet, Franklin McDuffee, 1921, for whom he had arranged a Dartmouth graduate fellowship and for whom he had high hopes as a future teacher of English at Dartmouth. Mr. Hopkins then sailed for home aboard the *Samaria*, which left Liverpool on September 6. During the homeward passage he had time to give some thought to his address for the opening of college later that month.

The Convocation address he delivered on September 21 was the most provocative of his career, setting off nationwide discussion of his assertion that, with the deluge of young people seeking to go to college, opportunities of higher education ought to be restricted to "an aristocracy of brains, made up of men intellectually alert and intellectually eager." The phrase "aristocracy of brains" caused the furor. Mr. Hopkins later said that he used it on purpose, in order to make an issue of the large number of students in American colleges with no serious purpose in being there. It is not unlikely that the phrase was prompted, in some degree, by his visits to Oxford and Cambridge, where attendance by another kind of aristocracy was a long tradition in the life of those famous universities.

This was the controversial portion of the Hopkins address: "It would be incompatible with all of the conceptions of democracy to assume that the privilege of higher education should be restricted to any class defined by the accident of birth or by the fortuitous circumstance of the possession of wealth, but there is such a thing as an aristocracy of brains, made up of men intellectually alert and intellectually eager, to whom increasingly the opportunities of higher education ought to be restricted, if democracy is to become a quality product rather than simply a quantity one, and if excellence and effectiveness are to displace the mediocrity towards which democracy has such a tendency to skid."

The foregoing had been preceded by the declaration: "Too many men are going to college! The opportunities for securing an education by way of the college course are definitely a privilege and not at all a universal right. The funds available for appropriation to the uses of institutions of higher learning are not limitless and cannot be made so, whether their origin be sought in the resources of public taxation or in the securable benefactions for the enhancing of private endowments. It consequently becomes essential that a working theory be sought that will operate with some degree of accuracy to define the individuals who shall make up the group to whom, in justice to the public good, the privilege shall be extended, and to specify those from whom the privilege should be withheld! . . .

"We hear much of men seeking an education, but too often they are only seeking membership in a social organization which has reputation for affording an education, from which reputation they expect to benefit, if they can avoid being detached from the association. The assumption would be humorous if it were not so serious, that enrollment with a college requires that the college shall either force education upon the individual man or surreptitiously bait him to it, rather than that he should crave and at the cost of any effort possess himself of the utmost which the college can give."

Elsewhere in his address, certainly one of the most purposefully prepared during his presidential years, Mr. Hopkins spoke of the "mental strength and moral fortitude" to which Dartmouth men should aspire; and he added that the principles he was about to enunciate "are involved particularly at Dartmouth in such policies as the restriction of enrollment, the selective process of admission, and the permanent elimination from the College membership of men incompetent or unwilling to qualify according to the standards the College seeks to maintain." This last part referred to the faculty's action of the previous fall, denying readmission to any man separated for scholastic failure.

The word "aristocracy" unleashed a flood of egalitarian rhetoric. President Hopkins' view was attacked as un-American, undemocratic, snobbish, and elitist, and as a denial of the equal chance to which American youth was entitled. The leaders of public-supported education pounced on him, and particularly strong criticism came from John J. Tigert, U. S. Commissioner of Education, and William H. Allen, director of the Institute for Public Service. The president's office had an incomplete count of the editorials devoted to the speech, but 180 were assembled by the president's staff, along with news stories and commentaries from Canada, England, and other foreign countries. Of Dartmouth's president, one editorial stated, ". . . he hurled a boomerang which is extremely liable to return and strike him on his learned pate." Along with the critics there were many who applauded President Hopkins. In considering the logic of his speech, it needs to be taken into account that only 3 percent of the population was college-trained at that time and going to college was not the inalienable right it is believed to be today.

At the invitation of the *Philadelphia Ledger*, Mr. Hopkins wrote a follow-up article for the issue of October 5, 1922. In it he stuck to his guns and said: "If one makes the statement that membership within a college is a privilege and not a right, he does not say that opportunity for education should be denied to any man. The statement simply suggests that varying kinds and varying amounts of education are due to varying groups, according to their respective abilities to absorb benefits. It would seem to be fairly obvious that there is no advantage to anybody in utilizing the college process for a man who cannot or will not benefit by it, to the impairment of its effectiveness for all those men who are capable of deriving advantage from it to become more serviceable citizens. . . .

"In order that the college may not be held accountable for that which it is not humanly or spiritually possible for it to do, let us not load it with the responsibility of meeting a dictum pleasant to the ear but without foundation in fact—that the college owes it to the idea of democracy to accept all men as candidates for its specialized form of education, regardless of their intellectual aptitudes. Let us not allow the argument to stand that in restricting its efforts within selected groups, who can most advantageously utilize it, the college is making higher education impossible to those who are entitled to it and is condemning vast numbers of those who are capable and ambitious to ignorance and hopeless social handicap."

Recalling 1922 as a particularly strenuous year in his life, Mr. Hopkins said, "I had three balls in the air at once—the Selective Process of Admission, the aristocracy of brains thing, and the Chicago presidency." The third ball was the effort of the trustees of the University of Chicago to persuade him to become their president, an effort which had become public knowledge to some extent. Mr. Hopkins had not shown any receptivity to the Chicago offer, but neither had he declined it firmly. The university was therefore pressing its invitation with tenacity. The approach had been made to Mr. Hopkins before he left on his European trip that summer, and he was not inclined to count it entirely a coincidence that a professor from Chicago occupied the stateroom next to his on the *Rotterdam*. Then, while he was visiting the Tucks, Harold Swift, chairman of the Chicago trustees, telephoned Mr. Tuck and said he was in Paris and would like to come to Malmaison to call on him. "What can he want?" Mr. Tuck wondered. "I can tell you," Mr. Hopkins replied. "He wants you to persuade me to be president of the University of Chicago."

Upon his return to the College from Europe, President Hopkins thought it best to bring the matter before the Dartmouth trustees. If he had ever had any serious inclination to move to another institution—he was at that time seemingly on every institution's list of prospective presidents and Johns Hopkins, Minnesota, and California actually sounded him out—Chicago probably would have been the place. The spirit of educational innovation was there, and large financial resources were available. Unquestionably the greatest attraction for Mr. Hopkins was the fact that many members of the university senate wanted graduate school funds used to humanize graduate education to a radical extent and to bring professional scholarship into closer relationship to men and life. The seriousness with which Mr. Hopkins considered the Chicago offer was indicated by his meeting in New York in early November with four of his closest friends—Natt Emerson, Clarence McDavitt, Joseph Gilman, and Thomas Streeter—to discuss what he ought to do. Mr. Rockefeller and the General Education Board wanted him to accept. A Chicago delegation, headed by Mr. Swift, met with him in Boston in November and told him that by vote of the Chicago trustees they were authorized to make a formal offer of the presidency. Other meetings were held with groups from the theology and medical schools, and on November 10 a third group including Julius Rosenthal sought to persuade him to take the Chicago assignment.

Mr. Hopkins finally decided he was not a "professional college president" and that he did not aspire to any greater position than being head of Dartmouth College, where he could devote himself to the mission of the undergraduate liberal college. He also felt that the Dartmouth trustees had taken the hazard of an unusual action in making him president and that he would be abandoning a trust and an unfinished task if he were to leave. The Chicago trustees in January 1923 elected Ernest D. Burton, sixty-three, president of the university, hoping Mr. Hopkins would reconsider after he had completed more of his program at Dartmouth.

The many expressions of relief and happiness over President Hopkins' Chicago decision were an indication of the place he had come to occupy in the life of the College and in the minds of Dartmouth men. He had not yet arrived at that period of his presidency when he was spoken of affectionately as "Hoppy" and considered the embodiment of Dartmouth by virtually all Dartmouth men, but he was, after six years, solidly in command as leader of the College, and he had established himself not only at Dartmouth but also among the most respected thinkers and doers in American higher education.

The pervasive influence that President Hopkins personally was having upon the College was observed by Christopher Morley, bookman and essayist, when he visited Hanover in the spring of 1922. Upon his return to New York, Morley wrote in a published article: "The virtues of colleges are peculiarly dependent upon the character of the man in charge; and it seemed to us that Dartmouth is excellently happy in its President. It is an outworn tag, we admit, and yet, for once, the old phrase 'a gentleman and a scholar' seems to fit the case. That singularly felicitous blend of intellectual tastes, business training and shrewdness, humane and humorous ease in personal relations—an unmistakable union of conscience and courage and sincerity—these are the qualities that any visitor must admiringly enjoy in Ernest Martin Hopkins."

On October 6, 1922, the sixth anniversary of his inauguration, President Hopkins received warm approval from *The Dartmouth*. "Short as has been his term in point of years," the student daily said editorially, "it has been throughout a period of change in the life of the College. Much progress has been made in all lines, owing in no uncertain measure to the constructive policies and able leadership of the president himself." After a catalogue of the gains made by the College on all fronts, the editorial concluded, "By his wise leadership and far-seeing policies in carrying on the notable line of the Wheelock Succession he is making of Dartmouth an enduring college."

If 1922 was an eventful and consolidating year for President Hopkins, it also was a year of great personal loss for him. General Streeter, the trustee to whom he was closest and on whom he depended most heavily, died December 11, 1922. General Streeter's death ended a very concrete tie with the Tucker administration; from that point on, the Hopkins administration became more an era of its own. Mr. Parkhurst and Mr. Thayer were to continue as trustees for some years to come, and the board was to acquire new members with whom Mr. Hopkins was to have close working and personal ties—notably, William R. Gray, 1904, John R. McLane, 1907, Victor M. Cutter, 1903, and Edward S. French, 1906—but a relationship such as the one with General Streeter was a unique thing, not to be duplicated. General Streeter, in writing to Mr. Hopkins, had customarily addressed him as "My dear boy" or "Dear Old Man," and had signed himself "Affectionately yours" or "Your faithful and admiring backer."

Knowing that General Streeter was seriously ill, President Hopkins had written to him in October 1922: "Dear Best of Friends, I want you to know, if it may be of interest to you, the depth of affection which I have always felt for you and always shall, and the extent to which any success of my administration here at Dartmouth has been enhanced by the knowledge that I had in you the same sort of militant and indefatigable supporter that reassured and strengthened Dr. Tucker. . . . No man can estimate what the value of your work has been to Dartmouth College, for it is beyond calculation." Shortly before his death, General Streeter sent for "Hop" and as his last words to him said, "I've never been a religious man in the ordinary way; Dartmouth has been a good enough religion for me." In his will he left $50,000 to Dartmouth College and $10,000 to Mr. Hopkins personally as a final mark of his fatherly affection for the man he was so sure would carry on the ideals of Dr. Tucker and be a great president of Dartmouth in his own right. Mr. Hopkins also inherited General Streeter's raccoon coat. Although it was several sizes too large for him and came down to his shoe tops, he wore it, almost as a ritual, to home hockey games for many years.

The Man and Administrator

I N their recollections of Mr. Hopkins, men and women are remarkably
unanimous in speaking of him first as a person and then as president
of Dartmouth College. He was a man of memorable character and
warm humanity, and the impress of his personality upon others was so
engaging that it is not surprising he is remembered, above everything else,
for the kind of man he was.

Someone has defined an intellectual as a person who loves all mankind
but cannot be bothered with people. Mr. Hopkins was seldom classified as
an intellectual, and according to that definition he would not have qualified
anyway; he cared too much about people. It was his interest in all manner
of men, his respect and consideration for them as fellow human beings,
that was the core element of his mastery of human relations. In his pioneer
work with industrial workers he had enunciated the principle that the only
humane way to deal with others is in units of one, and he never deviated
from it during all the succeeding years which took him into other fields of
endeavor. A natural gift for human relations is by no means uncommon,
but there was something special about that innate quality in Mr. Hopkins.
It came from his sensitivity to the individuality and self-respect of the
other person, whatever the other person's status in life, so that conversing
or working or being with him was never an ordinary experience. This
democratic spirit did not make him an egalitarian, for he believed a man
had to earn his place in life and that leadership and preference belonged to
the intelligent and the competent; but, even so, every person was a fellow
human being deserving of understanding and consideration.

His ability to establish an immediate personal relationship combined
with his other qualities to give President Hopkins a remarkably varied
circle of friends. One of his fellow college presidents once remarked to
him, "You know the damnedest people." Mr. Hopkins had a special liking

for colorful persons. It was characteristic of him, as a baseball fan, to be interested in the Brooklyn Dodgers and the Gashouse Gang of St. Louis, as well as the Boston Red Sox, closer to home. At the same time, there were critics who thought he associated too much with captains of industry and the very rich. He liked the company of business executives, partly because he had been on his way to being one himself and perhaps had never completely shaken off regret that that part of his career had not taken its natural course. His many erudite friends in the world of education were balanced by the Pullman porters and dining-car waiters whom he got to know in his frequent travels and whose everyday views about American life he found interesting. Although his gracious and open manner made it easy to have a friendly relationship with him, one did not presume familiarity. Without any outward display of it, there was an inherent dignity about him, and one readily sensed it. Even his closest friends, who knew him in his most relaxed moments, recognized an element of reserve in all his moods and actions. One of them described this as "a controlled ebullience, a quiet gaiety."

President Hopkins was one of the least pretentious of men. It was natural for him to be himself in all circumstances, and since he repeatedly said that being president of Dartmouth College was the most honorable position to which he could aspire, he had the kind of modesty that derives its genuineness from self-assurance and happiness with one's lot. In his case, it became almost a refrain to have others say that it was a pleasure, and something of a surprise, to meet a college president who was so far from being a stuffed shirt. Intimates of the family recall that Mrs. Hopkins was a salutary influence when her husband got out of character and showed the slightest sign of arrogance or pomposity. With laughter or a quip she would bring him back to his normal self. One manifestation of Mr. Hopkins' avoidance of pretension was his rule against the title of "Doctor" before his name, although he had the right to use it. One year the Hopkins family had the help of a Jamaican houseboy, who took leave from his graduate studies at Columbia University in order to earn money. Mr. Hopkins, after hearing him answer the telephone with "Dr. Hopkins' residence," asked him to say "Mr. Hopkins" in the future. "But you have several doctoral degrees, don't you?" the houseboy asked. Mr. Hopkins admitted that he did, but pointed out that they were "all honorary and not earned." "I understand," the houseboy replied, with new respect for his employer, but he probably did not understand that Mr. Hopkins had used this simple explanation to cover his ingrained dislike of any show of importance. As a railroad director, he frequently was offered red-carpet treatment when word went ahead that he was to travel on a certain train, but he invariably refused this and preferred to be treated as an ordinary passenger. This was sometimes a disappointment to traveling companions from his office, who were curious about the sort of blessings that V.I.P. status would produce.

Had he been aware that he was creating disappointment for his associates, Mr. Hopkins unquestionably would have suffered the special privilege. Thoughtfulness was another of his virtues. Untold numbers of Dartmouth faculty members, students, and others at the College were pleasantly surprised, and heartened, to receive on occasion a personal note from him. Russell R. (Cotty) Larmon, who was his assistant for seven years, remembered leaving the office at the end of the working day and coming back at 6:30 or so to find the desk light burning in the president's office and Mr. Hopkins busily penning notes and short letters to be mailed out by his secretary the next morning. These were messages of appreciation or congratulation or encouragement, and they were always personal and graciously expressed. The pleasure a professor or staff member got from such a message was sometimes increased by the enclosure of a College check and a word from Mr. Hopkins that he believed, from what he had heard, that the recipient could find use for it.

In appearance, Mr. Hopkins, at five-eleven, gave the impression of being taller than he really was. He had an erect and vigorous bearing and looked more the man of affairs than the academician. He had a high forehead devoid of hair, dark and heavy eyebrows, and a mouth that was slightly askew because of a deep cut he had received on his upper lip as a boy. His manner of walking was aptly described by Professor Stearns Morse, whose house at the north end of the campus President Hopkins passed almost daily on his way to the office: "He had a distinctive walk, which I can best describe as a sloping walk, throwing in leisurely fashion his weight from one foot to the other."

It has been mentioned that Mr. Hopkins did not fit Mr. Tuck's preconception of a college president, when they first met in Paris. Mr. Tuck was a gentleman of the old school, courtly in manner and always elegantly attired, although the spirit underneath was anything but formal. Elegance was not for Mr. Hopkins, but he had his own personal style, and as his presidential years went on, he became more and more a man of distinction in both appearance and presence. That distinguished air is well caught in a Bachrach photograph taken in 1931, showing him seated in the living room of the President's House with Bruce, his Scottish deerhound, at his feet. He was partial to big dogs and later had an English bull mastiff and also a husky. Mr. Hopkins dressed well and had a large wardrobe. He owned all the business suits, dinner jackets, and full evening dress required by his position, but he appeared most characteristically in sporty tweed suits, one or two of them with plus-fours. When the outfit was right for them he wore spats. On special occasions he appeared in striped trousers and cutaway, with which his bowler went well. He was a man who could carry a cane without affectation, and one usually hung on his arm when shipboard photographers showed him sailing for Europe or arriving back in the States. Nothing was more a sartorial trademark, however, than his gay and colorful neckties, betokening a youthful spirit. Most of his ties were custom made by a lady in Chicago. She sent him swatches of material in bright colors and swirling patterns, and some of Mr. Hopkins' bolder choices could be attributed, according to his daughter Ann, to the fact that he was partially color blind. He sometimes gave these handmade ties as Christmas presents, and recipients wore them with an air of bravado.

The chance to get into old clothes was enjoyed almost as much as the companionship when Mr. Hopkins was with his fishing cronies at the St. Bernard Club in Canada or in Maine. He had no interest in hunting, although in the earlier years of his presidency he sometimes went gunning for rabbits. One faculty member thought rabbit hunting was undignified for the president of Dartmouth College, but Mr. Hopkins remarked that he had no taste for killing deer and that he couldn't afford to go to Africa to shoot lions and tigers. One day when he was driving to Canaan, near Hanover, and was dressed in his old hunting clothes, he picked up a freshman between Hanover and Lebanon. When asked why he was on the road, the student answered that "the old women in the administration" didn't allow freshmen to have cars and he therefore had to keep his in Lebanon. Upon being deposited in Lebanon the young man somehow became aware that it was President Hopkins who had picked him up, and for the next two years he avoided Mr. Hopkins by crossing to the other side of the street each time he saw him coming. Finally, Mr. Hopkins sent a note telling him there was a statute of limitations and that he should drop by the office for a chat and reassurance that the freshman-year incident was not being held against him. Another student anecdote Mr. Hopkins liked to recount had to do with a sophomore who got him out of bed late one night and, as part of a fraternity initiation, asked him to autograph an egg. The student was shaking so that Mr. Hopkins had to tell him, "Look, if you don't hold still, the egg will break and this night's work will be wasted for both of us."

President Hopkins' sense of humor was one of the things that attracted people to him. He laughed easily, took delight in hearing stories and telling them, and saw the humorous side of happenings that others might take too seriously. The sort of personal incident which greatly amused him was one that took place in Cleveland when he and Fletcher Andrews, a prominent Dartmouth alumnus in that city, went bowling. A group of working girls arrived to engage in a league match, and one of them approached Mr. Hopkins and said, "Move over, baby, we need this alley." That was the high spot of the evening for him.

Life was meant to be enjoyed, President Hopkins told the Dartmouth students on many occasions. In his Convocation address of 1929 he advised them that being serious did not necessitate being solemn or dull, and his prescription for surviving life's difficulties was a sense of humor. His own enjoyment of life was immense, and although he was gregarious and had most fun while in the company of others, he found pleasure in contemplative things, as well. His greatest joy was books. His father started him reading at an early age, and the first money Mr. Hopkins earned as a boy was invested in a book. At Dartmouth the influence of Professor "Clothespins" Richardson so greatly enhanced his love of books and reading that they became an indispensable part of his life. Neighbors saw the light burning in his study in the old president's house on College Street long after midnight. Later in life, when bronchial asthma afflicted him, he could breathe more easily if propped up in bed, and in that fashion he did a tremendous amount of night-time reading. As his interests broadened, he favored non-fiction over fiction, but nothing attracted him as much as a good mystery story. In a memo to Dean Bill in 1926 he recommended three books as indispensable for the time—Walter Lippmann's *Public Opinion*, James Harvey Robinson's *The Mind in the Making*, and Alfred North Whitehead's *Science and the Modern World*. He told the trustees they would find *Jurgen* stimulating to thought. The one writer he favored above all others was William James, whom he described as "one of the most fascinating and one of the most convincing writers I have ever read." Robert Louis Stevenson was another great favorite. His experience with Ruskin is enlightening as to his reading habits. As an undergraduate, he had found Ruskin incomprehensible, and ten years later he had no better success when he tried to follow a friend's enthusiastic recommendation and made a new attempt. Five years after that, as he told it, he picked up the volume *The Seven Lamps of Architecture* in order to verify a quotation, and all of a sudden he found Ruskin lucid and inspiring. For the next ten nights he read Ruskin with the zest with which he devoured mysteries. The passion he had for books and the life of the mind was not as generally known as were some other facets of his character, but it was a deep and enduring part of him. Despite all the reading he managed, he felt that he was not doing as much as he should. In a letter to an alumnus, he wrote that a multitude of duties were making the modern college president illiterate. This was far from true in his case.

In his reading, as in nearly everything else, President Hopkins followed his own path. This spirit of independence was one of the most pronounced aspects of his character. It existed primarily because he had the courage to do what his own common sense told him to do, not what custom or established consensus suggested he should do. Trustee Philip S. Marden, who knew Mr. Hopkins intimately, wrote in one of his newspaper editorials, "If I had to select a single outstanding characteristic of President Hopkins, I should without hesitation name that most uncommon of all human qualifications—common sense." Mr. Hopkins' natural inclination to do his own thinking made him a fence-jumper and a difficult man to label—which was fine with him, because he hated labels on people. Although generally and deservedly considered a liberal, he was at times attacked as an arch-conservative for his views. Whatever he happened to think, he was honest and open about it, which got him into hot water often enough.

President Hopkins was more influential as an educational philosopher than he gave himself credit for, but he viewed his job as primarily that of administrator, in which role he was extraordinarily successful. He earned a great reputation for administrative skill, a mastery that was invariably mentioned when the press or others praised him. Mr. Hopkins' executive ability was made all the more effective by the human qualities that came into play in the exercise of his leadership. When he spoke at the inauguration of his brother Louis as president of Wabash College, he warned that anything tending "to dehumanize or make impersonal the work of the college president should be held to be anathema."

All of Mr. Hopkins' experience led him to the conviction that people are the most valuable asset of any enterprise. He chose his associates with care, and he had a sixth sense in picking men. He was a good judge of their potential, and often saw inherent possibilities that others missed. He was willing to gamble in the choice of faculty and staff associates, as he was in other areas of the president's responsibility. Writing to Franklin McDuffee at Oxford in 1922, he declared, "A college president's success, after all, is perhaps more essentially determined by the intelligence with which he gambles on men than in any other way, and I insist that one who deals with men must gamble, because the thing can never be reduced to a science."

Once his administrative associates had been selected, Mr. Hopkins gave them his trust and left it entirely up to them to conduct their day-by-day operations. If he kept an eye on them, it was in a way that protected their feelings. "Cotty" Larmon recalled that when he was a young assistant in the president's office, Mr. Hopkins made plans to be away for two weeks and astounded him by saying, "You run things while I am gone. Just use your own good judgment and don't bother to telephone me unless there is some urgent need of it." It was President Hopkins' standard practice to let his administrative associates read all his correspondence, without restriction, and to be completely open about what he was up to. In his taped reminiscences he said, "If you're going to command the loyalty of your subordinates, they need to be completely in your confidence. And that would be my first specification in regard to that. . . . Somebody's got to be head of the organization, but I don't think being head of the organization needs to be so secretive that you have some group not knowing what you're trying to do and why you're trying to do it. . . . Actually, I always felt of my own administration that I wanted an oligarchy rather than a monarchy, and I tried as well as I could to make it that." He put it another way by saying he always felt that he was working with associates and not with subordinates.

It was part of his sagacity to understand that appreciation of another's efforts was essential to that individual's morale and was a way of encouraging him to do his very best. Mr. Hopkins had the art of appreciation to an exceptional degree. He was thoughtful and generous in his awareness of the work his associates were doing and in expressing commendation and appreciation. The recipient sometimes felt he was getting more than his due, which was no hindrance to his trying to live up to the president's good opinion. "If a man is not willing to assume very much more generosity toward his associates than they necessarily do toward him," Mr. Hopkins said, "he ought to remain a subordinate and not take a principal's job."

Despite his readiness to delegate responsibility, President Hopkins was not reluctant to exercise presidential authority when the circumstances called for it. He had a strong sense of organizational structure and of the need for central authority. One of his clearest statements on this subject was made in a 1933 letter to Lloyd K. Neidlinger, to whom he outlined his administrative philosophy while proffering the job of dean. "I am theoretically and by conviction a centralist on the subject of authority," Mr. Hopkins wrote, "and I believe that no organization, governmental, industrial, or educational, can fulfill its highest obligations or meet its greatest responsibilities without there being existent and occasionally utilized the power of central authority." That authority, in his view, rested in the group of officers known as the administration, and he added, "Somewhere in the administration of the College there must again be a central and final authority, open-minded, I hope, and receptive to the points of views of others, but nevertheless ready in the last analysis to accept the burden and responsibility for final decision and for requiring that members of his symphony play the same tune and with some regard for the necessary requisites of rhythm and other matters. In other words, I should feel that it was a false modesty and a lack of stamina which would lead the president of a college to hide from himself or from his fellows the fact that in him resided the final authority and that under stress he should be expected to use this from time to time."

It was not like President Hopkins to be assertive about his powers, but this could happen when the faculty occasionally gave indication of believing his authority stopped at the educational line. One such instance occurred when Dean Bill proposed that the three divisional chairmen, appointed by the president, should be ex-officio members of the Committee on Educational Policy. The social science faculty turned the proposal down on the grounds that it would give the president too much influence in educational matters. In a disgruntled memo to Dean Bill, Mr. Hopkins declared that it would be well for the faculty to read the College charter, which states that the trustees "shall elect, nominate, and appoint so many tutors and professors to assist the President in the education and government of the students belonging thereto as they, the said Trustees, shall from time to time and at any time think needful and serviceable to the interests of said Dartmouth College." He added that he valued good morale among the faculty too highly to enter into any fight that could be avoided, but if they wanted a fight about the president's right to help determine educational policy he was ready for it.

In his administrative philosophy and his conduct of College affairs Mr. Hopkins held nothing to be more incontrovertible than that ultimate authority in all Dartmouth affairs rested with the board of trustees. "I think it is the prerogative of the trustees to say what kind of a college it is going to be," he stated. Trustee authority applied especially to approval of faculty appointments, in his view. It would be the final abdication of the college administration to faculty control, he once wrote to Dean Bill, if departments were to dictate faculty appointments. All the ineptitudes of trade unionism would prevail in those circumstances, he declared, and the college would become pedagogically controlled rather than educationally administered. To the occasional suggestion that the faculty should be represented on the board of trustees he answered that "operating men in any job do not make good directors and specifically this is true of college organizations."

President Hopkins could play the part of boss in a most agreeable way. When Felix Frankfurter spoke at Dartmouth's sesquicentennial celebration, he said of Mr. Hopkins, "I take it that I am not the only one who has experienced that subtle, almost unscrupulous talent of his, by which he gives you orders by seeming to agree with you." Mr. Hopkins never used the peremptory approach, choosing instead to explain the background of a situation and then asking the other person if he would be willing to undertake a certain action along suggested lines. There was never any question about what the president wanted done, but the doing of it somehow took on the character of a joint enterprise—and one felt pleased to be allowed to do it for him.

As concerned as President Hopkins was with the individuals on his staff, it was their pulling together as a team that was of first importance to him. To that end, he believed that loyalty to Dartmouth as an institution was imperative and that his staff should therefore be made up predominantly of Dartmouth graduates. He felt that such men should also form a substantial part of the faculty. In the history of the College, the Hopkins years probably have had no equal as a period in which Dartmouth had a clear sense of its institutional identity and distinctiveness and in which loyalty to the College was as pronounced among the faculty as it was among the students, administration, and alumni. This feeling for Dartmouth College derived some of its strength from President Hopkins' encouragement of it and was a major reason for the unity prevailing among all segments of the College. But loyalty to Mr. Hopkins himself was also very much a reason for the *esprit de corps*. He stated, after he retired, that he expected dedication to the College, not to himself—"with that kind of spirit you're pretty safe"—but the force of his personal leadership was so strong and so pervasive that loyalty to him was inevitable.

When he was engaged in industrial personnel work, Mr. Hopkins wrote, "The final measure of a man's accomplishment . . . is not whether he has been acclaimed a hero, or has been adjudged a worthy candidate for martyrdom. It is rather his success in acting as a coordinating, harmonizing, energizing, stimulating force upon diverse ambitions in an organization, which, if left to themselves, would too often become neutralized in conflict with one another." Without knowing it, he was describing, as well as anyone could, the measure of his own success as administrative head of Dartmouth College.

The Twenties

THE first six years of the Hopkins presidency, culminating in the events of 1922, have been viewed as a period devoted mainly to defining the College's role in a changing world and establishing a new administrative structure and a new order of leadership. During the remainder of the 1920's the momentum of those early years accelerated in remarkable fashion to give Dartmouth a solid financial footing, an enhanced educational stature, and a national reputation and popularity such as it had never known before.

The dominant reason for all this growth was Ernest Martin Hopkins. His personality, his ideas and vitality, his liberal and independent spirit were all-pervasive. Few other colleges or universities of the time were so completely linked with their presidents in the public mind as was Dartmouth. One result was a sharpening of the distinctive institutional character that the College had always enjoyed. "What American college has such a pronounced individuality as Dartmouth, that is so *sui generis*?" the *Manchester Union* asked in an editorial in 1928. "What a lot of things there are that are distinctively 'Dartmouth.' Physically, intellectually, spiritually, Dartmouth stands by itself."

In that same year, an alumni-sponsored communication to all Dartmouth men stated that Dartmouth College was enjoying conditions of exceptional promise and gave major credit to President Hopkins' leadership. "Its President is at the zenith of his capabilities," said the report. "He is vigorous enough to insure unity of effort within the organization. He is wise and sympathetic enough to win fullest support from the faculty, alumni, and students alike. His is the prophetic vision that sees the long future in the fleeting present; his is the courage to build for the morrow regardless of the timidities of today."

The statement was tinged with alumni loyalty and enthusiasm, but it also spoke the truth. The zenith of the Hopkins presidency did come in that second chapter of his administration, the period from 1923 to 1930, when achievement followed achievement in dizzying succession. Especially notable were the curriculum study resulting in a new educational program, still in effect today in its broad outline, and an eighteen-building expansion of the college plant, capped by the construction, at long last, of a splendid library worthy of the College. Financial support was provided in million-dollar figures—a new experience for Dartmouth; a better compensated faculty continued to grow; applications for admission under the Selective Process mounted steadily and undergraduate enrollment finally burst beyond the 2,000 limit the trustees had set for it; and alumni organization and support marched forward, exemplified by bigger Alumni Funds and by record attendances as President Hopkins continued to make his annual visits to alumni centers throughout the country.

More personally, Mr. Hopkins acquired a national prominence that resulted in amazing press coverage of his views on national issues, as well as on education. He was at that time the most quoted college president in the country, especially with regard to academic freedom and undergraduate liberal education. The *Chicago Journal* in 1926 said, "He has become the recognized spokesman for those who believe in the liberal evolution of the modern college and the sympathetic recognition of the inquisitive student." Never one to sidestep a controversial issue or hide his thoughts in platitudes, Mr. Hopkins won the respect of reporters and editors for his candor and level-headedness, and they turned to him constantly for his views. In the words of one New York editor, he was "good copy" and this carried over to Dartmouth as well. Any public address was reported at length, and his Convocation address each fall was a news event in New England and usually beyond, giving rise to editorial comment. President Hopkins' talk to the Dartmouth students on "The Goals of Education" in October 1923 was printed in full in the Yale student newspaper. Just as unexpected as this approbation from the *Yale Daily News* was a compliment from the president of Smith College. William Allan Neilson, who earlier as a university scholar had been less than approving of the academic quality of Dartmouth, was quoted in February 1925 as saying that educational thinking in the country was being given more of a stimulus from

Dartmouth than from any other college. A few years later, Roswell Magill, 1916, of the Columbia University faculty, wrote, "From all we hear here, Dartmouth is the most interesting college in the country."

The Neilson statement was made shortly after Dartmouth's Faculty Committee on Educational Policy had completed its survey of the liberal college and had proposed the adoption of a new curriculum that would better achieve the educational goals of the College. The colleges and universities in this country and Canada, and many abroad, had great interest in the Dartmouth study, especially in the 282-page printed report, *A Study of the Liberal College*, written by Professor Leon Burr Richardson, chairman of the Committee on Educational Policy, and submitted to President Hopkins in October 1924. Formal adoption of a new curriculum was voted by the Dartmouth faculty in May 1925 and was ratified by the trustees the following month, to become effective with the Class of 1929.

Prior to the developments of 1924 and 1925, changes in the College's educational program during the Hopkins administration had not been undertaken in any major way. A one-year faculty study had led to the 1919 revision of the curriculum, which changed some details of the major and introduced the required freshman courses in Citizenship and Evolution. In 1921, President Hopkins instigated a faculty review to see if the academic requirements for graduation should not be stiffened, and in 1923 he raised with the Committee on Educational Policy the question of whether the best students in the senior class couldn't be given tutorial guidance in place of the regular class work.

Both the faculty and an influential segment of the student body in the early twenties were pushing for improvement in the educational work of the College, and there was much campus discussion. Chaplain Frank L. Janeway told the alumni class secretaries, "This is not yet an institution whose atmosphere is charged with scholarship. Nevertheless, the men are thinking." For those desiring change there was some encouragement in the results of a survey by *The Dartmouth* which showed that students considered a Phi Beta Kappa key a greater honor than a "D" won in athletics.

Matters were brought closer to a head in May 1923 when the Committee on Educational Policy distributed to the faculty a special report that painted a picture of basic educational failure on the part of the College.

"We believe that higher standards should be set in most courses," the report stated; "that the teaching should be more stimulating and more thorough; that exactness of knowledge and clearness in thinking should be demanded; that 'loafing through college' should be made impossible; that every help should be extended to the earnest and willing student, and that none other should receive the honor of a degree; and finally that there should animate the entire teaching body of this institution a whole-hearted insistence on all those elements that make for a real 'aristocracy of brains.' "

Then, in January of 1924, President Hopkins encouraged his trustees to authorize an investigation of educational methods here and abroad to help determine what the College's purpose should be and, once that was defined, what methods should be adopted to carry it out. Professor Richardson was granted leave of absence for the second semester of 1923–24 to conduct the study. At the same time, in order that undergraduate thinking should be given due weight, Mr. Hopkins appointed a committee of twelve seniors to conduct their own study and make their own report on desirable educational objectives and policies.

On the basis of visits to nineteen of the leading colleges and universities in this country and fourteen others in Canada, England, and Scotland, Professor Richardson wrote his individual report, which still holds a high place in the literature about the liberal college. He discovered no consensus as to what constitutes the ideal curriculum, but he was impressed that in Britain each university graduate must know some one thing well, that the student is expected to do much by himself, and that never is the man of exceptional ability neglected in order that students of low ability may be pulled through. President Hopkins, while abroad in the summer of 1924, also visited Oxford and Cambridge.

The report of the student committee, headed by William H. Cowley, 1924 (later president of Hamilton College), was published in June of 1924. Its maturity and intellectual quality were widely commended, and requests for copies came from institutions all over the country. Among the seniors' propositions were the need for defining the College's educational goals, a change on the part of the faculty from lecturing to guidance of students in independent work, a revision of major study so that reasonable mastery of a subject could be tested by a comprehensive examination, and greater freedom and fewer courses in the last two years, especially in the case of outstanding men. Not all the detailed recommendations of the report were judged to be practical, but the general propositions of its preface were not far from the thinking of the faculty committee.

Particularly commended was the students' definition of Dartmouth's purpose: "It is the purpose of the college to provide a selected group of men with a comprehensive background of information about the world and its problems, and to stimulate them to develop their capacity for rational thinking, philosophic understanding, creative imagination, and aesthetic sensitiveness, and to inspire them to use these developed powers in becoming leaders in service to society."

With the Richardson and undergraduate reports in hand, along with other evaluations and proposals from the departments of instruction, the Committee on Educational Policy devoted several months to fashioning a new curriculum. The educational program finally approved by the committee, and then by the full faculty, focused upon the major as the heart of each student's course of study. Distributive requirements during the first two years had the aim of giving the student an orientation in various fields of learning before he decided upon his major subject. The major itself was enlarged and modified in ways that would make it a unified, coherent whole, subject at the end of senior year to a comprehensive examination calling for independent thought rather than mere memorization of facts. For men of superior ability the departments were called upon to institute honors work, to be done individually or in very small groups, and without the requirement of regular class attendance. The new curriculum dropped the awarding of both the A.B. and B.S. degrees and made the A.B. the degree awarded to all men completing the Dartmouth undergraduate course.

The honors courses, giving men the chance to acquire education largely through their own efforts and at a pace faster than possible in the regular course, was surely the part of the new curriculum that pleased President Hopkins most. One of the cornerstones of his educational philosophy was that a man could never be handed an education, that he must educate himself under propitious conditions and guidance provided by the college. He was not even convinced that college was necessary, so long as self-effort was exercised. In a letter in February 1926, he wrote, "I have said again and again that colleges and universities were by no means the only instruments through which to secure an education, but that the real argument for them was that an education could be secured more easily and more quickly through them than through self-effort." He added that a man who acquires an education on his own often has it more completely and more understandingly than does the man who has the advantage of a college course.

The expectation that a man would secure his own education through his own effort was the one thing about Oxford and Cambridge that most impressed President Hopkins—unless it was the college bells, which he remembered when it came time to build the Baker Library. The visits to the English universities in 1922 and 1924 reinforced a feeling he had long had about a form of instruction that would involve less rules and regulations and would at the same time put more of the burden of college work on the student himself. He realized, however, that as American colleges were constituted, the best that could be expected was to give this freedom to really capable students who were eager to make use of it.

President Hopkins succinctly expressed this point of view in 1928 when discussing the honors method of instruction. "It has been a constantly recurring criticism of the college of liberal arts," he said, "that in its endeavors to meet the needs of its students in general it has not been able to do justice to those whose mental capacities and intellectual interests raise them above the average of their fellows. . . . There is little dissent to the advisability of separating, in the later years of the college course, students of proved capacity from their fellows, of relieving them of technical requirements which seem necessary for the college at large, of separating them entirely from formal courses, the pace of which is determined by men of inferior capacity. Such gifted students may well be given a degree of freedom which is not advantageous for others; their intellectual progress may best be forwarded by methods and judged by tests in keeping with their capacities; and they would profit by receiving a degree of personal attention by instruction, individually or in small groups, which it would be difficult to justify in the case of others. Only the difficulty of financing the special and relatively expensive type of instruction adapted to this group prevents a general application of the honors method."

The great expense of the tutorial method of instruction was one stumbling block to the full adoption of honors courses at Dartmouth, once the new curriculum had gone into effect. Finances were not entirely the reason, however. The slowness with which the faculty departments, with only two or three exceptions, were moving into honors work was another deterrent. In March 1928 President Hopkins wrote to Professor Richardson expressing his discouragement and wondering whether it was worth proceeding with the effort to secure funds from the General Education Board or the Carnegie Corporation for endowing the extra faculty needed for honors teaching. In the letter he wrote: "Unless we can make a definite break with the study of subjects by courses, the requirements for credit on the basis of compulsory attendance, the measurement of achievement by rigid marks, and the whole attitude of acute specialization as a criterion of scholarship, I am not justified in going ahead with the proposition on the basis on which I have argued it heretofore."

President Hopkins had stated his wish to add thirty members to the faculty and to obtain $3-million of endowment money to finance them. He had asked the General Education Board to make half of this possible with a grant of $1.5-million. After drawn-out consideration, the Board, at one of its meetings, informed him it would provide half of the $1.5-million if Dartmouth could match it from some other source. Finding $750,000 elsewhere was not going to be easy, and Mr. Hopkins hesitated in making reply. He happened to be sitting next to John D. Rockefeller Jr., who whispered, "Accept it, accept it." Mr. Hopkins then said yes, with appropriate thanks, and in June 1928 the College made public announcement that it had received $1.5-million for the support of honors work, one-half from the General Education Board and the other half from an anonymous donor. Much later that anonymous donor was identified as Mr. Rockefeller.

A further step in granting freedom to students of exceptional ability was taken in 1929 with the establishment of the Senior Fellowships. This move was pure Hopkins. He repeated the procedure he had used in bringing about the Selective Process of Admission and went around the faculty's flank by having authorization for the fellowships come directly from the trustees. The Senior Fellows, originally five men chosen by the president near the end of their junior year, were allowed to study whatever they pleased in any way they pleased during their final year, as long as they remained in residence and in good standing as members of the College. The faculty would have preferred more control, but President Hopkins was adamant on complete freedom for the fellows. "The faculty has an insatiable desire to get their hands on that sort of thing," Mr. Hopkins later recalled, "and I did more of the picking myself than they thought good for the College." Professor Richardson was not pleased, and asked, "What right do you have to establish a separate educational sovereignty?"

The Senior Fellowships got their initial impetus from a conversation between Mr. Hopkins and Beardsley Ruml, 1915, about giving the really good student more freedom. Mr. Hopkins said he could easily pick a dozen juniors who were already better educated men than the average college senior would be at the end of four years, and it didn't make sense to tell them what to do in senior year. "Well, why do you?" Ruml asked. The more they talked it over, the more convinced Mr. Hopkins became that something could and should be done.

The problem of how to carry out the idea was made easier by the fact that St. John's College at Annapolis had adopted a fellowship plan the year before. The Senior Fellowships at Dartmouth were an almost exact copy of the St. John's scheme. President Hopkins stated that he had no compunction about stealing it "to make it the capstone of our honors work." If any defense of the theft were needed, he added, it would rest in the fact that the author of the St. John's plan was a Dartmouth graduate, Raymond Pearl, 1899, a noted biologist at Johns Hopkins University.

In describing the Senior Fellowships to Mr. Tuck in April 1929, Mr. Hopkins wrote: "I think this is still another step toward untying somebody's apron-strings from around the waist of the Dartmouth undergraduate and turning him loose on his own sense of responsibility. We have had more laws and regulations and rules than were necessary to run a principality; and for thirteen years now I have spent a large part of my time in knocking these down and getting rid of them. . . . So far as my educational interest lies, my whole objective is to get the College recognized as a place where men are expected to stand on their own feet and, if they cannot do this, to take responsibility for falling down. . . . I prize this particular project because it is at least an eloquent gesture."

It was a disappointment to Mr. Hopkins, after he retired, to see the Senior Fellowships come more and more under faculty control and to lose the unrestricted freedom that he considered the *raison d'être* of the plan. It is doubtful that the faculty would ever have been as free-wheeling in educational methods as Mr. Hopkins was willing to be with outstanding students. He was even ready, he wrote, to guarantee admission to some portion of the freshman class at the end of junior year in preparatory school, allowing the men to study whatever they pleased in the final pre-college year, as long as they remained in good academic standing.

President Hopkins was, of course, far from a pedagogue in his educational ideas. His faculty friend, Leon Burr Richardson, found him "a bit exuberant in his enthusiasm for certain men and measures." Professor Richardson would have had that reaction to something Mr. Hopkins wrote in April 1929 to Louis P. Benezet, 1899, then superintendent of schools in Manchester, New Hampshire: ". . . the ideal college in my estimation would be sufficient plant and facilities to provide a proper atmosphere and a proper environment for learning, a group of healthy-minded and intelligent human beings with educational training and a zeal for learning who should constitute a faculty, and a group of undergraduates who should have been selected solely on the basis of whether they had any embryonic understanding of what learning was and a desire for it.

"I would pour this whole crowd on Hanover plain, stir them up together by various agencies, and let the mixture settle for a while. After this, I would let nature take its course and on one basis or another I would find out which men were seeking to educate themselves by establishing contact with men from whom education could be received on one basis or another and would try to get some sense of the intangible factor of who was profiting by this procedure and who was not, and I would hold on to the former and dispense with the latter, and some time later I would give those who survived the process a diploma, if the price of parchment had not gone up too high."

President Hopkins frequently expressed his skepticism about the course system in higher education. For him, the content of any course was less valuable than the ability to think. As stated in his Convocation address of 1929, he believed that "the major emphasis of the college is to teach men how to seek knowledge rather than to state what knowledge is." On the other hand, he recognized that the ability to think and the willingness to follow the logic of thought through to conviction presupposed the acquisition of certain fundamental knowledge. And there came a time, later in his presidency, when he advocated a greater knowledge of the social sciences as essential to every college man.

To President Hopkins, another demerit of the course system was the danger of encouraging pockets of specialized knowledge without concern for the unity and interrelatedness of all fields of learning. The effort of the new curriculum to make each major more of a unified and coherent whole was only a little less satisfying to him than was the introduction of honors work. One idea among the many he tossed off in his voluminous correspondence with alumni and friends in education and business was the setting up of "a Master's degree concerned with the unity of knowledge and with the relationships among diverse fields." It would be unlike anything in American higher education, he wrote.

Another of his unconventional ideas was expressed to Wallace Wright of Stanford University. "Sometimes," he wrote, "I would like to have the resources to set up a fifth year at Dartmouth where men could come back and operate with the utmost freedom and flexibility in the study of subjects rather than courses, under guidance, as informal as you please, of competent men who would advise them."

President Hopkins never really forced his educational ideas upon the faculty, recognizing that the academic program was their province. But he was a member of the Committee on Educational Policy and exercised his influence there, particularly with regard to educational philosophy. With the chairman of that committee, he carried on an extended discussion about how to run a college. As an intimate, Professor Richardson had the prerogative of ribbing the president about his interest in football, fraternities, and other extracurricular pursuits, which the good professor viewed as a mild form of insanity and a hindrance to the achievement of scholarly excellence by Dartmouth men.

While Professor Richardson was engaged in his curriculum investigations President Hopkins had written to him about this difference of opinion. "The alumni, the outside public, and the undergraduates have been oversold on the value of intercollegiate athletics, extra-curriculum activities, and many of the external attributes of college life," he said, "and I have not felt that there was any danger of too much of a reaction in emphasizing the other point of view. I have given up practically all of my time at the alumni meetings in the attempt to puncture their theories and to show the desirability and necessity of proper appreciation and admiration for intellectual achievement.

"At the same time, I am not at all convinced that healthy, normal young males do not require a lot of this outside interest in order to be perfectly safe subjects for the development of the intellectual capacity to the limit. Of course, this statement applies only to the exceptional few, but the more I survey undergraduate bodies the more clear I am in my own conviction that it would be impossible to have a college made up of 'Rufus Choaters' and to escape a degree of smugness and self-esteem that would render our latter estate worse than our former. . . .

"All in all, the whole question of balance in the college is, to my mind, the primary problem for the administration, and it seems perfectly clear to me that it is up to us to recognize the fact that developing the ability to think is a primary responsibility while, on the other hand, we ought to accept the obligation for the development of body and soul so that this thinking shall be done responsibly."

Although he left the details of Dartmouth's educational program to the faculty, President Hopkins was constantly interested in seeing that the conditions of campus life contributed positively and not negatively to the primary purpose of the College. The practice of fraternity pledging in freshman year was something that he found detrimental to the academic work of first-year men. To Natt Emerson, in the fall of 1924, he wrote that after holding off for five years waiting for someone else to act, he intended "to move fast and hard" to rule fraternities out of the freshman year. Shortly after, when pledging had been completed, he released an open letter to the Interfraternity Council ordering fraternity pledging in the future to take place in the sophomore year.

"The interpolation of fraternity interests into the freshman year at Dartmouth is a maladjustment," he wrote. "Its processes are harmful to the class, demeaning to the fraternities, and injurious to the morale of the

College." For both fraternity men and freshmen the rushing system was taking up too much time, "time needful to many of these men if they are to qualify in their college work," he said. Moreover, non-fraternity men had a right to protection from the disorganization of college work that resulted from more than two months of rushing each fall. President Hopkins left the devising of a new system to the Interfraternity Council, but he recommended elimination of all arbitrary rules restricting the natural contacts between upperclassmen and freshmen, and the common adoption by fraternities of a pledging date as early as possible after the start of the sophomore year.

The change in fraternity pledging was by presidential fiat, and was another of what Mr. Hopkins called his "free and easy actions." The move was approved unanimously by the faculty and also by an overwhelming majority of the students. Three years after the change, upon being questioned by *The Dartmouth*, President Hopkins said that there was no chance at all of returning to freshman pledging. Since adoption of the new rule, he added, the number of freshmen separated or placed on probation had steadily declined.

In his taped reminiscences, Mr. Hopkins recalled that his successor as president, John Sloan Dickey, had come to him to say that he couldn't find any trustee or faculty record having to do with the adoption of sophomore pledging. "There isn't any," Mr. Hopkins told him. "It was one of those things I just went ahead and did. I got a trustee vote of approval after the action—that validated things."

Some months before the fraternity edict, in the spring of 1924, compulsory chapel was abolished. This was not done by presidential order, but Mr. Hopkins fully backed it. The requirement that students attend early morning chapel "had got to the point where its only advantage was that it got students up in the morning," he said. Although the morning service was made voluntary, the requirement of attending nine Sunday vesper services each semester was retained for 1924–25. In June 1925 the Sunday service also became voluntary, and daily chapel was rescheduled at 5:30 in the afternoon. A further change occurred in February 1927 when the 5:30 service was shifted to 10 o'clock in the morning, with a chapel break between classes.

Many alumni had strong feelings in favor of compulsory chapel, but the decision to drop it was made without alumni consultation. The older alumni remembered the daily chapel of President Tucker's day, but both the size and the changed conditions of the College were against sustaining such intimate and effective services. President Hopkins was convinced that religious views had changed among the rank and file of the alumni, just as they had among the students. Compulsory chapel, he said, was not consonant with the life the students led in their own homes, where family prayers were a bygone practice. Belief can never be bred by compulsion, he maintained, and besides, while chapel services should be held for those who wanted them, the religious influence of the College was more likely to come from the whole educational program than from chapel.

President Hopkins recalled that the discontinuing of compulsory daily chapel was the one thing of his administration that Dr. Tucker told him he disapproved of. "You will live to regret it," Dr. Tucker said, but late in life Mr. Hopkins jokingly remarked that if he didn't have a change of mind pretty soon, the prediction was not going to come true.

Mr. Hopkins throughout his years as president, and later, spoke of the importance of the religious spirit in higher education. In one of his clearest statements of this belief, made as part of the baccalaureate address to the Class of 1933, he said: "Any conception of education which holds that it can attain its ultimate possibilities unrelated to religion or exclusive of it is a fallacy. Like objectives pertain to both; namely, to know the truth and to live in accordance with it. Jesus' assertion of His right to the confidence of mankind was in His insistence that He was the truth, and that through truth alone could men know God. It is difficult to believe that educational processes have been effective, or even advantageous, if these have left men without something of the humility of one who recognizes the vast extent of knowledge outside the realm of that with which he can become acquainted, and who acknowledges his dependence upon a power beyond himself and far greater than himself, the existence of which is not to be doubted, even if its form cannot be defined."

He was not convinced, however, that the college man needed to show his religion in conventional forms; and to a friend he wrote, "I am absolutely without any interest in compelled religion." His liberal attitude brought

President Hopkins with Ernest Fox Nichols, whom he succeeded, on Inauguration Day in 1916.

Hopkins as an undergraduate.

Mr. Hopkins, then in business in Boston, and Mrs. Hopkins on Easter Sunday, 1914.

While assistant to President Tucker, Mr. Hopkins often rode at Perkinsville, Vermont, where his parents lived.

m left, Governor John H. Bartlett, Ralph D. Paine, President Hopkins, and Frank S. Streeter
)over Point, N.H., in August 1920 for a meeting about state education.

ert Hoover, Gov. Huntley Spaulding, and
dent Hopkins discuss work of European
f Committee in Manchester in 1920.

Mr. Hopkins with Athletic Director "Rip"
Heneage (l) and Head Coach Jess Hawley at
football practice in the fall of 1928.

President Hopkins and Edward Tuck at Chateau
Vert-Mont, near Paris, looking at plans for new
Tuck School in 1929. H. L. Burke, lifelong
secretary to Mr. Tuck, in center.

Mr. Hopkins and daughter Ann on steps
of the new President's House in 1928.

The Dartmouth Board of Trustees, one of the strongest in the College's history, in front of Parkhurst
Hall at Commencement in 1929. First row: Brown, Parkhurst, Hopkins, Thayer, Little. Back row:
Knight, Tuttle, Gray, Howland, McLane, and DuBois.

President Hopkins with Franklin D. Roosevelt, then Governor of New York, who
received an honorary degree in June 1929. They became friends during World War I.

Mr. Hopkins in living room of the President's House with Bruce, his Scottish deerhound.

President Hopkins, wearing his favorite McGill cap, greeting honorary degree recipient Adolph Ochs at 1932 Commencement. At right, Ray Lyman Wilbur, also a recipient, and Mr. Thayer.

...amily photograph of Mr. and Mrs. Hopkins ...d daughter Ann, taken in the early '30s.

Mr. Hopkins aboard the *Conte di Savoia* in 1934, on the trip that led to warning about Fascism.

The annual ceremony of matriculation, this one in 1936.

Stag party for football coaches at Manset, Maine, in the late '30s. Relaxing at "The Teahouse" on Sutton Island are (l to r) Trustee Edward S. French, Coach Harry Ellinger, Professor Charles Proctor, President Hopkins, William Miller, and Head Coach Earl Blaik.

him under attack by the Fundamentalists, and a Dr. Massee of Boston asserted that "Dartmouth is deliberately striving to make its men free thinkers." William Jennings Bryan, after speaking in Hanover and being subjected to critical student questioning, called Dartmouth the most irreligious college in the country, and others picked up and spread this glib verdict. President Hopkins in 1927 insisted that there was more genuine student interest in religion than there had been in earlier years but that there was less acceptance of creed and form. Interviewed by Drew Pearson in Hanover and asked about Fundamentalism, Mr. Hopkins replied, "I am a crank on that subject. There is no sense in holding to doctrine taught centuries ago. Our whole method of life has changed since then." Recalling the visit by Bryan and his subsequent denunciation of the College, he added, "Our theory is that a man who has no understanding of the belief he holds and no ability to defend it against attack is very little benefited by possessing it."

The tolerance and modernity of Mr. Hopkins' religious thinking might lead some to misjudge the depth of his faith, acquired during his boyhood as a minister's son. For the essence of that faith one should turn to "A Layman's Prayer," which he wrote for a Christmas carol service in 1941, and which was so widely admired that it was separately printed:

To Thee, Creator, and Almighty Ruler of the Universe, to Whom men have given the name of God and to Whom mankind has always turned at last in time of trouble, we pray for understanding and for guidance how to seek truth and how to know truth when it be found.

We recall with longing that in earlier days when men had more wisdom if less learning, and more fortitude if less culture, they saw Thee in days bright with Thy sunshine and in nights beaming with Thy heavenly fires, and that Thou then didst walk upon the earth with them in a companionship that only faith can give. Help us, dear God, to simplify our lives and to clarify our minds so that again we may know where Thou art and how to find Thee.

Listen now, we beseech Thee, to our prayer and forgive us our imperfections. For sins consciously committed, grant us strength that we shall not repeat them. Of our unconscious transgressions, make us conscious that we may shun them. And if in the clamor and turmoil of life, like Thy servant of old, we look for Thee and find Thee not in the strong winds of humanity's passions unloosed, or in the upheavals of a shaken world, or in the searing flames of human revolt, grant that we shall yet stand and listen until we hear that still, small voice in which ever Thou speakest to the souls of men. Amen.

In the light of President Hopkins' conviction that religion and higher education have a common objective—to know the truth and to live by it—one can better understand the fervor with which he defended freedom of thought and freedom of speech. His answer to the Baptists in 1921, it will be recalled, was described in one editorial as a broadside well in excess of what the target required. The role of defender of academic freedom was one that came to be indelibly identified with Mr. Hopkins. He repeatedly used the adjective "untrammeled" to describe what the search for truth should be, and over the years there were many addresses and articles in which he defined this philosophy, just as there were many occasions when he defended the faculty and students against those who wanted to restrict what they could teach or hear.

One of the most celebrated of these occasions, reported in the press from coast to coast, occurred when President Hopkins spoke at the first Dartmouth Alumni Pow-Wow in Chicago in February 1924. There, at a time of rampant anti-Bolshevist feeling, he made the startling statement that if Lenin and Trotsky were available, he would be glad to have them come and speak to Dartmouth's students. This was an interpolation in his remarks on the main theme that "the College must be ever watchful that it stands for freedom of thought and, incidentally, that which is essential to freedom of thought—freedom of speech."

The press, demonstrating its penchant for being sensational rather than accurate, quoted Mr. Hopkins as saying that he would welcome Lenin and Trotsky as members of the Dartmouth faculty. What he actually said was: "Recently after we had brought a certain man to Dartmouth for a talk, I received a letter from a man who said we might just as well have brought Trotsky or Lenin. I wrote back to that man and told him that if Trotsky or Lenin were available, we should be very glad to have them come to Dartmouth. If a man starts a new movement, if a man raises some question in regard to the validity of some belief which we have regarded as sure, men will flock to that theory. There is no place in the world where fallacies in thinking will be so quickly punctured as in the college group."

The speaker at Dartmouth whose visit had caused the protest from the father of an undergraduate was William Z. Foster of the Communist Party, who discussed "The Left Wing of the American Labor Movement." He came at the invitation of The Round Table, a student organization to which the College gave funds and full responsibility for picking the speakers for an annual lecture series. The Round Table at that time had also invited Scott Nearing, a Socialist banned on some other campuses; and such liberals as Bertrand Russell, Paul Blanshard, Whiting Williams, and Roger Baldwin. Its list was not one-sided, however, and other guest lecturers were Williams Jennings Bryan, Clarence Darrow, Norman Angell, and W. E. B. DuBois, the Negro leader. In the course of a college year the campus heard a great many speakers of all shades of opinion, and President Hopkins strongly supported the program as an invaluable part of the Dartmouth undergraduate's education. One of his first moves after becoming president had been to remove the choice of speakers from the president's office and place it in the hands of the students themselves.

While the conservative observer might fear that an impressionable young student would be won over to an extremist point of view by listening to these representatives from the outside world, Mr. Hopkins had no such fear. In an article printed by *Scribner's Magazine* in February 1928 he wrote:

Truth has nothing to fear from error if truth be untrammeled at all times and if error be denied the sanctity conferred upon it by persecution or concealment. The method of the educational institution in its search for truth calls for diversity in points of view and emphasis upon all capable of stimulating the student's thought. The great obligation of the College is to inspire men to think rather than to tell them what to think. . . .

Outside opinion to the contrary, the American college undergraduate is as competent to determine between reality and fallacy, between truth and error, between sincerity and hypocrisy, as he will be at any later time. Whatever temporary pose he may purport to take, it is nevertheless during this period of adolescence that the technique of acquiring belief is established and that there is offered the most ample opportunity for that reflective thinking which is necessary for soundness of belief.

The Lenin-Trotsky statement gave the editorial writers a golden opportunity to dwell on the subject of academic freedom and on President

Hopkins in particular. It also produced a flood of crank mail, inspired by the American Defense Society, and a rejoinder from Father Jones I. J. Corrigan, S.J., who said, "That's not academic freedom; that's insanity." The attacks on Dartmouth's president were more than offset, however, by praise and support.

Uncle Dudley, who signed a popular editorial column in *The Boston Globe*, wrote: "This is not the ordinary language of ordinary college presidents. It betokens a man who has been down cellar with lantern and hammer rapping the foundation walls of our national mentality to see whether they are solid, and has found a hollow sound. That hollow sound is—to put it politely—intellectual timidity. We are afraid of ideas."

For some time after his Chicago Pow-Wow appearance Mr. Hopkins' working days were lengthened by the need to elucidate and expand upon his headlined remarks. To one correspondent he wrote, "I know of no man and no interest I would not present if it would stir up the minds of the undergraduates. . . . Open-mindedness and the ability to think are, I believe, among the most cherished aims of the liberal college, and the greatest need of the hour." To another: "I am perfectly certain of my ground when I say that the safety of the Republic and the ideals of democracy can never be permanently protected by taboos. . . . I do not see how an educational institution can argue that it will conserve its ends and create leadership in the world of knowledge by concealing knowledge." And to another: "It is all nonsense to think you are going to train youths to be good Americans by withholding facts from them, or by presenting them with only one side of the case."

It was some time later, in November 1925, while speaking before the Alumni Council of Amherst College and describing certain of the administrative policies at Dartmouth, that President Hopkins also had this to say about freedom of speech on the campus: "Believing definitely that the function of an educational institution is to allow men access to different points of view, and to secure their adherence to conclusions on the basis of their own thinking rather than to attempt to corral them within given mental areas, I was bound to hold to the theory that freedom of speech, even for the presenting of pernicious doctrine, is not antagonistic to the college purpose so long as like access is not denied the student to other points of view, and so long as stimulation is given to his mind to weigh conflicting data for himself. However, I believe that as a matter of practice, entirely aside from the theory which I have enunciated, repression and censorship never work within an intellectually alert group of boys such as constitute the college."

It was because of President Hopkins' acts and declarations at that time that a Professor Moore, before the American Association for the Advancement of Science, defined the radical as a Columbia man, the hidebound conservative as a Yale man, and the open-minded man in the middle as a Dartmouth man.

The reputation he was gaining as one of the country's staunchest liberals was not an unalloyed satisfaction to Mr. Hopkins, for he was basically a moderate man, and his championing of freedom and openness misled some to think that he was espousing the views of those to whom he was willing to provide a platform. The *Dartmouth Alumni Magazine* summed it up well in March 1925: "The one serious drawback to the position taken at Dartmouth with respect to hearing the apostles of liberalism set forth their doctrines to the top of their bent, has been the headlong desire on the part of some of the wildest extremists to rush up to President Hopkins and kiss him with fervor on both cheeks, as a reward for his kindness and hospitality. This has been embarrassing at times because it betokened an exaggerated idea of what such hospitality implied."

What the magazine in exaggerated fashion termed "wildest extremists" were only a fraction of the guest lecturers to whom Dartmouth was extending hospitality at the time of the Lenin and Trotsky episode. The Round Table leaned toward political and social thinkers, but another student group, The Arts, played host to the country's leading authors, playwrights, poets, and critics. Then there was the visit in 1925 of the Oxford University debaters, which may have provided some impetus to the decision to go ahead with the building of Dartmouth's new library. One of the Oxford speakers, acknowledging the students' welcome, said that he had a special interest in coming to Dartmouth because he had heard that the College had the largest gymnasium and the smallest library of any college in America. "That burned me up," said Mr. Hopkins.

Without any stimulus from the Oxford debaters, however, the trustees were on the verge of deciding to go ahead with the construction of a million-dollar library, even though the funds for doing so were neither in hand nor in sight. In order to meet Dartmouth's most pressing need "we were going to borrow the money, or beg it, or steal it," Trustee John R. McLane said later.

The trustee vote, at the October 1925 meeting of the board, authorized that measures be taken immediately for the construction of a library, and instructed President Hopkins to appoint a committee to study all questions related to the matter. Mr. Parkhurst headed this trustee committee, which worked closely with the Faculty Committee on the Library, headed by Professor Charles N. Haskins. In addition, Mr. Hopkins named a special committee to determine the needs that the library was to meet and also an undergraduate committee to propose features that the students would like.

With the exception of decades of abortive planning for a student social center, no building at Dartmouth had such a long gestation period as did the library. Talk about it began early in the administration of Dr. Tucker, who expressed the hope to live long enough to see three new buildings at Dartmouth—a gymnasium, an administration building, and a library. He saw two of them, and although the library was not built before his death in September 1926, he at least knew that it was assured through the gift of one million dollars from George F. Baker. At President Hopkins' inauguration, Mr. Parkhurst said he would be bold enough to prophesy that early in the new administration the College would succeed in building "a college library which shall be the crowning glory of all the buildings we have put up here," and he even went so far as to name it the Tucker Library.

Wilson Hall, erected in 1885 for a student body of four hundred, was grossly inadequate as a library for two thousand students, and architecturally it was an unattractive building. It had run out of space, and books were stored in basements and scattered in departments all over the campus. President Hopkins in 1917 had stated that he was opposed to solving the library problem on any minor scale. A cost of one million dollars seems to have been in his mind from the very beginning, and although a building of such magnitude delayed things for nearly a decade, his foresight once again was vindicated. Tentative library plans had been sketched over the years by a variety of architects, including Charles A. Rich, John Russell

Pope, and Jens Fredrick Larson, the College architect, who did the final design. The trustees in 1919 had decided to locate the new library "in the center of the square north of the College Green with its principal face to the west." At the time of their 1925 call to action, this decision was re-affirmed, but subsequent planning swung the library's principal face to the south and set the building back so there would be a large expanse of lawn. Mr. Hopkins was proud of the fact that a long period of planning had taken place before the architect went to work.

Mr. Baker's million dollars was announced as an anonymous gift on May 17, 1926. The story of how it came about is one of the most fascinating of the Hopkins administration, although in its frequent telling apocryphal bits have crept in. The three main characters, aside from the donor, were Mr. Tuck, Mr. Thayer, and Mr. Hopkins, and a very effective team they were. In the sequel, Mr. Hopkins and Mr. Thayer had to move deftly and persuasively to save a $1.6-million bequest of Edwin Webster Sanborn, 1878, who had wanted to give the library in memory of his father and was bitterly disappointed when Mr. Baker's gift killed his dream. Mr. Sanborn had been unwilling to make his gift until he died, and with funds for the library so desperately needed, the president and trustees decided to go along with Mr. Baker's more timely and more certain offer, come what may.

Mr. Tuck and Mr. Baker were friends of long standing, having first known each other as young men in banking in New York. Both were men of wealth, with an interest in philanthropy, although Mr. Baker as one of the founders of the First National Bank of New York was many times richer than his Paris friend. After his first visit to Mr. Tuck in 1922, Presi-dent Hopkins mentioned Mr. Baker in a letter to Mr. Tuck, and the latter reported a month or so later that he had written to Baker urging an in-terest in Dartmouth. In June 1923, Mr. Thayer, another close friend, was in touch with Mr. Baker, who told him that he intended to do something for Dartmouth in memory of his uncle, Fisher Ames Baker, an alumnus of the College, Civil War soldier, and New York lawyer. Baker was devoted to his uncle, who was only three years his senior, and he had walked all the way from his home in Troy, New York, to see him graduated from Dart-mouth in 1859. Further discussion of a memorial gift took place when Mr. Baker visited Mr. Tuck in Paris in the summer of 1923. The sum of $50,000 was mentioned and Mr. Tuck, by letter, expressed the hope that he would "double the ante." There was some thought of giving a concert organ for Webster Hall, but by October 1925 Mr. Thayer and Mr. Baker were talking about an endowment fund.

This was the background for the meeting between President Hopkins and Mr. Baker which took place at a Cornell alumni dinner at the Hotel Roosevelt in New York on November 14, 1924. Mr. Hopkins, the principal speaker, sat at the right of President Farrand of Cornell, and Mr. Baker, a trustee and benefactor of the university, sat at Farrand's left. There was not much opportunity for conversation, but after the dinner Mr. Baker invited Mr. Hopkins up to his room, where he brought up the subject of a memorial to his uncle. In his reminiscences late in life, Mr. Hopkins recalled that Mr. Baker asked him what the College could do with $25,000. "Not much," Mr. Hopkins replied. "Why, I thought anyone could use $25,000," said Baker. "Yes, they could," Mr. Hopkins answered, "but that amount wouldn't provide the sort of memorial that would be worthy of your uncle or of you."

The story is told that Mr. Baker sat down the next day and sent Dartmouth College a check for $100,000. The amount is correct, but the fact is that it was a month later, December 16, 1924, when Mr. Baker wrote to President Hopkins saying that he was sending securities worth $100,000 to establish the Fisher Ames Baker Endowment Fund for educational purposes. Mr. Hopkins recalled that in thanking Mr. Baker he decided to press his luck and wrote that he was turning the securities over to the College treasurer "on account." Mr. Baker is reported to have got in touch with Mr. Thayer and asked, "How much is it going to cost me to buy my way out of this situation?"

Mr. Baker now became, in the minds of both Mr. Hopkins and Mr. Thayer, the most promising solution to the problem of how Dartmouth was going to pay for the new library that the trustees had just authorized. While in London in November 1925, Mr. Thayer wrote to Baker suggesting that he might want to consider giving the library in memory of his uncle. Three months later, President Hopkins wrote to Mr. Tuck, "Mr. Thayer's project, about which I wrote you, moves along gradually, with at least this encouragement, that he hasn't been turned down. . . . If your own influence is exerted and gets time to have effect, I am allowing myself the indulgence of high hope." And three months after that, the good news was made public. The identity of the donor of a million dollars was kept secret until November, when the *Boston Herald* made a good guess as to who he was, and Mr. Hopkins confirmed it. The year before, Mr. Baker had given $5-million to the Harvard Business School. He was told, or at least was under the impression, that he was providing a home for the oldest graduate school of business in the country, but Mr. Tuck took delight in claiming that distinction for the school he had founded at Dartmouth in 1900, eight years before the Harvard school was founded, and he never let Mr. Baker forget it.

Construction work on the Baker Library began in the late summer of 1926 and partial use of the building began early in 1928, with the official dedication held in June of that year. George F. Baker, because of illness, was unable to be present at the dedication. He had come to Hanover the previous June to receive Dartmouth's honorary Doctorate of Laws, the first trip he had made to the College since his uncle's graduation sixty-eight years before. In September 1928, however, he made a special visit to see the library, and as he was taken through the building in his wheel-chair, with President Hopkins and Mr. Thayer as guides, he expressed himself as delighted with it in every detail. In 1930, the year before his death at the age of 92, Mr. Baker asked to see the library again. Baker Library was a benefaction in which he took great satisfaction and pride, and Mr. Hopkins remembered the tears in the financier's eyes as he looked out at the campus from the library colonnade and spoke of the uncle whose name was now perpetuated in the finest undergraduate college library in the country. On that occasion he said, "Dartmouth is a good college. Everybody speaks well of Dartmouth."

As a banker Mr. Baker was pleased that the cost of the library was right on target—$1,132,000, made up of his million-dollar gift, the earlier fund of $100,000, and $32,000 gained in the sale of his securities. Not so happy was his experience at Harvard, where the cost of the business school ran considerably beyond estimate. He therefore felt that Dartmouth was deserving of something more, and when both Mr. Tuck and Mr. Thayer urged him to provide for the proper maintenance of his building, he was quite receptive and gave another million dollars for its endowment. Announcement of this second large gift was made in February 1930.

The happy outcome of the library project, in its planning for the educational work of faculty and students, its design, and its financing, was due to a remarkable group of men, all working together smoothly and as one in their devotion to Dartmouth. In addition to the Tuck-Thayer-Hopkins team, the work of the Faculty Committee on the Library, and especially that of its chairman, Professor Haskins, was superlative. But the leading role of all must be granted to Trustee Henry B. Thayer, 1879, who was of key importance in the relations with Mr. Baker and who, as chairman of the special Committee on the Construction of the Library, spent innumerable days in Hanover overseeing the progress of the work. After he retired as chairman of AT&T in 1927, he gave most of his time to the library and to other plant developments for which he felt responsible as chairman of the Trustee Committee on the Physical Plant. Mr. Thayer was the spiritual successor to General Streeter on the board of trustees, and he and President Hopkins had a mutual affection and harmonious working relationship similar to that of the Streeter-Hopkins alliance from 1916 to 1922. Their one disagreement about the library was over Mr. Thayer's wish to eliminate Wentworth Street at the north end of the College Green. Mr. Hopkins thought this would be detrimental to the town, and no effort was made to close off the street. Butterfield Hall, "the best building on campus," had to be razed and eight other structures had to be moved or torn down to make room for the library, but Wentworth Street survived.

President Hopkins also vetoed somebody's idea that a statue of Diana be placed atop the library tower. His idea of a weathervane with a Dartmouth theme was adopted instead. The one feature of the library for which Mr. Hopkins was clearly responsible was the chime of bells in the tower. After his visits to Oxford and Cambridge he talked so much of his desire to have more bells at Dartmouth that one of the trustees said he would put up the money to get some for Mr. Hopkins' sake. The sum of $40,000 was given anonymously in the fall of 1927, and later the donor was identified as Clarence B. Little, 1881. The original idea of having a carillon gave way to the simpler and less expensive idea of a chime of fifteen bells. The bells, ranging in weight from 200 to 5300 pounds, were specially cast by the

Meneely Company in Troy, New York, under the supervision of Professors
Fred Longhurst and John Poor, who spent the better part of a year learning the art and mechanics of ringing changes on them. Not everybody in
town was delighted at first when the Baker bells loudly rang the hours, and
later the changing of classes, but now they are an ingrained part of Hanover life and a nostalgic memory for most Dartmouth men.

In a letter in July of 1926, Mr. Hopkins expressed his thoughts about the
importance of place and local color in the affection that Dartmouth men
have for their college. "My own belief has always been," he wrote, "that
in our location, in our history and in our daily life we were susceptible to
influences that many another college could not respond to, and that the
devotion of alumni was dependent to a degree beyond what they quite
realized on the environment and the isolation which gave a special flavor
and a special atmosphere to Dartmouth life.

"Personally, I want to give the color of our local life all possible hues and
to make associations with the College in the subconscious minds of men
who come here fixed and pleasant. I want to see the College filled with
visible symbols of spiritual and intellectual things, and for the same reason
that I want a beautiful Gothic chapel on Observatory Hill, I want a sunset
carillon to play just as the sun falls below the Vermont hills and just before
dusk comes on."

For what it contributed to the educational work and intellectual life of
the College, it would be difficult to exaggerate the importance of the arrival
of Baker Library on the Hanover scene. President Hopkins had a justi-
fiable sense of satisfaction and achievement in the library. In his reminiscences, he said, "Achievement of Baker Library was the fulfillment of a
large part of my dreams as president of Dartmouth. I came pretty near
thinking that my career as a college president, all that I could be expected
to do, had been accomplished when we got the library."

When Baker Library opened in 1928 as the repository of the College's
280,000 volumes, no one was thinking of a million volumes or of running
out of space. The *Dartmouth Alumni Magazine* editorialized: "Dartmouth
now has the space to harbor her needful volumes for many years to come,
if not for all time." The euphoria of the period is understandable, for never
in the history of the College had its primary educational program received

such a shot in the arm. The way was clear to implement the goals of the new curriculum, with its emphasis on independent study. One of the peaks of the Hopkins presidency had been reached.

The solution of Dartmouth's library problem left in its wake the disappointment of Edwin Webster Sanborn of New York, who as early as 1917 had sent a copy of his will to President Hopkins disclosing that he planned to leave his sizable estate to Dartmouth for the purpose of erecting a library in memory of his father, Edwin David Sanborn, 1832, for nearly fifty years a member of the Dartmouth faculty and College Librarian from 1866 to 1874. (Professor Sanborn's wife, Mary Webster Sanborn, was the daughter of Ezekiel Webster, brother of Daniel.) President Hopkins, who had maintained a steady stream of correspondence with Mr. Sanborn from the beginning of his administration, wrote immediately after the Baker gift to inform him that an anonymous donor was providing a million dollars for the library. Mr. Sanborn, angered by what he considered almost a breach of contract on the part of the College, made a tentative offer of $300,000 to preserve the Sanborn name on the library; but Mr. Hopkins replied that the library would have to bear the name of the Dartmouth graduate in whose memory it was being given.

Mr. Sanborn's lawyer, Charles Albert Perkins, was privy to Sanborn's plan to leave his entire estate to Dartmouth, and it was the College's good fortune that he used his influence to bring that about in spite of the library development. Perkins wrote to President Hopkins in June of 1926 that Mr. Sanborn was thinking of changing his will. In this matter, as in his intention to provide Dartmouth with a library, Sanborn was a man of extreme caution who vacillated and then ended up by postponing action. In Hanover, meanwhile, much thought was being given to the idea of having some part of the library named for Professor Sanborn, but this was finally dropped as being unpalatable to both Baker and Sanborn. Mr. Hopkins wrote to Perkins wondering if a Faculty Club would appeal to Mr. Sanborn. Then Mr. Hopkins and Mr. Thayer got their heads together and came up with the winning idea. A library without books is no library; why couldn't Mr. Sanborn fulfill his dream and appropriately honor his father by endowing the purchase of books for all time? Many meetings with Mr. Sanborn ensued, and in the end he was won over to the idea of a book fund.

However, he still wanted a building to bear the Sanborn name. Mr. Thayer, ever resourceful, proposed a building for the Department of English, in which Professor Sanborn had served as Evans Professor and later as Winkley Professor. Mr. Sanborn's reaction was enthusiastic, especially since there would be incorporated into the Sanborn House a replica of the study in which Professor Sanborn had extended hospitality to students at all hours and to men of letters visiting the College.

Mr. Sanborn died March 18, 1928, and left his entire estate to the College, with President Hopkins and Treasurer Halsey Edgerton named as executors. The total amount that came to Dartmouth was $1,655,555. The sum of $10,000 was left to the Dartmouth Outing Club, $344,000 was used to build the Sanborn House, and the remainder went to establish the Sanborn Library Fund. Since the book fund was the principal memorial to his father, Mr. Sanborn left instructions that the English House should be a memorial not only to his father, but also to his mother, Mary Webster Sanborn, and his two sisters, Miss Kate Sanborn and Mrs. Mary Webster (Sanborn) Babcock.

Dr. Tucker had characterized Mr. Hopkins as a gambler, and the whole Baker-Sanborn episode was an example of what he had been wise enough to foresee. President Hopkins took chances, at what seemed to him to be reasonable odds, and the outcome in this case was a magnificent library, a million-dollar fund to maintain it, another endowment fund of approximately $1.3-million for purchasing books, and an attractive home for the English Department. That was an excellent piece of presidential work.

Sanborn English House was built at the southwest corner of the library and was dedicated in September 1929. Three months earlier the College had dedicated, at the northwest corner of the library, the Carpenter Fine Arts Building, made possible by a gift of $305,000 from Frank P. Carpenter of Manchester, New Hampshire, holder of Dartmouth's honorary A.M. and LL.D. degrees. If the plan for completing the library square had been carried out, a music building would have been built at the southeast corner of the library and a home for the foreign language departments at the northeast corner.

The mushroom growth of new buildings in the 1920's was almost too rapid to keep up with. No comparable period of concentrated plant expansion has since been experienced by the College, and in the earlier and poorer years that preceded it, the thought of eighteen buildings in seven years would have been regarded as sheer fantasy. Twelve of the plant additions were built with funds given by alumni and friends of the College. The other six were dormitories authorized by the trustees, who adopted a "full speed ahead" philosophy under the heady leadership of their president. The new residence halls built with College funds were Gile in 1928, Streeter and Lord in 1929, and Ripley, Woodward, and Smith in 1930. Another dormitory, Russell Sage Hall, had opened in 1923; with Memorial Field, it marked the start of the great plant expansion of the twenties.

For its contribution to the comfort and dignity of Mr. Hopkins and his family, the new President's House was a plant addition of special importance. Mr. Tuck, who provided the money for it, had brought up the matter of a fitting residence for Dartmouth's president early in the Hopkins administration, but the war intervened and the project was put aside. He discussed it again during Mr. Hopkin's first visit to Paris in 1922, and shortly after the second visit, in the spring of 1924, agreement was made to go ahead. Following his definite offer of funds in May 1924, Mr. Tuck wrote, "The home must be both worthy of the College in appearance and sufficiently commodious never to prove an inadequate one. I shall foot the bill with entire satisfaction." President Hopkins thought that $50,000 would be an adequate sum, but Mr. Tuck was doubtful that the kind of house he had in mind could be built for so little. The final amount he contributed for the house, grounds, and furnishings was $132,000, and he enjoyed spending every penny of it, for he had no keener wish than that the president of his college should be splendidly housed.

Where to locate the house was the subject of much correspondence between President Hopkins and Mr. Tuck. The president's first choice for a site was the Dewey farm, where the Dartmouth Medical School now stands, but there was no chance of obtaining any of that land. The three Dewey sisters, all spinsters, were at odds with the College. They would scarcely speak to President Hopkins when he called upon them, and it took Mrs. Hopkins to ferret out the cause of their hostility. They were angry because students were running across their field in their underwear—which was their interpretation of the daily workouts of the Dartmouth cross-country team. One of the sisters said, "How would it look if I ran across the campus in my drawers?" When Mr. Hopkins passed this comment along to the trustees, Mr. Parkhurst wrote back, "Please keep me informed as to when it is going to happen. I don't want to miss being there."

Second choice for the site of the President's House was Observatory Hill, not far from the residence then in use, but it was finally decided that this had the drawback of noisy traffic and also that it lacked sufficient privacy. A site off Tuck Drive was therefore chosen, and in view of the identity of the donor of the President's House, this selection had a certain fitness. Since the address of the President's House is One Tuck Drive, Hanoverians have never been certain whether the front entrance is on the Drive or on Webster Avenue, the entrance commonly used. President Hopkins preferred the Tuck Drive entrance, with its view of Mt. Ascutney in the distance, and this was the one he used when he set out for the office and when he returned home each day. Reporters from *The Dartmouth* once asked him why he used that entrance when everyone else used the other one. "I go out that way in the morning," he replied, "so I won't have to step over *The Dartmouth*." This quip so upset the editors of the student paper that they asked President Hopkins to meet with them to explain the reason for such aversion.

Work on the President's House began in the spring of 1925, and the Hopkins family moved in late in the summer of 1926. In the very careful planning that went into the house Mrs. Hopkins took a leading part. Mr. Tuck had written to President Hopkins, "I don't care what you prefer. I want Mrs. Hopkins to be happy." With her new home, Mrs. Hopkins, who was a gracious and thoughtful hostess, was able to entertain on a more fitting scale, and one of the first social events in the new President's House was a reception for several hundred members of the faculty and staff. The new quarters, including a large social room on the lower floor, worked admirably and were greatly admired. As they settled into their home, Mr. and Mrs. Hopkins and daughter Ann gradually adopted a large bedroom on the second floor as their family gathering place. With a fireplace and space for easy chairs and tables, this family room was where their closest friends were entertained.

A personal meeting between Mrs. Hopkins and Mr. Tuck did not take

place until the spring of 1929, when she and President Hopkins made a
trip to Europe to visit Lord Dartmouth in England and Mr. Tuck in Paris.
Mrs. Tuck had died the year before, and since the Tucks had no children,
relations between Mr. Tuck and the Hopkins family became even closer
than before. Between Mr. Tuck and Mr. Hopkins the rapport and bond of
affection were complete. Intertwined with the solicitude Dartmouth's
greatest benefactor had for the College was a fatherly affection for Mr.
Hopkins as a person. In his letters to his older friend, Mr. Hopkins usually
ended with "my love to you." In 1927 Mr. Tuck was vexed because Mr.
Hopkins was unwilling to have Dartmouth join with Columbia, Princeton,
and Yale in urging a reconsideration of France's war debt to the United
States, but there seems to have been no other point of disagreement between the two men in the sixteen years of their deep and abiding friendship.

Mr. Tuck's benefactions to the College continued unabated during the
twenties. In four separate gifts he added $1,035,000 to the Edward Tuck
Endowment Fund, and through his custom of sending year-end checks to
supplement the income from this fund he contributed another $50,000. In
the spring of 1928, Mr. Hopkins wrote to him to tell him that he had the
idea of moving the Tuck School from its location on the west side of the
College Green so the central campus could be entirely undergraduate. The
trustees had feared that Mr. Tuck would be upset, but on the contrary, he
thought that Mr. Hopkins was right, and he added that if the College were
willing to take over the old building at a fair valuation, "it is possible that I
could furnish the additional funds required to complete the new and large
structure." He did not wish, he said, to have outside capital contribute to a
work which he thus far had taken care of financially himself. In December
1928, Mr. Tuck gave the College six hundred shares of Chase National
Bank stock, valued at $575,000, and this plus the $125,000 from the old
Tuck School (later named McNutt Hall) provided the funds for the business school's new home. Completed in 1930, the Amos Tuck School complex consisted of the central Edward Tuck Hall; two dormitories, Chase
and Woodbury; and Julia Stell Hall, the refectory, named for Mrs. Tuck.
Next to Baker Library, the new business school at the west end of Tuck
Mall was the most important new addition to Dartmouth's plant in the
twenties.

To show their appreciation for all that Mr. Tuck had done for Dartmouth for so many years, the trustees in October 1929 voted to send him a gold replica of the Wheelock punch bowl. The bowl was made by Tiffany's in New York, with Mr. Thayer seeing to its execution. Suitably engraved, it was taken to the French Embassy in Washington and then by diplomatic pouch to Mr. Tuck in Paris. The gift, made personally by the members of the Dartmouth board of trustees, was one of Mr. Tuck's prized possessions for the remainder of his life.

A new facility of special charm and usefulness was Dick's House, begun in 1926 and dedicated at Commencement the following year. To build this infirmary in memory of their son, Richard Drew Hall, 1927, who had died in his sophomore year, funds totaling $297,655 were provided by Edward K. Hall, 1892, a trustee from 1915 to 1923, and Mrs. Hall. In the loving care the Halls gave to planning the infirmary they were desirous of creating a place which Dartmouth boys, when ill, would look upon as second only to their own homes for comfort, care, and cheerful atmosphere. Dick's House was connected to the Mary Hitchcock Hospital, so that the best of medical care would be immediately available. Each volume in the infirmary library was a personal gift inscribed by its donor. Calvin Coolidge gave a copy of his book *Have Faith in Massachusetts*, and in it he wrote, "To Edward K. Hall, in recollection of his son and my son, who have the privilege by the grace of God to be boys through all eternity."

The trustees in October 1926 voted to build a new natural science building. This was ready in 1928 and was named for T. Julien Silsby of Brookline, Massachusetts, who by gifts and legacy had earlier and anonymously given Dartmouth more than $400,000. For use in connection with the natural science building the trustees also authorized the building of the Clement Greenhouse, named for Orson C. Clement of Corinth, Vermont. It was ready in 1928, and in that same year the Class of 1900 offered the funds to build the Dartmouth Outing Club House, which was dedicated in January 1929. In deciding what facility to give to the College, the officers of the Class of 1900 had for some years engaged in an exchange of ideas with President Hopkins. It was one of Mr. Hopkins' fondest hopes to have a literary center on campus, similar to the Elizabethan Club at Yale, which had impressed him. The class officers were won over to the idea, but when it was proposed to the members of the class it was criticized as too "aesthetic" and the more rugged Outing Club House was approved instead. In this choice the men of 1900 showed that President Hopkins hadn't completely won his battle against the old alumni thinking.

A literary club was on the list of plant needs that President Hopkins had prepared for the trustees in the fall of 1924. Also on his list were a library, student union, fine arts building, infirmary, faculty club, Gothic chapel, and a hockey rink "without ice machinery, which we do not need in this country"—a gross miscalculation about the dependability of natural ice, as it turned out. Before the twenties were over, the library, fine arts building, and infirmary had been realized; and the hockey rink also came into being thanks to the generosity of Howard Clark Davis, 1906, of Boston. Before he pledged the $60,000 for the hockey rink in September 1929, Mr. Davis had already given $138,000 to build the Varsity Field House bearing his name, which was dedicated in the fall of 1926.

The major additions to the Dartmouth plant during the seven-year period from 1923 to 1930 have been mentioned. The trustees also authorized a new wing for the Hanover Inn, which was ready by June 1924, and an extensive program of renovation. Four dormitories were remodeled—Middle Fayerweather, Middle Massachusetts, Richardson, and Wheeler Halls —and renovation of Thornton Hall and Wilson Hall, converted into a museum, was also carried out. Faculty housing for eleven families was built in the summer of 1928.

In his ebullient way, President Hopkins had no end of ideas about desirable facilities for the College, and at the rate financial support was pouring in, everything seemed possible. Although he never got his literary club, the Sanborn English House library and the Tower Room of Baker Library were to some extent substitutes for what he wanted. A million-dollar Gothic chapel on Observatory Hill was another Hopkins dream that never came true, and later he admitted that lack of funds at the time saved him from a serious mistake. Ralph Adams Cram, the noted architect of Gothic structures at Princeton, West Point, and elsewhere, had on his visits to Hanover declared that the Observatory Hill site could give Dartmouth the most impressive Gothic chapel in America, and for some years Mr. Hopkins had this chapel on every list of plant needs he drew up. He was willing to do away with Rollins Chapel, which had been erected in 1885, and it was another of his ideas to move the Old White Church (before it burned in 1931) from its location at the northwest corner of the campus to the Rollins site, thus balancing Reed Hall in the row of white buildings on the east side of the College Green. He also had it in mind to enlarge Webster Hall to seat 2,100 persons, and to construct a Greek theatre, seating five thousand, on the hillside behind Tuck School leading down to Tuck Drive.

Mr. Hopkins played with the idea of a separate freshman quadrangle with its own living and dining units, and before the Harvard house plan was adopted, he considered the possibility of breaking up the entire College into similar units. He finally decided that Dartmouth was uniquely suited to be one big unit, and that all that was lacking was a central student union which would have social and educational advantages. In the spring of 1929, the president named a special committee, headed by his executive assistant, Robert C. Strong, to make a study of student unions at other institutions and to define the role that such a center could fill at Dartmouth. (This was the first of a series of ill-fated planning groups that worked periodically for more than thirty years until the Hopkins Center was built during President Dickey's administration.) Mr. Hopkins wanted the student union plans prepared well in advance, as had been done with the library, and it was his intention to gamble on the financing, again duplicating the trustees' library action. To provide a central site for the union building, College Hall was to be razed. All these plans were sent into limbo by the Great Depression.

Dartmouth Personified

THE extraordinary development of Dartmouth's physical plant in the twenties is one of the most compelling examples of the vigorous leadership President Hopkins was capable of providing. The progress of that period serves equally well to demonstrate the productive working relationship he had with his board of trustees. The board was by no means a rubber-stamp body. It was, in fact, one of the strongest and ablest boards in the College's history. So great was the trustees' confidence in the president, however, and so thoroughly attuned were they to his formulation of Dartmouth's purpose and its needs that they gave him their backing without a quibble.

In addressing the Dartmouth Secretaries Association in the spring of 1924, Lewis Parkhurst, senior member of the board, said of Mr. Hopkins, "We as a board not only believe in his ideas, respect his judgment, and follow his leadership, but we love him as a brother; and you may be sure of one thing, that whatever else we may do or whatever we may fail to do, we shall stand by Hoppy to the last ditch."

The members of the board at that time were an impressive group of men, and they admirably complemented President Hopkins in his finest years. Lewis Parkhurst, 1878, who had been a trustee since 1908, was a partner in the publishing firm of Ginn and Company. He was the financial watchdog of the board and the originator of the College's budget system. Deficits were anathema to him, and if his fellow trustees showed any excess of exuberance in approving President Hopkins' ideas, he could be counted on to interject a cautionary note and to bring the discussion around to hard financial facts.

Mr. Parkhurst's classmate, Albert O. Brown, came to the board in 1911, and during his twenty years of membership served as New Hampshire's governor from 1921 to 1923. Governor Brown, a lawyer and banker, was a progressive in spirit and one of President Hopkins' staunchest backers. It was his ambition to leave Dartmouth College a million dollars, and when he died in 1937 he thought he had. The estate actually came to about half that figure, but the trustees voted that his fund should be allowed to accumulate until his wish came true. Today, the Brown Fund of more than a million dollars provides support to the Hopkins Center.

Henry B. Thayer, 1879, began twenty-one years on the board in 1915. As previously pointed out, he took over, in personal relationship with President Hopkins, the place that General Streeter had filled up to the time of his death in 1922. Mr. Thayer, president of Western Electric Company and then of American Telephone and Telegraph Company, was a sagacious business leader who had a great knack for getting things done. He and President Hopkins were the two driving forces on the board, and affection as much as mutual respect and admiration drew them together. It was natural that they should make several trips to Europe together and that one of the bedrooms in the President's House should be "Mr. Thayer's room."

Clarence B. Little, 1881, a banker from Bismarck, North Dakota, became a trustee in 1921, and William R. Gray, 1904, Dean of the Tuck School, in 1926. These two men, with Mr. Parkhurst, Mr. Brown, and Mr. Thayer, were Life Trustees. John R. McLane, 1907, a lawyer from Manchester, New Hampshire, who eventually served as a Life Trustee for many years, was elected an Alumni Trustee in 1926. The four other Alumni Trustees he joined were Fred A. Howland, 1887, president of the National Life Insurance Company of Vermont; Charles G. DuBois, 1891, president of Western Electric Company; Morton C. Tuttle, 1897, president of a Boston construction company bearing his name; and Edward W. Knight, 1887, a lawyer from West Virginia.

It was a board of trustees made up of businessmen, bankers, and lawyers. Yet their interest in undergraduate liberal arts education and their support of President Hopkins' progressive policies could not have been stronger. Paul Blanshard in the September 7, 1924 issue of *The Nation* wrote that the list of Dartmouth trustees read like a page from Upton Sinclair's *The Goose-Step*, a critical study of American education. But he cited Dartmouth as one private institution controlled by businessmen trustees that nevertheless was notably liberal. Mr. Hopkins was comfortable with his trustees from the business world and the professions, and if they did not fully have his liberal spirit to begin with, they soon absorbed it. "I think the theory is all bunk that you get a greater interest in academic affairs and in the purposes of education from ministers and teachers than you do from business men," Mr. Hopkins wrote in January 1924. This was reminiscent of the advice the Rev. Francis Brown had given President Hopkins at the time of his inauguration. "Don't ever let yourself be misled by a hue and cry for ministers and educators on the board of trustees," he had admonished him.

President Hopkins once wrote to Percy Marks, author and former Dartmouth English instructor, that the principal need in a trustee was the ability to deal with large things; and to the extent that he had a say in the election of each new trustee, this was the quality he sought. He was fortunate in having a succession of trustees of such caliber throughout his administration, but a particularly strong constellation happened to come together in the expansive twenties. There is no question but that these board members enjoyed working together, pooling their brains and their energies for the greater good of Dartmouth College. The unity created by their solicitude for the College was matched by the unity that came from their feelings about Mr. Hopkins as a person and as a leader. They looked upon him as indispensable to the continuing good fortune of Dartmouth College and as an asset to be safeguarded. They expressed their appreciation in resolutions and by raising his salary to $20,000, plus a $2,000 maintenance fund, and also by telling him that he was working too hard and that he should adopt a program of regular periods of rest and relaxation.

In April of 1926, the trustees decided there should be greater public knowledge of the national importance of helping Dartmouth College to render its fullest service. The needed financial support would be more readily given, they agreed, if an account were made of the accomplishments of the first ten years of the Hopkins presidency. The board asked the Alumni Council to be responsible for preparing such a printed statement "for the purpose of enlightening that portion of the public which is receptive of plans and investment in education." The Council in turn placed the responsibility mainly in the hands of Mr. Hopkins' friend, Natt Emerson.

The desire of the trustees and Alumni Council to focus this ten-year review on President Hopkins' leadership gave him some concern that people would think he was seeking personal aggrandizement. To Council member Clarence McDavitt he wrote, "... though I am no blushing violet, and though my feelings are not inordinately hurt by the thought that my presence at Dartmouth may not have been harmful, nevertheless, I care too much for the College to believe it either true or desirable to argue that any individual can be thought of in comparison with the College itself."

He made the same point in correspondence with Mr. Emerson, but he recalled the advice that Mr. Vail had given him when he left AT&T to accept the Dartmouth presidency. Mr. Vail had told him to remember that an institution was dependent for its reputation and its progress upon the extent to which its administration was personalized in a single individual. It was altogether desirable, he said, to have the credit devolve upon a single administrative leader, just as it was necessary for blame to rest upon him when things went wrong. It was only in that sense, Mr. Hopkins said, that he was willing to be the individual in whom the College administration was symbolized in the Alumni Council brochure.

Continuing the letter to Mr. Emerson, he wrote:

I have welcomed the public approval and the alumni enthusiasm and the official confidence expressed in regard to the administration, and my pleasure in it is partly because it is mighty pleasant to have such things so, but as much, I believe, because the existence of these facts indicate that the College is prospering and is maintaining its momentum.

I would greatly dislike to have any situation arise which implied a lack of appreciation on my part of all those other factors which are involved in the present-day reputation of the College. I would dislike to see any trace in myself of belief that my part in this was anything except a cooperating part, and I would, as much, dislike to have other people feel that they saw any trace of such a spirit within me. . . .

On the other hand, externally, I understand perfectly well, be it for good or ill, that the College has got to be represented through some individual, signified by some person in whom the College administration will be symbolized.

I have no knowledge as to the extent to which this can be done justifiably and desirably. I want anything done which will be helpful to the repute of the College in the outside world. On the other hand, I want nothing to be done that would seem to imply that I am unconscious of how dependent the College is upon the loyalty and effort of the faculty, upon the wisdom and the courage of the Trustees, or upon the cooperation and confidence of the alumni.

The Alumni Council's ten-year review was published in 1927. In addition to an account of the advances made by Dartmouth, it contained a list of the College's greatest needs for more progress, among them $10-million for endowment, a biology building, a student union, an auditorium-theatre, and, once again, a Gothic chapel to symbolize the religious spirit of the institution. President Hopkins' role in Dartmouth's progress was not as "blurred" as he had wished, but even modest adherence to the truth required that he be given a large measure of the credit.

Mr. Hopkins had worked at a strenuous pace during his first ten years in office and was not yet taking the long summer vacations that were to become a regular fixture a little later. In 1926 it began to be clear that he would have to slow down. He suffered occasionally from neuritis and lumbago, and an infected jaw from an abscessed tooth kept him from giving the Convocation address in September. In March of 1927, with Mrs. Hopkins and Ann, he took a three-week trip to the Caribbean aboard a United Fruit Company steamer, which relieved some bronchial trouble. The following year, at their June meeting, the trustees expressed their concern about the president's load and urged him to take a half-year's leave of absence and to reduce his public engagements. This Mr. Hopkins did not feel able to do, with so many irons in the fire, but he promised to take more short respites from the office and to lengthen his summer vacations at Manset, Maine. On a trip to Boston during the 1928 Christmas holidays he became ill and had to return home, where he was confined for three weeks. The newspapers carried stories that he was seriously ill, which led to a flood of mail from concerned friends. In late January the Hopkins family went to Bermuda, but cold weather made the trip less salutary than it was intended to be. In April, President and Mrs. Hopkins sailed for England to visit Lord Dartmouth and then went to France to visit Mr. Tuck. Their trip had originally been planned for January but had been cancelled because of Mr. Hopkins' illness. They returned to Hanover in early June, in time for

Commencement, and soon after had a chance to go to their place in Maine for a long summer rest.

One reason he got colds and bronchitis, Mr. Hopkins was told by his friendly faculty critic, Professor Richardson, was that he was foolish enough not only to go to football games but to stand around on Memorial Field watching practice. Personal concern for his health was not likely to impel any change, however, for Mr. Hopkins was too ardent a football fan, especially in that era. The Dartmouth teams of the mid-twenties, coached by Jess Hawley, were some of the greatest in the College's history, and the undefeated 1925 team, with Oberlander, Parker, Tully, and Sage, was ranked as the top team in the nation.

At that time when Dartmouth happened to be riding the crest of the wave there was nationally great agitation for deemphasis of football. Students from thirty-two institutions met at Wesleyan University in the fall of 1925 and proposed a season of only four games. What particularly incensed President Hopkins was an air of self-righteous superiority adopted by Harvard, Yale, and Princeton, and their unconcealed feeling that if Dartmouth had had their ideals and high standards a team as good as the 1925 national champions could not have been produced in Hanover. That was sour grapes, President Hopkins asserted, and at a Boston alumni dinner in January 1926 he lashed out at the innuendos that Dartmouth's Selective Process of Admission was a means of enrolling athletes and that it had taken athletic success to lift Dartmouth from insignificance. Mr. Hopkins' best show of belligerence was certain to be called forth by any attitude of superiority on the part of the so-called Big Three. And when there was talk of incorporating Dartmouth into a Big Four, he beat everyone else to a rejection of the idea, saying that Dartmouth desired to maintain its singularity and to continue to go its own way.

Shortly after his return from a trip to Europe with Mr. Thayer late in 1925, President Hopkins had addressed a meeting of the National Collegiate Athletic Association in New York. In discussing "The Place of Athletics in an Educational Program" he had intended to dwell on some of the faults of the system but, as he put it, he decided to reverse his field when he discovered that criticism of intercollegiate athletics had become so extreme as "to kill the patient as a cure." In his December 30 address he therefore came to the defense of intercollegiate athletics, claiming that they had a desirable place in the colleges and that their virtues outweighed their evils, real or imaginary. "Personally, I have not found the well-bodied, emotionally normal, physically active, and sports-loving college man less capable mentally nor less sensitive morally than his fellows who have lacked these attributes," he said. "No agency of undergraduate life so powerfully binds the college community together, nor, on the whole, so advantageously permeates the ideals as do the undergraduate sports. Hence, let us not deny them either the consideration or the credit which is rightfully theirs."

Support of athletics did not go so far, however, as to lead Mr. Hopkins to agree with Dartmouth's California alumni that the 1925 team should accept a bid to play the University of Washington in the Rose Bowl. In his stand he had the backing of both the Athletic Council and the Dartmouth coaches. In March of 1927 he shook up the football world and drew far more national publicity than he had with his NCAA speech when he proposed a drastic modification of college football. In a letter to Lemuel G. Hodgkins, president of the Dartmouth College Athletic Council, he urged consideration of a plan whereby varsity football would be limited to sophomores and juniors, all coaching would be done by seniors, and two Dartmouth teams would play an opponent on a home-and-home basis on the same day. He suggested that a conference of colleges and universities be called to consider the whole range of football reform, saying, "I do not want to see it exalted to its ruin by uncomprehending forces outside the college life, nor do I want to see it stifled to its death by exasperated forces within."

Sports columnists and editorial writers had a field day with the Hopkins plan. The spirit of the proposals was praised, but there was almost universal criticism that the details were impractical. *The New York Times* called the plan "somewhat fanciful and overrefined." The *Harvard Bulletin* said the suggestions "carry authority because they were put forth by one of the wisest, most progressive, and far-seeing college presidents of which this country can boast," but there was no rush in Cambridge to adopt them. Among college leaders, only President Marsh of Boston University gave unqualified approval to the plan. Dartmouth's Athletic Council made official answer that it did not consider the proposals practical for Dartmouth, and after a short-lived flurry of publicity and debate, the Hopkins plan was filed away. One concrete result did come about when the University of Michigan announced that it was adopting a two-team plan for the 1928 season. And a surprising by-product for Mr. Hopkins was an invitation, not accepted, to go on the lecture circuit debating Knute Rockne on the merits of intercollegiate football and professional coaching. To make the proposal attractive he was offered a minimum of ten debates at $450 each.

That he did not have any real expectation his football plan would be accepted is indicated by a letter President Hopkins wrote to Trustee Fred Howland at the time he made his proposals to the Athletic Council. "I will not attempt to argue the matter," he wrote, "because under any conditions that I can foresee I am not going to ask for any official legislation in the matter. The most that I shall do will be to get the plan out as a constructive suggestion and allow the public to take pot shots at it, which, of course, they would do to extensive degree.

"However, I believe that in the final analysis this would not be harmful and would be likely to be helpful in that it would indicate that Dartmouth was thinking upon the problem and was willing to be cooperative if any group would get together to modify the intensity of the modern sports program."

Athletics at Hanover was back in the news in October of 1929 when a special report by the Carnegie Fund for the Advancement of Education included Dartmouth, as well as Harvard, Princeton, Pennsylvania, and Navy, among the Eastern colleges accused of subsidizing athletes. Dartmouth's crimes, it was charged, were the maintenance of athletes at certain private schools until ready for college and the employment of a member of the athletic staff to handle correspondence with prospective students. While the other colleges issued flat denials of the charges, Mr. Hopkins publicly said, "I pass the report over as inconsequential at this time. On the basis of statistics carefully compiled, it would appear that Dartmouth attracts men of athletic ability in rather less degree from the great preparatory schools than do several others of the Eastern colleges. As a result of the selective process, it might easily be true that we should have increased the number of men of athletic ability. I confess to a hope that this may come to be true."

Confidence in President Hopkins' ability to get an exceptional educational return from Dartmouth's comparatively limited resources was a large factor in the financial support that began to flow to the College in the twenties. Dartmouth's total assets stood at only $7,296,000 in June of 1920. They had grown to $12,120,000 midway through the decade, and at the close of the 1929–30 college year they amounted to $21,956,000. Because of the great expansion of physical facilities, plant assets more than tripled to $6,781,000. But even more impressive was the decade's growth in endowment, from $5,287,000 to a little over $15,000,000. There was a two-year spurt that was especially striking: in 1927–28 the College received total benefactions of $5.2-million—more than its total assets of fifteen years earlier—and in the next year another $3.6-million was added through gifts and bequests. The Sanborn bequest of $1.3-million for library books and the $1.5-million given jointly by the General Education Board and John D. Rockefeller Jr. for honors work were the major additions to endowment in that two-year period. The College in those two years also received, by bequest, $500,000 from Jeannette I. Cummings, $360,000 from Randolph McNutt, $242,000 from Helen L. Bullard, $232,000 from Edmund Hayes, $123,000 from Charles F. Brooker, and $100,000 from Florence L. Johnson. Gifts of similar size, made just before or after that two-year spurt, were $250,000 from Francis L. Town, $228,000 from Thomas P. Salter, and $185,000 from R. Melville Cramer.

The annual Dartmouth Alumni Fund had a steady growth throughout the twenties, rising from $55,000 in 1920 to $129,000 in 1929. More heartening than the increase in dollars was the increased interest and loyalty of the alumni, as evidenced by contributions from 46 percent of the alumni body in 1920 and 71 percent in 1929. The Alumni Fund money, doubly helpful because its use was unrestricted, and income from the College's growing endowment made possible a dramatic increase in the instructional budget. Also contributing to this advance were two tuition increases, in 1923 and 1925, raising the fee from $250 to $400. President Hopkins early in the twenties had expressed the aim of adding $500,000 to the instruction budget in the next ten years. Actually, it was added in six years. From

$519,000, or 55 percent of the total budget for 1921–22, the expenditure for instruction rose to $1,012,000, or 68.2 percent of the total budget for 1927–28. Two years later it had grown to $1,244,000, or 68.7 percent of the budget. Mr. Hopkins had no hesitation in allocating as much as possible of Dartmouth's growing revenues to instructional purposes. The higher instructional outlay represented not only better faculty salaries, but also a larger faculty to teach the new curriculum. While enrollment had increased by one-third in the first ten years of the Hopkins administration, the faculty had grown by three-fourths.

President Hopkins had a low opinion of his ability to raise funds for Dartmouth College, and without much doubt this was a part of the president's job that gave him little joy. In a letter to Adelbert Ames in April 1926 he wrote, "Perhaps it is time for the College to have a president who has the genius to solicit funds from the public and special donors. I do not have it. Neither officially, in behalf of the College, nor personally, am I able except awkwardly to present the claims of the College for public support or for private benefaction."

Perhaps he was right about himself when it came to asking for money point-blank, but he was remarkably effective as a fund-raiser in indirect ways. For example, William Pierce Johnson, 1880, was an alumnus who was outraged when Mr. Hopkins was elected president of Dartmouth but who later met with him in California and ended up giving $100,000 "because of my interest in you and your very unusually competent administration as President of one of the oldest and in my opinion soundest colleges in America and because I wholly endorse your ideas in regard to properly educating boys at Dartmouth."

John D. Rockefeller Jr. once told Mrs. Hopkins that her husband was the only college president he knew who had never asked him for money. "Why do you suppose he hasn't?" he asked her. To which Mrs. Hopkins replied, "Well, he thinks it's a privilege to be a benefactor of Dartmouth College and he doesn't ask people for money." This astute answer greatly impressed Mr. Rockefeller. In recounting the incident, Mr. Hopkins added, "I never did ask him for anything. He volunteered everything." Although Mrs. Hopkins' answer may have had its influence, Mr. Rockefeller's admiration for President Hopkins and his close friendship with him were the real reasons for his support of the College. At the Commencement luncheon in June 1930, when his son Nelson was graduated, Mr. Rockefeller was one of the speakers. In tribute to President Hopkins he said, "If a boy comes to me for advice on what college to attend, I should suggest that he find out what college Dr. Hopkins is president of and go there."

President Hopkins was not averse to pulling his oar in cooperation with others when a prospective donor hove into sight. But he was uncomfortable in making a head-on approach and preferred, as a method of stimulating the interest of a possible benefactor, to talk in relaxed fashion about the goals and achievements of Dartmouth or about his own educational ideas. "It's not pleasant work, even when you think you've got the right to raise the question," he said. "I'm not a salesman, haven't the remotest instinct for salesmanship. There's the assumption on the part of some of my friends that I like salesmanship, which is entirely wrong." His dislike of the go-getter approach in fund-raising was expressed in a June 1928 letter to Allan L. Priddy, 1915, then Alumni Fund chairman, who had agreed to take on the additional job of canvassing a selected group of wealthy non-Dartmouth men. "The idea has to be planted and the merits of the idea made evident," Mr. Hopkins wrote in definition of his fund-raising philosophy. "After that, though one may occasionally water the budding plant, the most successful technique I have found is to let it alone. So much for my theory about gifts and my consequent concern that you should feel that there had been any special misfortune in the fact that we got only $5,000 instead of $500,000." (The final part was a reference to the outcome of an approach that had aroused high hopes and had ended with a miniscule result.)

Although urged by some alumni to mount a major national campaign to raise money for the College (a dinner at the Waldorf, at which Mr. Thayer would play host to the business tycoons of America, was one idea), President Hopkins opposed the notion. Financial support would come, he believed, if Dartmouth were made preeminently good as an undergraduate college. In telling Mr. Sanborn in 1925 that he hoped to add $10-million in endowment over the next decade, he said, "I am determined that the College shall be kept out in front, even at the expense of deficits, if these have to come. Men are much more interested in contributing to support a college preeminently good than to salvage a derelict." Among non-Dartmouth men, he said, "my argument was here is a college on the move and there would be some distinction in being identified with it."

The rejection of an all-out effort to raise big money for Dartmouth and the preference, instead, for a steady, continuing effort to win the interest and support of wealthy individuals who would be attracted to excellence was the philosophy to which President Hopkins adhered throughout his administration. This produced its disappointments, as in the case of Mr. Hopkins' friend Andrew Mellon, whose interest in Dartmouth led him to express an intention of making a major gift, but which never came about. As for a major capital fund drive among the alumni, Mr. Hopkins was opposed to that also, feeling the time had not yet come for such a campaign and that such a move might damage the Alumni Fund, which was just beginning to realize its great potential.

President Hopkins kept his sense of humor, even about fund-raising. To Victor M. Cutter, 1903, who became a trustee in the thirties, he wrote of his impatience, before his own death, to experience the benefits to be provided by prospective benefactors, and he added, "There is nothing which so insures maximum vitality and prolonged years as making Dartmouth the beneficiary of one's fortune." He suggested that Mr. Cutter make this a selling point with his millionaire friends.

Whatever the differing opinions about the most effective way to raise funds, Dartmouth's financial fortunes took a decided upturn in the twenties. Eliminated for good was the kind of threadbare existence the College had been forced to lead for so many years of its history. By October 1929 the investment assets of the College had become large enough to make it advisable for the board of trustees to establish a committee on investments. The committee was created to advise and assist Treasurer Halsey C. Edgerton, who up to that time had been doing the work all alone. Not only had he been in charge of the College's investments, but as chief financial officer he had kept a tight rein on operating expenditures and had brought the College through a succession of years without a deficit. For this accomplishment he had endeared himself to Mr. Parkhurst and also to Mr. Tuck.

President Hopkins was happy to give Mr. Edgerton a full measure of the credit for the successful financial management of the College during his presidency. They took office together in 1916 and for the full twenty-nine years of the Hopkins administration they enjoyed an effective partnership. As a sometimes parsimonious guardian of the College's pocketbook, Mr. Edgerton was not Dartmouth's most popular administrative officer. But President Hopkins in 1927 paid tribute to him for what he meant to the College: "I do not know how we could have lived through the period since the war and avoided bankruptcy excepting for the very qualities which have given rise to these sentiments towards Halsey." In January 1930 he added more praise, writing, "I believe that there is no college treasurer in the country superior to Mr. Edgerton as a treasurer, and I doubt if there is any other one so versatile as he in qualities which make him ideal as virtually the business manager of the institution."

Interest in Dartmouth College among the prominent citizens of the country was certainly enhanced by President Hopkins' enormous circle of personal friends. Either socially or as board member or speaker or participant in national affairs, he had come into contact with the leading figures in government, industry, education, and the professions. He was sometimes accused of being too impressed with notables and men of wealth, but the simple fact was that he enjoyed their company, their dynamism, and their ideas, as they enjoyed his. And without being scheming about it, he was aware that these outside activities and contacts were contributing to the reputation and the general good of the College. Besides, his friends were by no means limited to the wealthy. He had a close acquaintanceship with three Presidents—Coolidge, Hoover, and Franklin Roosevelt. He had a special friendship with Wendell Willkie, and he knew Charles Evans Hughes, John W. Davis, Alfred E. Smith, and Thomas E. Dewey among others who ran for the Presidency. There is no point in trying to give an exhaustive list of his friends who were prominent in American life, but some idea of the sort of acquaintanceship he enjoyed can be had from mention of Lincoln Filene, Felix Frankfurter, Walter Lippmann, Learned Hand, Dwight Morrow, John Winant, George Moses, Sinclair Weeks, Philip La Follette, Harold Swift, Admiral Peary, Adolph Ochs, Arthur Sulzberger, Owen D. Young, William Allen White, Admiral Byrd, Clarence Darrow, Arthur Vandenberg, Elmer Davis, Kenneth Roberts, and

Ellery Sedgwick. To this group must be added, of course, many of the leading man and women in education.

In an era when the individuality of college presidents was more pronounced than it is today, Mr. Hopkins was probably the best known college president in the country. It was the time of Lowell of Harvard, Angell of Yale, Hutchins of Chicago, Butler of Columbia, Wilbur of Stanford, Frank of Wisconsin, Little of Michigan, Meiklejohn of Amherst, Garfield of Williams, Farrand of Cornell, and Faunce of Brown. One reason for the particular distinction Mr. Hopkins enjoyed among college presidents was the unusual amount of publicity given to his views by the national press. If his opinion was solicited, and he had one, he was willing to state it. He staked out the undergraduate liberal arts college as his special province and public responsibility—mainly, as he said, because there was a vacuum that needed to be filled. His defense of academic freedom was always quick and forceful. And since he believed that higher education needs to be in closer touch with the world of affairs, he accepted many outside responsibilities and was willing to take part in the public discussion of national and international issues. The press decided that here was a college president who did not fit the mold, and he became of more than routine interest to them.

For this public role and the attendant publicity, President Hopkins was taken to task in the November 3, 1925 issue of the *Christian Register*: "When this idea took root that a college president must say something snappy and put his college over with a bang of type, no man knows. We sometimes suspect that it originated in its present potency in Hanover, N.H. They say Dartmouth is the 'best press-agented school in the country.' At any rate, Ernest Martin Hopkins, a gifted leader, manages to keep out in front, and in the center, and in some newspaper offices he is a darling. But does it help Dartmouth in the dignified and highly serious problems of education? Would more assiduous collaboration on the academic problems and less press notices for the publicity man's album be good advice for colleges in general?" Although Mr. Hopkins was singled out, the attack was directed, as well, at several other college presidents, including Glenn Frank of Wisconsin and A. Lawrence Lowell of Harvard. If Dartmouth and its president were faring so well in the press in the twenties, it was not because of any studied effort to bring this about. It was not until 1933 that

President Hopkins acquired on his staff an assistant who would give most of his time to public relations.

To the censure from the *Christian Register* was added the criticism of a few alumni and others who thought that being in public print was somehow undignified. Mr. Hopkins' rejoinder to all this comment was that his critics ought to be told about all the publicity opportunities he had passed up. He was not unduly concerned, nor did he relinquish the belief that his activities in the world beyond the campus were part of his job and of benefit to the College.

President Hopkins had to restrict himself to acceptance of only a few of the invitations that poured in upon him. In 1923 he became an Elector of the Hall of Fame at New York University and also was chosen the first president of the Woodrow Wilson Foundation, which was established to make an annual award to the person or institution judged to be making the most conspicuous contribution to the ideals of public service. The following year, Mr. Hopkins became a trustee of the Laura Spelman Rockefeller Memorial and a member of the board of the National Committee for Mental Hygiene. In 1926 he was elected a trustee of Phillips Academy at Andover and of the Brookings Institution. In the remaining years of the decade he became a trustee of Industrial Relations Counselors and a member of the Rockefeller Foundation, the New England Council, the General Education Board, and the National Industrial Conference Board.

Among his non-organizational activities, President Hopkins gave his support to the Permanent Court of Justice and other programs fostering international cooperation. In 1925 Governor Winant named him vice chairman of the New Hampshire World Court Committee. The year before, he was part of a group, headed by Franklin D. Roosevelt, who met in New York to start a movement to establish a graduate school of international relations at Johns Hopkins University. That same year, he joined President Emeritus Eliot of Harvard and the heads of other leading colleges and universities in condemning Congress for passing the anti-Japanese immigration bill; and he was one of a group of prominent Americans urging all political conventions to adopt an anti–Ku Klux Klan plank. Newton D. Baker in 1926 asked him to serve with him on a committee of the National Crime Commission to study the causes of crime.

Several efforts were made during the twenties, as they were in the thirties, to get President Hopkins to run for the United States Senate. But his interest in state and national politics, which was considerable, did not go so far as to give him an appetite for holding public office. Mr. Hopkins was a liberal Republican and consistently threw his support to candidates who favored international cooperation. His backing was considered influential at both state and national levels, and candidates were happy to receive his endorsement. In each campaign it was customary for Mr. Hopkins to announce his choice, which was duly reported in the press. In 1928 he served as Republican Presidential Elector from New Hampshire, which he characterized as one of the most unexciting events of his life.

As part of his busy schedule of outside activities and interests, Mr. Hopkins continued to accept speaking engagements, but the number was considerably reduced from those of the earliest years of his presidency. Invitations now came more frequently from the educational world, which involved more arduous work in preparing his speeches. In April 1925 he inaugurated the annual lectures of the Henry LeBarre Jayne Foundation in Philadelphia, giving a series of three addresses on the theme "Philosophers and Kings." They were published later that year by the Princeton University Press under the title *Man and His Fellows*. The theme developed in the Jayne lectures was the changing relationship of the individual to the group, which Mr. Hopkins considered one of the fundamental developments in the postwar world. He spoke of "the obligation to work outward and not inward, to work for mankind and not for individual ends." But while attacking self-centeredness and advocating group concern and cooperation, he used the talks to make known his disapproval of the growing centralization of social responsibility in the federal government. Writing about this to Professor Frank H. Dixon of Princeton, he said, "I purposely overstated my case and overemphasized the extent to which I believe we should have reversion to local government, for it seems to me the swing is so far in the other direction, or at least has been, and so far as I can see is likely to continue."

Some months before his Philadelphia lectures President Hopkins gave one of the best received addresses of his career. He appeared at the Harvard Union in December of 1924, speaking to five hundred Harvard students on "The Relation of College to Life." His advice to his Cambridge audience was to avoid specialization in the undergraduate years and to look upon college not as a preparation for earning money in life but as a time to be used in acquiring breadth of knowledge and interests to which access would be largely denied them once they embarked upon postgraduate careers. The address attracted unusual attention and was printed in full in the *Harvard Bulletin*, which prefaced the text with the statement, "There is nothing hackneyed or commonplace about the address on 'The Relation of College to Life' which we print in this issue. It proves that President Hopkins is not only abreast of the times, but in some respects a little ahead of them, which is where a successful educator ought to be. He has seized upon some of the most vital problems of the American college and illuminated all of them in his own interesting way."

Writing to Mr. Tuck shortly after his Harvard appearance, President Hopkins said the Harvard Union talk and the Cornell alumni dinner of the month before were occasions for the two greatest ovations he had ever been given, and that he took this as a sign of the growing respect for Dartmouth as an educational institution. The Cornell dinner he referred to was the November 1924 gathering in New York where he had begun the friendship with George F. Baker that led to the Baker Library. In his Cornell speech, President Hopkins spoke about the value of the alumni to an institution, saying that their value was in direct proportion to their understanding of the changing responsibilities of higher education. What made the headlines, however, was his balancing statement that "the emotional alumnus, harking back only to undergraduate days, is an incomplete alumnus of minimum value at best and a positive detriment at his worst." It was a typical press performance, in covering Mr. Hopkins, to take a provocative nugget and make it into a news story that was picked up by papers across the country, with a headline such as "Dr. Hopkins Says Alumni a Liability."

In February of 1925, Mr. Hopkins gave the noon address at King's Chapel, Boston, which prompted a complimentary editorial in the *Boston Globe*, and later that year he delivered the Convocation Address at McGill University, where he received the honorary Doctorate of Laws. A speaking engagement with special meaning for him was associated with the inauguration of his younger brother Louis as president of Wabash College in December of 1926. In his address on "The College President" he passed on to his brother the advice given to him at his own inauguration—not to take himself too seriously but at the same time not to underestimate the vital importance of the work on which he was embarking. Continuing his brotherly advice, he said that the boldness of the college administrator must be used to offset the inclination of the institution to hold back when it should move ahead. And lest there be any thought that the job of college president is not a happy one, he concluded: "Participation in college work is a task to be undertaken joyfully, in happiness at the associations it offers, in gratification at the ideals which govern it, and in elation at the range of territory yet unsubdued over which dominion may be acquired. The tears of Alexander for lack of new worlds to conquer can never be shed by the college teacher or by the college administrator." Recalling, some years later, his visit to Wabash, President Hopkins said he had been surprised to encounter among Western educators such a distrust of the liberal arts idea. The prevailing belief in that section of the country was that higher education should have some professional or utilitarian end in view.

Mr. Hopkins was the guest speaker at the annual Exeter Academy alumni dinner in Boston in December 1927, and in the next few months he appeared at Union Theological Seminary, Bowdoin College, and the University of Michigan where the subject of his Honors Convocation address was "The Amateur Scholar." At a University Club luncheon in Boston in January 1928, he dwelt on the lack of public understanding of what education is all about, and again drew public attention by answering the charge of Clarence W. Barron that the colleges of New England were not contributing enough to the economic development of the region. Colleges were not training schools for business, Mr. Hopkins declared. "I am not convinced," he said, "that the college has anything to do with the current aspirations that prosperity shall become our sole objective as a people. These are all desirable conditions for mankind, but they are not primarily the concern of the college. The concern of the college is, first, more and better thinking; that mental processes shall be disinterested, that they shall be true, and that they shall contribute to the ennoblement of man's soul as well as to the indulgence of his body. It is no rare thing in life to see comfort destroy power." The press made much of the fact that this was the view of a man who had a business background and who was sympathetic to the economic aspirations of New England.

The honorary degree he received from McGill in 1925 added to President Hopkins' academic wardrobe a bright scarlet gown and a velvet cavalier hat, in both of which he took great delight. The "Henry the Eighth" hat was much preferred to his gold-tasseled mortarboard, and he wore it on most academic occasions thereafter. The scarlet gown, however, required rather more willingness to be conspicuous than Mr. Hopkins could muster. He told Robert Hutchins that he intended to be a sartorial sensation by wearing his McGill grown at Hutchins' inauguration at the University of Chicago, but unfortunately illness prevented him from being present. When informed by Mr. Hopkins of what he planned to do, Hutchins replied, "Good Lord, they will think you are the one being inaugurated." He may have been aware that Mr. Hopkins had actually been offered the Chicago presidency a few years before, but apparently Mrs. Hutchins was not. Later, when the Hopkins and Hutchins families were spending a day together at Palm Beach, and the two men had gone into the ocean for a swim, Mrs. Hutchins said to Mrs. Hopkins, "Why didn't you ever tell me that Mr. Hopkins had been offered the president's job at Chicago?" Mrs. Hopkins considered the question for a moment and then replied, "I guess I didn't think it was important." Recalling this incident, Mr. Hopkins said, "It didn't make our relations with the Hutchinses any warmer."

In addition to the honorary degree from McGill, President Hopkins in the twenties received a Doctorate of Laws also from Pennsylvania, New Hampshire, Yale, Williams, and Harvard. Part of the citation used at Yale has often been quoted about Mr. Hopkins—"the mind of a scholar, the courage of a soldier, the heart of a boy." The ceremony at Yale is recalled also because one of the best Hopkins anecdotes attaches to the conferring of that degree by President Angell. Since the joke was on him, Mr. Hopkins took special delight in telling how, in the midst of the awarding of his degree, an elderly Yale alumnus near the front of the audience was seized by a fit, creating a great uproar. The ceremony had to be stopped while the unfortunate man was carried from the hall. During the delay Mr. Hopkins said to President Angell. "I am sorry to be the occasion for such irritation to

one of your valued alumni." To this Angell quickly retorted, "Very frequently we receive protests from our alumni at our judgment in the award
of these degrees, but never has one come to us so vociferously, so emphatic,
and so *immediate* as this one."

None of the honors paid him by other colleges meant quite so much to
President Hopkins as his honorary Doctorate of Laws from Harvard. It
was a sentimental event because, as he said in his talk at the alumni luncheon following the ceremony, it gave him an official tie with his father's
college; and it was an event he enjoyed in relaxed fashion because he was in
the company of a great many Harvard friends, President Lowell among
them. The Hopkins-Lowell friendship was more personal than official. At
the very first gathering of New England college presidents Mr. Hopkins
attended after his election in 1916, President Lowell took him in hand and
said, "Come sit by me and I will tell you who the stuffed shirts are." From
that first meeting their friendship blossomed, and they saw each other
frequently in addition to carrying on a steady correspondence.

President Hopkins always stood up for Lowell when he heard him criticized as being aloof or not the intellectual star that the head of Harvard
ought to be. In a letter to Percy Marks in May 1926 he called this kind of
criticism unfair, saying, "My own belief is that President Lowell is a bigger
man, a sweeter man, and a more intellectually preeminent man than Harvard is likely to get, even with all her resources upon which to draw. . . . I
have, in all my relationships with President Lowell, found him big and
generous and kind to his professional associates." Mr. Hopkins liked to
tell how Mr. Lowell sat on the floor and played with young Ann when he
was a visitor at the President's House in Hanover. And Harvard's president captivated Ann by telling her about a secret staircase at his home in
Cambridge. Shortly before the academic procession was to begin for the
1928 Harvard Commencement at which Mr. Hopkins received his honorary degree, President Lowell suddenly asked if Ann was there. When told
she was nearby with her mother, he said, "I want to take her to my house
to show her the secret staircase." To Mr. Hopkins' protest that there
wasn't time, Mr. Lowell replied, "It makes no difference when an academic
procession starts, and it makes all the difference in the world whether a little
girl sees a secret staircase." So off he and Ann went to the president's
house, close by, to see the "secret staircase" in a closet off the entrance

hall, which enabled him to climb directly upstairs without encountering visitors in the ground-floor rooms.

President Hopkins had a rather odd ambivalence about Harvard. He admired the university and had warm feelings towards it, partly because he almost became a Harvard man, and also because his Boston associations and his summers at Mt. Desert Island in Maine had given him many Harvard friends. Yet any display of Harvard superiority or condescension, especially towards Dartmouth, would put him in a belligerent mood and lead to colorful descriptions of how hard it was to live with those people in Cambridge. A touch of Hopkins one-upsmanship was provided when he went to Harvard to receive his honorary degree. Only Harvard men, by custom, wore caps and gowns at the Commencement ceremonies; honorary-degree recipients were expected to show up in business suits—"because Harvard men think they are the only ones who are educated," Mr. Hopkins quipped. But Mr. Hopkins felt that as the president of Dartmouth College he had as much right to wear a cap and gown as anyone else, so he purposely attired himself that way for the ceremony. He marched beside Dwight Morrow, who said, "My God, you've got your nerve."

During those years, disgruntled Harvard alumni in the Boston area kept saying the university needed "someone like Hopkins" as president, and this went on to such an extent that it became embarrassing to Mr. Hopkins. After the success of his Harvard Union talk, other groups there wanted him to come back as a speaker, but he carefully avoided anything that would look like an intrusion into President Lowell's home territory. The Harvard alumni talk was nothing more than that, and Mr. Hopkins knew it, but in a letter to Natt Emerson, to whom he expressed himself in more uninhibited fashion than to anyone else, he wrote, "I wouldn't touch the Harvard presidency with a ten-foot pole. . . . With all of my admiration for Harvard and my friendship with Harvard men, it irritates me that they feel it to be a compliment to discuss me in this connection."

Members of the Harvard faculty and administration were part of a sizable academic colony which assembled at Mt. Desert Island in the vacation months. President Emeritus Eliot of Harvard had gone to this beautiful Maine spot for many years and others from the university had also taken up summer residence in Bar Harbor or in Northeast Harbor or Seal Harbor on the island. President Gilman of Johns Hopkins, President Little of Michigan, and President Angell of Yale were other academic notables, in addition to President Hopkins, who found the Maine resort a restful and congenial place.

The Hopkins cottage was in Manset, a small village in the Southwest Harbor section of the island. Southwest Harbor was informal and not at all fashionable like the Bar Harbor and Seal Harbor sections, and its residents took fierce pride in that fact. The Hopkins family had first gone to Manset in the summer of 1922, after vacationing for some years at Rye Beach on the New Hampshire coast. They occupied what was formerly a farmhouse, owned by Henry Teague, a Dartmouth graduate. When they told him how much they had enjoyed their first stay in it, he suggested that they buy it, and this they did in 1923. The cottage was moved back from the water's edge and remodeled, and later it was considerably enlarged into a comfortable and attractive summer home. During his early years at Manset, President Hopkins commuted back and forth to Hanover while Mrs. Hopkins and Ann remained in Maine for the summer. He gradually spent more and more time there himself, and in order that he might do all his College work at Manset from early July until Labor Day, a small office was built not far from the main cottage.

President Hopkins loved Manset and was especially happy that he could dress as he pleased and could shed the role of college president and be just like any other villager. Some years after the Hopkins family had taken up summer residence there, John D. Rockefeller Jr. offered Mr. Hopkins a piece of property near his own place at Seal Harbor, but Mr. Hopkins was reluctant to give up the informality of Manset or to get involved in the social life that such a move would have entailed. The Hopkins-Rockefeller friendship began at Mt. Desert a couple of years after Dartmouth's president first went there, and the two families regularly exchanged visits thereafter. Mr. Rockefeller, who found Mr. Hopkins a congenial companion and admired both his personal qualities and his thinking, liked to stop off at the Hopkins cottage, called Dartholm, when he was out for a drive. No doubt he too enjoyed an escape to the simplicity and informality of the little village across the bay from Seal Harbor.

A description of life at Manset was given by Mr. Hopkins to the *Boston*

Transcript in 1926 when the paper was making a survey of what New England college presidents did in the summer. "If, as I suspect, what you really want is to know the avocations of the summer," Mr. Hopkins wrote, "we have a place on Mt. Desert Island at Manset, Maine, which is not the fashionable part of the island. I play golf when I can find congenial partners, play with a motorboat somewhat, eat sea food three times a day, and wear old clothes all of the time. Incidentally, in the desire and attempt to do something out of the ordinary routine of the year, I do some reading, and a good deal of loafing around doing nothing at all. Somehow, this does not seem to me very likely to breed confidence in the administrative policies of Dartmouth College, but I cannot help it. I am trying to be truthful —another avocation of the vacation period."

Manset was proud of the fact that it too had a distinguished college president as a summer resident, and when President Harding died and the word went out that Bar Harbor was to hold a memorial program, the village leaders got in touch with Mr. Hopkins, who was then away, and urged him to come back and give a memorial address in Southwest Harbor. Mr. Hopkins obliged them, but admitted later that his opinion of Harding did not make it an assignment into which he could put his heart. On another occasion he was invited to give the sermon at the Congregational Church in Manset, and it was with amusement that he told the story of what happened afterwards. Mr. Hopkins was part of a double foursome that played golf every Sunday morning, but on the Sunday he was to deliver the sermon the match was called off and the other seven members of the golfing group came to church to give him their moral support. The sermon went well, and sometime later the lady in charge of signing up guest speakers pressed Mr. Hopkins to take the service again. He demurred, but she was insistent and kept asking him during the next two years. Finally, Mr. Hopkins asked her why she was so anxious to have him give another sermon. "That Sunday when you spoke and your rich friends came was just wonderful," she told him. "We had the biggest collection in the church's history."

Mr. Hopkins' frequent golfing companion at Mt. Desert was President Angell of Yale, whom he had known back in the days when Angell was Dean at the University of Chicago. The two men had a great deal in common, particularly a sense of humor which led to much friendly bantering. Their association was very enjoyable for both. Mr. Hopkins played a consistently good game of golf, usually scoring in the eighties, sometimes in the high seventies. He won the championship of the Southwest Harbor Golf Club, where medal play was the rule for summer tournaments.

President Hopkins became a member of the exclusive Pot and Kettle Club, a group of Bar Harbor and Seal Harbor men, and was the first member to be invited from his side of the island. Among his club mates were Walter Lippmann, Walter Damrosch, Clarence Little, and Arthur Train, all of whom, along with Mr. Hopkins, were part of an inner circle of a dozen or so who met every Sunday night for chowder and discussion of "everything under the sun." It was indicative of Mr. Hopkins' unassuming nature that he enjoyed the stimulation of such intellectual company and yet, at the same time, took pleasure in the more homespun friendship of a number of Manset natives. An especially colorful character among the latter was Derby Stanley, who was signed on as captain of the Hopkins boat, which was a small cabin cruiser built in Manset. Derby was a regular companion and helper, and also a sort of guardian and adviser for the whole Hopkins family. At eighteen he had gone to Dartmouth as a football prospect, but after only three days he had departed for Bowdoin. His stay at Bowdoin was also short-lived, but in the two weeks he was there he had become a member of Delta Kappa Epsilon and thus a fraternity brother to Mr. Hopkins. When the Bowdoin football coach had berated him with profanity, Derby deposited him head first in a water bucket and left for Manset and home. Prohibition gave Derby a chance to put his seagoing experience to use, and he became Mt. Desert's cleverest and most dependable bootlegger. He was reputed to have no equal in the use of strong language or in the coining of colorful new words. He and Mr. Hopkins got along beautifully, with mutual respect and good humor.

Another touch of Mr. Hopkins' exuberant spirit is to be found in a letter he wrote to Mr. Tuck from Manset in July of 1929. "I am the proud and exultant owner of a LaSalle convertible coupe geared up somewhat higher than in the stock cars." he wrote. "I tried it out on the cement road between here and Ellsworth the other night and quit at 78 miles because I didn't dare to drive faster than that even on a perfectly smooth roadway."

He added that he was out to beat the driving time to Hanover set by "that gay young blood, Dr. H. B. Thayer." Mr. Tuck was appalled and wrote back that killing himself was not going to do Dartmouth College any good.

One of the things President Hopkins usually did at Manset was to begin work on his address for the opening of college in the fall. Although the audience for the annual Convocation address was primarily undergraduate, he consistently put more thought and effort into this speech than into any other he would give during the year. He never spoke down to the students, and his Convocation addresses in total comprise the most considered and profound expression of his thinking about higher education in general and about the liberal arts college in particular. Few Dartmouth undergraduates fully comprehended what their president was trying to tell them, partly because his speaking style on those occasions was formal and not easy to follow. But the responsibility he was urging upon them, the worth of education, the opportunity being offered to enrich one's personal life and to serve society, the definition and spirit of the liberal college, and the unique role of Dartmouth itself—these were things the students could absorb, along with the idealism and the vision with which President Hopkins spoke to them and challenged them.

In the twenties, Mr. Hopkins gave a particularly impressive series of opening addresses. At the end of the decade, Harland R. Ratcliffe, writing in the *Boston Evening Transcript*, praised Dartmouth's president for not running with the herd and for giving as much attention to his student addresses as he did to those prepared for academic gatherings beyond the campus. "The opening addresses in Webster Hall at Hanover have been uniformly outstanding," he wrote, "so thoroughly worth while, that those of us in the newspaper 'game' who are especially concerned with college news have come to look upon the Dartmouth opening convocation addresses as an annual feature, one of the big guns of the autumn campaign."

At the opening exercises in the fall of 1923, President Hopkins chose to speak on "The Goal of Education," the address that was picked up and printed in full by the Yale newspaper. He followed this in the next two years with "Some Attributes of Education" and "Understanding." Kept from giving the 1926 address because of an infected jaw, he resumed in 1927 with "Today's Responsibility of the College," and then in the next two years he took up "The Undergraduate and His College" and "Orientation."

The best way, perhaps, to give some idea of the character and substance of the opening addresses of that period is to offer a few brief quotations:

The goal of education is cultivation and development of our mental powers to the end that we may know truth and conform to it. Knowing truth requires something more than an occasional disposition to seek it out. No nodding acquaintanceship or good-natured willingness to be friendly with it will give us real knowledge of truth. To know it requires unceasing effort to learn its lineaments in order that it shall be recognized when found, unremitting vigilance that it shall not pass by unseen, and the cultivation of high respect and deep affection for it and all its works. Moreover, education cannot be held to have been of large avail if it simply creates an attitude of passive acceptance of truth without inspiring likewise a devotion to the spirit of truth which shall breed a definiteness in the loyalty which we offer. They in whom the spirit of education has at all approximated its reasonable function must be doers of the word.

.   .   .   .   .

To understand life and to seek genuine satisfaction from it is to accept responsibility and to meet the demands of responsibility. Vital among the factors which comprise responsibility is that which considers the needs of the lives of others and denies to no other man and to no other groups of men the opportunities essential for self-respect and self-satisfaction. If for no nobler reason, this is essential as our contribution to a condition in which others shall not deny us like opportunities.

Mankind has never been entirely free from this obligation. Today, however, it exists to a degree unprecedented in the history of the human race. The boundaries of the space within which men live have been so greatly compressed, and the formerly existent prescriptions of time necessary for contact among men have been so largely removed that such words as freedom and liberty become practically meaningless except as they be redefined and become more inclusive. Freedom to disregard others and liberty to think only of self have become impossible now, regardless of whether they can ever have been desirable.

Education, then, has to do not only with our lives individually but with our lives collectively. Education, if it is to be justified, must help us to know better how to live together.

.   .   .   .   .

It is as true today as it was in the days when the Book of Proverbs was written that knowledge and wisdom are incomplete without understanding. No fact is of much consequence ultimately except in relation to other facts. It may truthfully be claimed, unfortunately, that faculties and administrations in colleges and universities fail as completely in recognizing this as do undergraduates; nevertheless, the need for understanding in one group is not abated because of the lack of this quality in another.

If all men of great knowledge had understanding, the establishment of pervasive educational ideals within this country and elsewhere would be a far simpler task. Arrogance, superciliousness and indifference are not infrequently associated with technical knowledge, but they are impossible in the man who has understanding, the fruits of which are humility and a spirit of neighborliness.

.   .   .   .   .

It is too little considered how greatly the background of life has been transformed even within the period of the youngest member of the College. Conditions have changed the nature of the home. The population of the country has become preponderantly an urban population and is on its way to becoming overwhelmingly so. Government has been removed from local centers and centralized to unprecedented degree. The adaptations of invention have largely increased the range of contacts of human beings and have added enormously to the interest of life, whatever have been their effects upon its satisfaction. Along with all these, everybody's expressed thoughts have become available to everybody else, until the intellectual ether has become as badly jammed as is ever the physical ether. We need a selective process for identifying good ideas even more than for choosing desirable freshmen.

.   .   .   .   .

If we conceive of leadership in terms of power, we are not lacking evidence in contemporary life that in individual men this quality still persists and that authority can be seized and held and exercised by a Mussolini or a Lenin. If we hold leadership to be influence that wins affectionate confidence and fires the imagination, we have for contemplation the figure of a Gandhi with a greater following than any man has ever had in his own lifetime.

In distinction from these, we have among all peoples men of discriminating judgment, intellectual power, and spiritual conviction, who have all the potentiality needful for great leadership but whose very greatness holds them from seeking it or seizing it. Meanwhile, ignorant or irresponsible constituencies withhold from conferring it upon them. One trouble with representative government, for instance, is that it is too representative. I have come, therefore, more and more to the conviction that it is not so much qualities of leadership in individual men that the world lacks today as it is the intelligence, the desire, and the will in the public to entrust leadership to qualified men.

Consequently, I have come to distrust the validity of much of what has been said, including much which I have said myself, in regard to its being the function of higher education to train for leadership. I ask permission to revise this statement to say that the first function of the college is to educate men for usefulness.

.   .   .   .   .

The college has the responsibility to cultivate the feelings as well as the minds of its membership. Its atmosphere is as important as its curriculum. The careers and accomplishments of its graduates will be affected not alone, nor perhaps most largely, by specific knowledge which they have acquired. Their disposition toward life, so far as college influence goes, will be determined by the extent to which their feelings have been refined and tinged with sense of responsibility during undergraduate years. Herein lie the incentives to action and the wellsprings of inspiration among college men.

In spite of the dangers of generalization, I, with deliberation, make this one. If the only options available to this college were to graduate men of the highest brilliancy intellectually, without interest in the welfare of mankind at large, or to graduate men of less mental competence, possessed of aspirations which we call spiritual and motives which we call good, I would choose for Dartmouth College the latter alternative. And in doing so, I should be confident that this college would create the greater values, and render the more essential service to the civilization whose handmaid it is.

.   .   .   .   .

I wish my final word today to be a plea to men of the undergraduate body not to fall into easy misconceptions of what the College wishes to accomplish or of the significance of the process by which it works. It seeks to be a stimulus to intellectual awakening and heightened mental power. It aspires to be an agency by which men may be induced to think. It cajoles ability, not to flatter it but to give it self-confidence. It flays ignorance, not in contempt for those condemned to it but in solicitude for those who may avoid it. It questions conventionality, not because convention is predominantly wrong but because convention is not always right. It challenges belief, not that belief shall be destroyed but that it shall be made strong.

. . . . .

New times bring new conditions, and the technique of educational method must keep pace with the changing status of the transforming world in which we live if the process we call education is to be actually educational. The undergraduate of today stands upon the threshold of a world whose problems would have staggered the imagination of generations past. The power development of the country has created a force equivalent to the work of 150 slaves for every man, woman, and child in the United States. All affairs of life have become larger in dimension and move at a greatly accelerated pace. This is a situation which demands realignment of all our physical, intellectual, and spiritual forces, if mankind is to adjust itself to its new environment. Here are the new conditions for education to meet.

. . . . .

Today, the American college has prestige, influence, intellectual vitality and consequent potentialities far beyond those which have been evident in any former time. Moreover, it has increasingly the openness of mind, the sense of responsibility, and the determination to utilize its opportunities and to render its desirable service. Its major obligation still is to human society and its principal solicitude is that civilization continuingly shall benefit from the absorption into itself of individuals who are better and wiser and more competent and more cooperative than they would otherwise have been. Specifically, this is today the principal concern of Dartmouth College.

In his formal addresses, and particularly those delivered at Convocation, President Hopkins tended to use a style that was not at all characteristic of the man. The sentences and paragraphs tended to be convoluted, with qualifying phrases tucked in, so that the real substance of a speech could be better grasped in reading it than in hearing it. In his mail a few days after one address, Mr. Hopkins heard from a critic who described what he had said as "a cadaver of bias clothed in the flesh of scholarly verbiage." He thought this a wonderfully graphic use of words and could not resist passing it around among his office associates.

One of his close friends in the English Department, Professor Stearns Morse, who wrote a sympathetic and perceptive character sketch of Dartmouth's president for *The American Scholar*, offered the theory that Mr. Hopkins had taken to heart a snide faculty criticism early in his administration to the effect that he talked just like a businessman, and that consequently for official occasions he had made a conscious effort to sound academic. If true, this was unfortunate, because in his extemporaneous talks, his informal conversation, and his correspondence he expressed himself easily and trenchantly, and often with humor.

Mr. Hopkins dictated his correspondence to a relay of secretaries, and in the long letters to which he was addicted he could toss off a logical, unified and vigorous exposition of his ideas. He was a masterful letter-writer, and alumni and others who heard from him invariably saved his letters. Writing to John K. Lord, who had complimented him on his Harvard Union speech, Mr. Hopkins confided, "My style . . . is a constant source of worry to me, and somehow it seems to get more and more involved all the time. I would give a great deal if I were able to present my thoughts more simply, and some of my closest friends do not omit to keep me reminded how advantageous this would be."

Public speaking, despite the surface appearance, was hard work for President Hopkins and he frequently said that it was a part of his job in which he took no pleasure, Something of the strain beneath the surface could be detected in the way he rubbed his moist hands or moved papers about while he was speaking. And yet he never resorted to perfunctory or "canned" speeches. To do so would have seemed dishonest to him. His friend, Robert Lincoln O'Brien, 1891, editor of *The Boston Herald*, once told him that he was foolish to prepare a new speech for each occasion, because nobody really paid attention to what was being said. O'Brien told how he had conducted an experiment by giving exactly the same speech three years in a row to the members of a club of which he was president. The second speech was praised as being much better than the one the year before, and the third was extolled as being the finest of these annual addresses. It just was not in character, however, for President Hopkins to take the easy way out, although he certainly dwelt on the same themes many times over.

Dr. Tucker told Mr. Hopkins he was wasting good material by putting too much into a single speech and that his hearers would get more of what he had in mind if he covered less ground. Writing about this to an alumnus, Mr. Hopkins said, "I suspect that if anybody ever takes the pains to discuss me at some later date, they will say that my speeches were diffuse, for more and more I have undertaken to string on a central thread thoughts of the College from different points of view and suggestions having varying appeals." Whether diffuse or not, President Hopkins could hold the rapt attention of his audience and end up with their admiring approval. His assistant "Cotty" Larmon recalled attending a Boston alumni dinner and, as the crowd broke up, hearing one Dartmouth alumnus say, "I couldn't understand everything that Hop was talking about, but I agree with him completely." And similar faith was expressed another time by Joe Gilman, who said, "I couldn't follow Hop's reasoning but I'm sure he's right."

In his Convocation addresses President Hopkins dealt with broad concepts of education and life. The specifics of national issues were usually saved for other occasions and for talks beyond the campus. In his opening address of 1927, had he chosen to do so, he could have taken up a very specific issue of prejudice versus justice in which the College had become involved only a few months earlier—the Sacco-Vanzetti Case. Dartmouth became involved through an act of conscience on the part of a member of the faculty. Sacco and Vanzetti, tried and found guilty of murder in 1921, were approaching the time of their execution in 1927, after unsuccessful attempts for a new trial or commutation of sentence. In April 1927, Professor James P. Richardson of the Political Science Department wrote to Governor Fuller of Massachusetts to report that the presiding judge, Webster Thayer, a Dartmouth graduate of 1880, had made remarks to him that indicated prejudice against the two Italian radicals. Although he had received Professor Richardson's charges in a personal letter, the governor made them public and a national uproar ensued.

Judge Thayer had approached Professor Richardson on the athletic field in Hanover, in the fall of 1924, and of his own accord had talked about the motion for a new trial that had recently been before him. "Did you see what I did to those anarchistic bastards the other day?" the judge asked, according to Professor Richardson's account. "Let them go to the Supreme Court now and see what they can get out of them. . . . They wouldn't get far in my court."

That Professor Richardson should have betrayed the confidence of another Dartmouth man was one of the reasons for the angry reaction of many alumni. From Randolph McNutt, in Hot Springs, Arkansas, came a wire saying, "Fire Jim Richardson and I will mail at once ten thousand dollars for the Tucker Fund." President Hopkins showed the telegram to Professor Richardson, who became agitated over it. "Calm down, Jim," Mr. Hopkins said to him. "If you go, I'll go with you, and we'll split the ten thousand." This story has become one of the standard anecdotes associated with Mr. Hopkins, with the usual embellishments—which over the years have got the McNutt offer up to fifty thousand dollars.

President Hopkins' reply to Mr. McNutt said indirectly that he was not taking him seriously: "I welcome your telegram just received as evidence that you are in good physical and mental vigor and operating with all of your old-time definiteness of opinion. I have been wondering in recent weeks where you were and how you were. Both of these queries are now taken care of."

President Hopkins had discouraged Professor Richardson from getting the Dartmouth faculty to make a group protest, but he was unbending in his defense of the right of any individual faculty member to express a personal opinion. Replying to Rolla W. Bartlett, 1894, who wanted a public apology to Judge Thayer or the dismissal of Professor Richardson, he wrote, "I do not want Dartmouth served by a tongue-tied or thought-repressed faculty, who stand in fear of losing their positions if they give expression to their convictions in regard to any subject upon which they are qualified to have an intelligent opinion. . . . So long as I have any connection with the College, there will be no change in the policy, hitherto prevailing, that an individual does not lose his rights to personal opinion or his privilege to an expression of these by becoming an officer of the College. . . . I think too much of Dartmouth College to see her demeaned among her sister institutions and bereft of respect among academic men everywhere by yielding to alumni pressure at this point."

In January 1928 the Boston alumni dinner took the form of a tribute to Judge Thayer. For participating in it, President Hopkins was chastised by Felix Frankfurter of the Harvard Law School, who was particularly critical of Judge Thayer in his book *The Case of Sacco and Vanzetti*. Mr. Hopkins responded that the dinner was a Dartmouth family occasion and that the tribute was given to Judge Thayer simply as a senior alumnus. But Frankfurter was not persuaded that the tribute was for anything but Thayer's judicial conduct which had been condemned by the Boston Bar and by leaders of the American Bar Association. What President Hopkins personally thought of the Sacco-Vanzetti verdict is not clear, but in a letter to Robert Lincoln O'Brien in April 1927 he wrote, ". . . the defenders of law and order in Massachusetts seem determined to hang Sacco and Vanzetti to indicate that this country is unsafe for radicals if there is any convenient crime around which can be pinned on them."

As the twenties drew to a close, another national issue was on its way to Dartmouth's doorstep. This was an issue about which President Hopkins had a very clear and definite opinion, resulting in publicity, denunciation, and praise—all in greater measure than had attended any of his other pronouncements about public issues. Mr. Hopkins took a stand against Prohibition, and so much importance was attached to it that it received a great play in the national press, and became the most noteworthy happening at the midpoint of the Hopkins presidency.

The Liberal College

IF any one thing can be said to epitomize the life of Ernest Martin Hopkins, it was his championing of the liberal arts college. It was his concern for the future of the historic cultural college and his desire to preserve Dartmouth's commitment to undergraduate liberal education that persuaded him to accept the presidency of the College when he had no inclination to leave the business career on which he was happily embarked. He believed that he alone among those being considered for the job could be counted upon, with certainty, not to take Dartmouth down the university road.

From the day he took office in 1916 to the day he retired in 1945 the liberal college was the central theme of his addresses and writings about higher education. He defended it vigorously, hundreds of times he defined it and its unique place in the hierarchy of American educational institutions, he interpreted its spirit and essential qualities, he bespoke its worth and its proud and indispensable role in the life of the nation. He admitted that he had been "harping along and plucking at this single string year by year," and he justified it by asserting that the liberal colleges were largely silent or inarticulate about their function and purpose, or possibly awed by the magnitude of the forces arrayed against them, and he therefore felt it necessary to fill the void. It was not so much the functional lineaments as it was the spirit of the liberal college that he expounded, and this was the greatest of his accomplishments as an educator.

In a memorandum to the Dartmouth trustees in October of 1940, President Hopkins referred to the effort he had made over a long period of years to define the liberal college. "It is not only among the public at large," he wrote, "but it is among many who make up our college constituencies that only the haziest sort of an idea exists of what constitutes the liberal college. On the whole I think that more attempts to explain what such a college is

157

have emanated from Dartmouth in the last twenty-five years than from any other institution of which I know, although more recently Harvard in particular and other institutions have gone into periodical and somewhat elaborate definitions and descriptions. It is, of course, always harder to define an idea than it is to define a fact, but in the course of making the idea of liberalism a fact at Dartmouth, the requirement has been upon us to make a lot of attempts at definition."

President Hopkins spoke of the independent liberal college as *sui generis* and as the historic college of this country, created and developed to meet the needs of a pioneer people. From it came all the other forms of American higher education—the technical school, the vocational school, the junior college, the college within the university, and the university with its myriad of professional schools. With the growth of the great universities and the professional schools, many said that the liberal college as an independent, self-contained unit no longer had a viable place in the system of American higher education. President Butler of Columbia early in this century predicted that the college would cease to exist if it insisted upon maintaining the four-year course. President Jordan of Stanford, at about the same time, declared that every successful college points toward the university. "As time goes on," he wrote, "the college will disappear, in fact if not in name. The best will become universities, the others will return to their place as academies." President Eliot of Harvard complained that the tradition of Harvard College was an obstacle to the progress of the University, and Professor Seligman of Columbia in 1916 said that the college was one of the perils of the real university and was a part of it only in the sense of being a threshold to the university.

Views such as these, plus growing disparagement of the liberal college because it did not provide a utilitarian education, aroused Mr. Hopkins' assertiveness about the unique values of the liberal college, which, he said, were needed in national life to offset the dangers of professionalism and narrow specialization. In a speech at Amherst College in 1925 he made one of his fullest and most militant statements about the liberal college and its deserved importance in American higher education. The great good that accrues to society from the college in its present form cannot be duplicated by any other institution, he declared. "For the sake of balance in our educational system the self-contained, individual unit college needs to be much more assertive in regard to its rights and prerogatives than has been its custom, and it needs to acquire a militant sense of self-respect which shall make it both feel and declare the dignity of its function as compared with that of any other kind of institution." To his Amherst audience he also said, "I wish . . . to assert the dignity, the worth, and the need in the American commonwealth of that kind of institution of higher learning which is known as the liberal college, and in much the form which natural evolution has given to it. With all due admiration and respect for the work of colleges of other sorts, I wish to emphasize my belief in the value of the existence of the self-contained, separate unit college, under control specifically interested in the college, such as Amherst or Dartmouth. Herein the needs of American youth of undergraduate age are a primary consideration. Such colleges are not only valuable to society, but likewise they are indispensable to any system of education wherein sense of the unity of knowledge is to be emphasized and wherein understanding of the scope of life, its atmosphere and its background, is to be held equally important as specialized study with its tendency toward the bulkheading of facts into idea-tight compartments."

One of the points about which President Hopkins was most insistent was that the liberal college must be independent and have full freedom to carry out its educational purposes in ways of its own choosing. The idea that the college was but the stepping stone to the university and should shape its program to that end was anathema to him. He drew a sharp distinction between the historic college, functioning as an individual unit, and the college maintained as the undergraduate department and feeder for the university. Moreover, he pointed out, the independent college course was the terminal point in the formal educational process for the majority of students enrolled—a state of affairs which prevailed at the time of the Hopkins presidency but which could not be claimed today. On this point, as on others, the views he held were inevitably shaped, of course, by the conditions of the time.

In taking on the role of advocate and interpreter of the liberal college President Hopkins never adopted a defensive posture. He often said that the college should take itself for granted, and his exposition of its virtues was always positive and self-assured. He was sincere in the respect he paid educational institutions of a different type, and he readily conceded their importance in the whole scheme of education, but he managed at the same time to convey the idea that they were somehow wanting and that true education was the province of the liberal college. Training is not education, nor is intellectual virtuosity the same thing as intelligence, he asserted. "I don't think much of the academic establishment," he said as he went his independent way. The academic establishment got its revenge by calling him an anti-intellectual and claiming that Dartmouth under his leadership was not to be taken seriously as a scholastic center. The success of the Hopkins campaign in behalf of the liberal college made it all the easier to bear such criticism with serenity. His efforts can be credited with creating a new awareness of the ideals and importance of the liberal college, and with giving undergraduate colleges everywhere a greater self-confidence and self-esteem. More important, popularity and public support were increased. In his Amherst speech he said that the college was the Cinderella among its sister institutions but that the American public was playing the part of the legendary prince.

Considering the hundreds of times that he either spoke or wrote about the liberal college, it is surprising that President Hopkins did not attempt at some point a comprehensive and definitive statement of what he conceived it to be. Perhaps he knew that such an attempt could not be entirely successful. He stated several times that a definition of the liberal college was difficult because of the intangibles. Consequently, his concept must be pieced together from what he said on numerous occasions. Two addresses that dealt with the liberal college *per se* and came closest to constituting a definition were those delivered in 1925 at Amherst and in 1944 at Bowdoin, both of which colleges were prime examples of what he was advocating. At other times he uttered striking phrases that would demand inclusion in any composite of the Hopkins concept. In his 1929 Convocation address, for example, he said:

"The liberal college is interested in the wholeness of life and in all human thinking and in all human activity. Its consideration is given mainly to the common denominators which make for fullness of life rather than with exclusive interests which ignore vital phases of human life. It is characterized as liberal because it recognizes no master to limit its right to seek knowledge and no boundaries beyond which it has not the right to search. Its primary concern is not with what men shall do but with what men shall be."

The phrase, "Its primary concern is not with what men shall do but with what men shall be" was one for which he apparently had special liking. He repeated it in his opening address of 1931, and it appears again in the address "The Faith of the Historic College," which was given at Bowdoin's sesquicentennial commemoration in 1944.

Another important piece of the composite definition comes from the opening address at Dartmouth in September of 1930: "No man can know all things. No man can even foretell what things it will in the immediate future be most important to know. Consequently, the desirable results are that he shall acquire facility in learning easily, that he shall acquire the will to learn accurately, and that he shall acquire the taste for learning continuingly. Recently, when occasion has arisen for discussing educational theory, I have been calling particular attention to what should be the central aim of the liberal arts college—to develop a habit of mind rather than to impart a given content of knowledge. This is, of course, but a variant of the statement, which the liberal colleges have reiterated often in one form or another, that their concern is far greater with how men shall think than with what they shall think. It is even more a responsibility of the liberal college to elevate the mind of man than to enlarge or sharpen it."

Although there exists no complete definition of the liberal college as President Hopkins conceived it, a scanning of his addresses and writings provides, clearly enough, the principal attributes he ascribed to it. The paramount obligation of the college is the development of the mental powers of its men and women. In that development of mental competence the untrammeled search for truth is of utmost importance. The liberal college is therefore the "free" college, as its name implies. In seeking the truth, openness of mind and freedom to think for one's self are to be prized above any body of specific knowledge or any set of beliefs. The concern of the liberally educated man is for the wholeness of life and the unity of knowledge, which he will come to appreciate from a learning that is neither narrowly specialized nor utilitarian. Instead of being trained for one special thing, he will be an adaptable contingency force capable of dealing with many things and with new problems as they arise.

Liberal education, while concerned with self-fulfillment for the individual, has the higher goal of inculcating social consciousness and social usefulness. Education until it is put to use is incomplete. Intelligent leadership is expected of those who are capable of it. Of those who may not have the attributes of leadership it is expected that they will choose intelligent, altruistic leaders and support them in their efforts for the public good.

Beyond mental ability, broad interests, and social responsibility, it is the purpose of the liberal college to develop the whole man. The college course comes at a time when youth is growing into manhood, and positive character should be the by-product of reflective thinking and of association with faculty and fellow students. Physical and mental health are also to be considered important in the development of the whole man, and the nurturing of moral and spiritual values through religious opportunities has its place among the functions of the college. Even social and community life has its educational value, and the college cannot be unmindful of this as an influence that is brought to bear upon the undergraduate.

His frequent comments on the desirability of developing the whole man —"man is not a disembodied intellect"—led some to underestimate President Hopkins' devotion to the life of the mind. In his address at Dartmouth's sesquicentennial observance in 1919, he said that the College's paramount obligation was "to develop the minds of its men, to expand the mental capacity of the individual man by its training, and to enlarge the area within which the individual mind shall be expected to work by the breadth and the comprehensiveness of the subject matter of its curriculum." But he did not consider this the whole obligation. "The function of the College," he went on, "is not primarily to develop intellectualism but intelligent men, and this purpose is not observed if consideration is given only to the mind, while the soul and the body are left to the whims of chance. . . . The College must preclude all that makes for impairment of physical well-being and must encourage all that makes for health. In short, while conceding and accepting the magnitude of its obligation to develop mentality of strength and accuracy, the College must, as essential corollaries of this, safeguard the physical and moral standards of collective living and offer individual inspiration for the development of spiritual excellence."

Much of what President Hopkins believed about the primacy of the life of the mind was expressed in the form of championing the search for truth, wherein he gave full play to his instincts for protecting freedom of inquiry and freedom of speech. "The goal of education," he said, "is cultivation and development of our mental powers to the end that we may know truth and conform to it." He also said, "The liberal college is the purest expression of the untrammeled search for truth from which change ideally comes." The search for truth is best conducted in a slow, reflective way, and he disagreed wholly with those who charged that students in a liberal college wasted time that could be used in practical learning. "In a world whose complexities become cumulatively greater year by year, and the interrelationships of whose activities become constantly more involved," he said, "the stress of a policy of 'hurry-hurry' should not be laid upon the one agency of higher education which exists primarily to develop capacity for reflective thinking. In a world where the need becomes more imperative daily that those of special skills, whether in politics or machine tooling, shall be men of deeper understanding, broader vision, and clearer insight, the liberal college should not abandon its thesis that the fruits of wisdom are more obtainable for him who saunters than for him who runs along the road of knowledge."

What President Hopkins believed about truth as "the Holy Grail of all untrammeled educational quest" was inextricably combined with what he believed about freedom in the liberal college. A succinct statement of that comes from the address he gave at the opening of college in September 1935: "The Anglo-Saxon tradition of education is that, though never attaining final perfection, we approach it nearer and nearer by ever increasing our store of knowledge; that by inquiry, discussion, and investigation we progressively acquire ability to distinguish truth from error; and that freedom to inquire, to speak, and to investigate is the essence of the liberty we prize. This is what is meant by a liberal education. It is an education that makes a man free; and only the free man can see reality."

In an exchange of correspondence in 1926 between Mr. Hopkins and Arthur Vandenberg, the future United States Senator from Michigan who was then editor of the *Grand Rapids Herald* and the father of a Dartmouth junior, the issue was raised as to whether the liberal college's emphasis on freedom to question anything and everything didn't lead mainly to criticism of existing values and the existing social order. Vandenberg wondered if it was not the responsibility of the college to see that this was balanced by defense of the existing social order and explanation of why people supported it. Mr. Hopkins' reply provided another piece of his composite definition of the liberal college.

"I am interested," he wrote, "in no trick method of getting the men to accept any specific point of view save that of social responsibility. The rigidly correct point of view of one day has been too often proved the handicap of a succeeding day for me to be willing to see the College become dogmatic about anything except the fundamental obligation of men to live in accord with the general interest of their fellows, and the enduring responsibility upon the individual man to recognize that he is, in due proportion, his brother's keeper. Your view of the importance of one type of nationalism or my view of another may, either one of them, be right or wrong. Certainly, it would be unfortunate for the country to have all of its citizens have a common view, even in regard to this. There are, however, as Macaulay says in his discussion of English public affairs, two forces always existent in the state, one of which makes for liberty and the other of which makes for order; one of which makes for progress and the other of which makes for stability; one of which is like the sail, without which there would be no motion, and the other of which is like the ballast, without which the sail could not safely be spread.

"This sums up the whole of my theory in regard to education, that the different philosophies of life should recognize the presumable integrity and value of other philosophies, and that men should interest themselves to find out what of possible value may lie in theories diametrically opposite to their own. This requires a tolerance and an openness of mind which shall not be passive and futile, but shall be active and dynamic, to uphold all that is strong and good in old theory, and to cut out and slough off all that is useless or possibly harmful, replacing this by so much of new doctrine as may appear to have value to the welfare of mankind at large."

Of all the attributes of the liberal college, as he saw them, it was the fact that the liberal college offered a general rather than a specialized education that Mr. Hopkins spoke of most often. This was a subject on which he expressed himself emphatically, especially when, with a sort of reverse twist, he was making his point by dwelling on the evil potentialities of excessive specialization and professionalism in education. The value and necessity of intense specialization and what he called "professional scholarship" were appreciated, but he wanted them kept in their proper place, which was the university or professional school. He conceded the responsibility of the liberal college towards those men who were preparing for graduate and professional studies, but it was his thesis that any specialized work in the undergraduate years should come late in the course, after the student had had a chance to sample varied fields of study and to develop a variety of interests. He was an advocate of the philosophy that a liberal education provided the best groundwork for any sort of specialization and that professional career training could advantageously wait until after the full four years of general education. He recalled his own experience in recruiting men for the Western Electric Company, and to bolster his point he cited the opinions of men he knew in the business and professional worlds, such as Dr. Anderson, economist of the Chase National Bank, who said that narrow practicality was self-defeating and that if the colleges would send out men with good general education, inquiring minds, and an understanding of basic principles, the business and banking world could quickly train them for the jobs they were to handle.

In supporting general rather than specialized education, President Hopkins did not want the liberal college to carry this to excess. "I would not underestimate the value of, nor willingly be without, the so-called practical courses," he said in his opening address of 1921. "They have their vital place in the college curriculum in association with the other courses. But grave mistake is made by him who forgoes, in those years of easy access to them, the resources of lifelong enjoyment made available through the influences of the cultural courses. In our preparation for life's work, it is proper and even indispensable that to some extent we bend our thoughts and direct our study to mastery of some of the material of practical affairs. In conjunction with this, however, no opportunity should be lost for securing those contacts that, come what may, give access to the great and eternal values of life." What he said in that address became the central theme of his Harvard Union talk in 1924, when he urged Harvard students to use their college years to gain understanding of the wholeness of life, not to limit themselves to specialized preparation for their postgraduate careers.

Too much specialization, in Mr. Hopkins' view, not only denied the student the chance to acquire those lifelong interests, but it killed the spirit of education for the public good. "I am a thorough and unmitigated bigot on the subject of overprofessionalization," he wrote, "and I think that one of the greatest evils in our civilization is that mankind almost invariably looks at the problems of society through the lenses of his professional connection." Another thing he held against the overly specialized man was the lack of understanding of the unity and interrelatedness of all knowledge. "Today the world is handicapped even more by lack of men with sense of proportion and sense of the relationship of one phenomenon of life to another than it is by lack of men of erudition in specialized branches of knowledge," he said in his address opening the 1927 college year. "Ignorance of the relationships of knowledge may be found as evident and as dangerous among men learned in specialized fields as among those who are ignoramuses in all fields." Within the system of formalized education, the liberal college was for him the only agency that was concerned about this condition and that was making an effort to correct it.

One other piece of the Hopkins concept of the liberal college that will bear some elaboration is the college's responsibility to develop character. "Scholarship as a product of the college is incomplete except as it be established on the foundation of character which is not only passively good but which is of moral fiber definite enough to influence those with whom it is brought into contact," he stated. "By as much as evil directed by intelligence is more dangerous than brainless badness, by so much is the college open to the danger of doing the country an ill turn if it ignores its responsibility to safeguard and develop character as it undertakes to stimulate mentality."

In his discussions of character Mr. Hopkins frequently spoke of "the good man" as the desirable product of the college. His concept of goodness was a combination of altruism, social responsibility, spiritual aspiration, and "moral fiber"—another phrase he used many times. The undergraduate years were a time for the individual to establish a code of moral conduct for his life, and indispensable to producing the good man of moral fiber was the religious content of the college's community life. "In my belief," said Mr. Hopkins, "a sense of personal, individual responsibility for making the world better, such as religion most completely gives, is an essential for any man who wishes to live a life worthy of the best within himself, or serviceable to those within the group of which he forms a part. . . . Education without the influence of the spirit of religion is incomplete education."

The greatest educational value of the college's community life came from the students themselves. Mr. Hopkins was fond of quoting Bagehot's statement that true education comes from "the impact of youthful mind on youthful mind." And he was convinced that the Selective Process of Admission, drawing outstanding young men from every geographical section and every economic level of the country, made Dartmouth the college par excellence where such youthful interchange could take place. He was delighted when his attention was called to something that George Washington had written to Alexander Hamilton in 1796, supporting the idea that there be founded in this country a college "where the youth from all parts of the United States might receive the polish of erudition in the arts, sciences, and belles-lettres . . . but that which would render it of the highest importance, in my opinion, is that in the juvenal period of life, when friendships are formed and habits established, that will stick by one, the youth, or young men from different parts of the United States would be assembled together." Such a cross section of the young manhood of the nation was exactly what the Selective Process had as one of its objectives when President Hopkins established it in 1921.

The foregoing effort to put together a comprehensive definition of the liberal college as President Hopkins saw it still falls short of being either exact or complete. The pervasiveness of intangibles, which he found difficult to put into words, is obvious. But the idealism and balanced functions of the liberal college come through clearly enough, and in the exposition of these Mr. Hopkins was masterful and convincing. In both spirit and practice, Dartmouth under his leadership was one of the best exemplifications of the undergraduate liberal college in American higher education.

What has been presented up to this point is a characterization of the liberal college itself. The fulfilling of its purpose depends primarily upon the faculty, and about this also President Hopkins had much to say. Paramount among the desirable qualities of a college faculty is commitment to teaching. "Appreciation of our function," he said, "will demand that men on the College faculty be teachers as well as scholars, interested in their students as well as their subjects, and solicitous for the College as well as for their departments of knowledge." The high value the liberal college places upon teaching is one of the things that most clearly distinguishes it from the graduate departments of the university. Good teaching in the undergraduate college has its base in thorough knowledge of a subject, but its goal is not so much the transmitting of detailed knowledge as the arousing of intellectual curiosity. The teacher of character and intelligence, who brings his personal influence to bear while working with the student in his special field of study, who has broad interests and in concerned with educating rather than training, is the priceless member of the college faculty.

The standard of excellence elsewhere in the hierarchy of higher education is usually otherwise. The impingement of the university scholar's priorities on the college—research, productive scholarship, and rigorous intellectual training such as leads to the Ph.D. degree—has been one of education's stormiest controversies ever since the methods of the German university began to have their influence in this country. The issue was not so heated in President Hopkins' time as it is today, but it was an issue he often discussed. His outspoken denunciation of any attempt to impose university standards on the liberal college led some to grossly misrepresent his real position and to claim that he was against research and against scholarship. There is still an echo of this misrepresentation today.

President Hopkins believed that the faculty was the foremost of the factors making for institutional excellence. "I hold it true beyond the possibility of cavil," he said, "that the criterion of the strength of a college is essentially the strength of its faculty. If the faculty is strong, the college is strong; if the faculty is weak, the college is weak." But the faculty of the liberal college must be willing and eager to teach. "Personally, my opinion would be that teaching ability is essential in all men who are to be permitted to meet undergraduate classes; and that the fact should be faced squarely that if men who lack proper respect for the service of teaching and fail to understand the glory of its service are to be associated with the institution, then they should be withheld from contacts whose opportunities they fail to grasp, and their work should be applied at points where it can be most productive. I would not be understood to be arguing for the elimination of desire for opportunities for research from the teacher's mind, for I recognize the inspirational value of such work to teaching. The emphasis, however, belongs on the teaching."

The denial to teaching of its full and deserved respect was the result, he held, of accepting the standards of the graduate schools which they, in turn, had adopted from abroad. "I know of nothing more unreasonable nor of anything more deleterious to the self-respect of the American college," he asserted, "than that so many men of ample training and of broad learning, with real enthusiasm for contributing to undergraduates not only of their knowledge but of their zest for life should, on the one hand, lack the complete respect of their associates or, on the other, be deprived of the satisfaction of reputation because of the great delusion which has pervaded the college world, to its loss, that a record of research only, if of sufficient profundity, more than compensates either for incomplete manhood or for incapacity or indisposition to recognize the real purpose of the American college. . . . Research is important, yes; production is important, yes; teaching ability is important, most emphatically yes. But, if it be conceded that all three are not indispensable in the individual, let us be honest enough to acknowledge that teaching ability is not the first to be sacrificed."

University standards got into the college mainly because the accepted way to prepare for college teaching was to undertake graduate studies leading to the university's Ph.D. degree. To Mr. Hopkins' way of thinking, it was wrong that a degree which was in no sense a college teacher's degree should be sought almost exclusively as the basis for college teaching. Some of his academic colleagues were scandalized that his faculty had a number of teachers without the doctoral degree. President Garfield of Williams once asked him if the reason for this was that Dartmouth lacked the money to hire Ph.D.'s. Mr. Hopkins hoped that some universities would institute graduate work specifically designed to prepare men for college teaching and certified with a degree equivalent to the Ph.D. In the absence of such a program, he favored the hiring of instructors after a year or two of graduate study, letting them get the feel of college teaching for several years, and then granting them leave of absence to complete the work for the doctoral degree. This interruption of the course in the graduate school had the advantage, he believed, of catching a potentially good teacher "before he has become wholly permeated by its ideals and subject to influences antagonistic to the college purpose."

This policy favored by President Hopkins, and followed by him to a considerable extent, gave rise to the idea that Dartmouth did not offer incentives to scholarly men. "In reply to this," Mr. Hopkins said, "I would simply say that it is all a matter of definition, and that it all depends upon who is defining scholarship and in what terms it is being defined, whether the work of any specific institution is called scholarly or not. If the work of the College continues to be as fruitful as it has been in arousing the interest of some of its men in mental effort, I am not concerned as to the nomenclature by which it is described."

President Hopkins was never seriously at odds with the members of his own faculty, because there was no difference of opinion about the first place accorded to teaching. He was fortunate also in having an instructional corps that, by and large, was loyal to Dartmouth as an institution and that supported its aims as a liberal college. There is some basis, however, for saying that President Hopkins and the faculty did not fully understand each other. He, while defending the faculty's freedom to teach as they pleased and conceding their responsibility for academic affairs, was wary of a substratum of "professional scholarship" which served the instructor's welfare rather than the student's. The faculty, while assured of their free choice to engage in research and to publish, were not entirely convinced that they really had the support of the administration in devoting time to such interests.

By "professional scholarship" Mr. Hopkins meant that kind of scholarly work that was done primarily for its own sake and had little or no bearing on the job of educating others. It was, in his view, a self-centered business and it was associated with his scorn for "the attitude that the student body exists in order that a faculty may be maintained." This criticism was perhaps deserved in some individual cases, but it would not stand up as a generalization. Even the liberal college teacher can have intense interest in providing new knowledge or new insights within his special field and may seek the approbation of his peers as a personal satisfaction.

President Hopkins, who was not afraid of "free and easy actions" when they expedited necessary administrative changes, was much more willing than his faculty to carry that same spirit over into the educational program; and this was the only fundamental difference that ever came up between them. The overriding objective of the College was to give undergraduates the best possible education, and Mr. Hopkins thought that if the way to do it, in some instances, was to forget departmental lines and disciplinary distinctions, then the faculty ought to be willing to forget them. But it was not in the nature of an academic faculty to be that free and easy. This was demonstrated in the mid-thirties when the Hopkins-backed proposal of a two-year, general social science requirement for all students was modified to preserve departmental courses in the second year.

President Hopkins' sense of humor usually came into play against, or in shared enjoyment with, those whom he liked. By this token, he was fond of his faculty. When Dean Laycock's notice of a June faculty meeting was accompanied by a request for contributions to the flower fund for faculty funerals, Mr. Hopkins replied, "You will forgive me if I don't get enthusiastic about your letter. I don't like, in perfectly cold blood, on a peaceful spring afternoon, to have to consider buying funeral flowers for most members of the faculty. There are, however, a very limited number to whose funeral expenses I would be willing to contribute heavily in the pre-Commencement season."

The faculty of which he was fond, and proud, could hold its own with any other faculty group when it came to teaching. "I would go to almost any extent to get a good teacher," Mr. Hopkins once told a reporter from *The Dartmouth*. During his presidency of nearly three decades, his record on that score was well above average.

The Thirties

I N September 1930, eleven months after the stock market crash, Dartmouth College began a new academic year with few visible signs of the Depression. The College had closed its books on June 30 with a deficit of $14,395, the first in nine years, but this was hailed as a very favorable outcome after the gloomy projections made earlier in the year. Undergraduate enrollment of 2,226 was larger than for the previous year, thanks to an entering class of 664 men and the fact that the job market offered no inducement to leave college before graduation. One sign of belt-tightening was an abrupt halt in the College's budget growth, for the first time in the Hopkins administration; but the faculty was being maintained at full strength and salaries were not being cut. Reduction of faculty and staff salaries was not to happen until three years later, by which time, it had been expected, prosperity would be back. Mr. Hopkins proved that economic forecasting was not his forte when he told a conference of New Hampshire state leaders, meeting in Concord in December 1930, that there would be an upturn in employment by the coming spring.

The national economy was not mentioned in the Convocation address with which President Hopkins opened the 1930–31 college year. Entitled "The College Mind," the address played new variations on the theme of the liberal college, and in a particularly interesting section it posed the question of what constitutes culture in contemporary times. True education, Mr. Hopkins told his audience, must be concerned not only with mental development but also with the external conditions which affect the mind. He suggested that the traditional concept of culture and aesthetic appreciation was too narrow in ignoring the new forms of beauty the modern world had to offer. "There are built and building in this country in these modern days great bridges as beautiful as anything wrought by the hands of man, and there are railroad terminals as inspiring, in their way, as cathedrals of old. There are ships which sail the sea the lines of whose hulls are poems, and there are great machines doing the world's work whose rhythms are sweet music to those who sense their song."

In a rare poetic mood, he became almost Wordsworthian in another passage, widely quoted at the time, extolling the beauties of the Hanover region. "I would insist," he said, "that the man who spends four years in our north country here and does not learn to hear the melody of the rustling leaves or does not learn to love the wash of the racing brooks over their rocky beds in spring, who never experiences the repose to be found on lakes and river, who has not stood enthralled upon the top of Moosilauke on a moonlight night or has not become a worshipper of color as he has seen the sun set from one of Hanover's hills, who has not thrilled at the whiteness of the snow-clad countryside in winter or at the flaming forest colors of the fall—I would insist that this man has not reached out for some of the most worthwhile educational values accessible to him at Dartmouth."

This descriptive flight, so unusual in a Hopkins address, could be appreciated by anyone sharing in the Dartmouth experience. But ascribing educational value to naturalistic emotions raised the eyebrows of some academic colleagues, particularly Irving Babbitt's New Humanists at Harvard, so that Mr. Hopkins' statement was picked up with derision as well as approval. The Hopkins conception of education was both broad and fluid, and by no means confined to the study or the classroom. He was not of a mind to leave the north country out of Dartmouth's educational assets. Support, had he needed it, would readily have been given by his friend, Admiral Richard E. Byrd, who visited the Hopkins family shortly after college opened that autumn and spoke to a huge audience of students, faculty, and townspeople in the football stadium.

Among the invitations that came to President Hopkins that fall was one from the National Temperance Council, asking him to attend a conference of officers of national temperance organizations in Washington in early December. He responded that he could not attend but that he was willing to state his own attitude about Prohibition, which he then went on to condemn not only as ineffective in the achieving of temperance, which he supported, but as pernicious in encouraging a disregard for law and subsidizing a criminal underworld. The letter must have been prepared with great care. President Hopkins had been under pressure for some time to state his views on Prohibition, and although it was not his intention to make public his letter to the National Temperance Council at the time it was sent, he recognized the conference invitation as an opportune context within which to make the statement he knew he was going to have to make sooner or later. Although rather long, the letter of December 1 to Dr. Ernest H. Cherrington, secretary of the Council, needs to be quoted in full if one is to appreciate its balanced analysis of the national situation:

DEAR DOCTOR CHERRINGTON:

It is impossible for me to accept your courteous invitation to attend the conference of officers of national temperance organizations, to be held in Washington, December 8 and 9. In deference, however, to your statement that the officers are desirous of having frank discussion of the present situation, I am perfectly willing to state my own attitude in the matter.

I have few convictions as strong as my belief in the value and indispensability of a theory and practice of temperance among a people which wishes to realize its best possibilities. I would not knowingly argue against or oppose any movement which made for temperance. For many years, in the assumption that practice might eventually show prohibition to be conducive to temperance, I have kept silent in regard to my belief that the whole theory of the Eighteenth Constitutional Amendment was pernicious. I felt very strongly that this Amendment gave too much justification to building up great new powers of the Federal Government as against holding local communities responsible for the conduct of their own intimate affairs. Nevertheless, I was not sure that the Amendment might not prove an exception to test the rule and might not develop benefits which I could not foresee.

Now, however, looking back over a period of time in which at least the tendencies developed by the Amendment can be shown, I cannot see, in the large, that advantage has accrued to anybody, except possibly to industrial efficiency, in the enactment of the Amendment and in the mass of legislation which has followed in its trail. I do not believe that it is a proper function of the constitution of a great federal government like the United States to devise sumptuary provisions for personal conduct. As little do I believe that detailed provisions for increasing the industrial efficiency of workmen belong in a national charter of any government except of one more frankly utilitarian than I am willing to see the United States become.

Personally, I believe that whether from the social, the educational, or the religious point of view, the greatest weakness in American society at the present day is the disposition of individuals to avoid responsibility and to delegate this to outside agencies, and particularly to the National Government. The effectiveness of attempted control shrinks rapidly to the vanishing point as responsibility for exercising this is removed to one center or another far distant from the locality wherein it is needed. A complementary weakness of almost as great importance is not only the willingness but the desire of a federalized and bureaucratic government to take over these responsibilities.

I feel so strongly in regard to the desirability of temperance in the use of alcoholic liquors, as in all other things, that, despite my objections to the whole theory of the Eighteenth Amendment, I would support it if I either had seen or was seeing at the present day any evidence to justify a belief that legislation enacted under the Amendment had worked or that it could be made to work. Instead of seeing this, my observation in traveling about the United States is that great areas which used to be wholly dry are now saturated, not only with alcoholic liquors but with a spirit of complete abandon in regard to the control or use of these. Likewise, the original attitude of resentment against the use of law for the support of this Amendment has given place to a complete indifference to the requirements of law, which to me is a more dangerous situation. Meanwhile, money which was originally collected in excise on liquor and paid to the National Government, plus the swollen profits of inflated prices on liquor and the further profits of cutting and cheapening liquor, has been made available to the extent of hundreds of millions of dollars for corruption. Thus the law has subsidized the building up of an underworld empire of enormous power backed by enormous financial resources.

I can see how men whose whole lives have been devoted to the single end of eliminating alcoholic liquors from national life may have become so fixed in their opinions as to make it impossible for them to modify these even for the sake of securing a national attitude of temperance. I can see how hosts numbered in the membership of Protestant churches, who believe that religious aspiration and the guardianship of public morals are synonymous, can conscientiously refuse to consider any compromise with convictions to which they have come to give greater allegiance than to social welfare or to public morals or even to the stability of government. Most of all, I can see how the official corps established to make effective the work of great organizations which have consecrated themselves to the upholding of all legislative enactment in behalf of the Eighteenth Amendment can feel an unwillingness to forgo any effort for the complete realization of the objectives to which they have committed themselves.

Meanwhile, on the other hand, I do not see how individuals or organizations whose solicitude is for building up a spirit of temperance can continue either to believe in or to support the theory or the practice of the Eighteenth Amendment as defined in current legislation.

Yours sincerely,

ERNEST M. HOPKINS

It is not clear how the letter got into the hands of the press. Copies of it must have been in limited circulation, but it is not unlikely that Mr. Hopkins himself took the initiative in making it public, especially since he was annoyed with the "devious and misleading" conference report implying a unanimity of opinion that the Eighteenth Amendment and the Volstead Act should be maintained and more rigidly enforced. In any event, in a memorandum to the Dartmouth trustees, dated December 20, President Hopkins advised them that the papers of Monday, December 22, would carry the story of his letter opposing Prohibition. He explained that he could not put off a public statement much longer and that he "preferred to pick the time and place rather than to run the risk of some garbled statement of this in some other connection." He added that he fully expected to be involved in a great deal of personal controversy and that he hoped this would not too greatly embarrass members of the board.

The Hopkins denunciation of Prohibition was front-page news all across the country. Newsreel men came to Hanover and the radio networks sent reporters for interviews. A surprising importance was attached to Mr. Hopkins' statement, explained perhaps by the fact that the tide was turning against Prohibition and here was a respected moderate joining the more ardent critics of the great American experiment. Editorials praised the restraint and reason of his analysis, and pointed out that his view was all the more persuasive because it was offered by a man who had wanted Prohibition to succeed and who still sought to promote temperance. Some papers, trying to make the Hopkins statement more dramatic than it was, described him as "a total abstainer," but that was not true.

The fact that his attack was made from such an impregnable position was perhaps the main reason the "drys" denounced Mr. Hopkins with such vehemence. The Anti-Saloon League organized a campaign against him, ministers of the gospel denounced his evil influence, and the mail poured in, much of it anonymous and vitriolic. President Hopkins sent several of the most abusive letters to his mother in Perkinsville, Vermont, and said he thought she might like to know what people thought of her son. Mrs. Adoniram Hopkins was a member of the Women's Christian Temperance Union and looked upon alcohol as one of man's greatest evils. Mr. Hopkins had supplied her with a bottle of bourbon, upon her doctor's prescription, but for years she had refused to touch it. Soon after she received the abusive letters from him, she telephoned her son to tell him how angry she was. "I have not only resigned from the W.C.T.U.," she told him. "but I have opened that bottle of whiskey. I find a little bit of it rather pleasant, and the next time you come to Perkinsville you can bring me another bottle." This, to Mr. Hopkins' mind, was a supreme act of maternal support.

Herbert Hoover was among those who were unhappy about the Hopkins anti-Prohibition statement. He invited Dartmouth's president to the White House and it soon became obvious that his purpose was to tell Mr. Hopkins how much the statement had disappointed him and to try to get him to reverse his position. Hoover indicated he had reliable intelligence that the country was 80 percent in favor of the Eighteenth Amendment, to which Mr. Hopkins replied that his own estimate of the situation was quite different and he thought the President was being given an inaccurate picture of the national mood. The White House visit produced no meeting of the minds, and although the friendship of the two men was put to some strain, it survived.

Mr. Hopkins had worked with Herbert Hoover on the food program after World War I and he had supported him in the presidential campaign of 1928. In his reminiscences late in life, Mr. Hopkins said relations with Hoover had never been pleasant during his White House years. This may have been somewhat overstated; Mr. and Mrs. Hopkins were overnight guests at the White House in June 1929 and in December 1931 they were guests at a dinner the President gave for members of his Cabinet. Later in the thirties, when President Hopkins was in Arizona to recuperate from an illness, Hoover heard he was there and called on him, and the two men had a friendly reunion.

Support for President Hopkins' stand was overwhelming within the College. Such was to be expected of the students, but the faculty, when polled by *The Dartmouth*, voted against Prohibition, 186 to 30. Student drinking had been a frustrating problem for the College ever since the Volstead Act was enacted in 1919, and Mr. Hopkins had gradually come to the realistic conclusion that as long as Prohibition gave drinking "an air of fictitious romance" there was not likely to be any satisfactory control. He had written, "I would handle the problem on the basis of the men's own sense of responsibility and on local option with good liquor." Long after the repeal of Prohibition, he revealed that he and the region's best-known bootlegger, operating from across the river in Norwich, had entered into a gentlemen's agreement that the College would not be a party to legal action against the bootlegger so long as he handled nothing but the best Canadian liquor, which he faithfully and consistently did.

The Hopkins attitude did not condone student drinking, but years of trying to halt it had brought him to the point of being as realistic and candid on the subject as any college president could be at the time. In a press interview in Chicago, three months after his much publicized statement, he declared that it was unfair to have a double standard which blamed college students for drinking and sanctioned raids on fraternity houses while turning a blind eye on drinking in American society in general and failing to raid the country clubs and other places where drinks were easily available. "College students are not a group apart among the citizens of the nation, to be treated and judged separately," he said, "and they should not be expected to have a code of morals different from that of the world beyond the campus."

From December 1930 on, until repeal in 1933, President Hopkins was looked upon as one of the pillars of the anti-Prohibition movement. He declined the active role that many invited him to take, but at the request of Senator Hiram Bingham of Connecticut he did make another statement of his views. This letter, printed in *The Congressional Record* of April 15, 1932, offered pretty much the same argument for repeal that had been made in his original statement.

Alumni support for any Hopkins action could be counted upon almost without fail, and this certainly held true on the Prohibition question. When it came to murals in the Baker Library, however, all hell broke loose. Mr. Hopkins, looking back upon that 1932–34 period, ruefully admitted that it was the only time during his presidency when he did not have the alumni solidly behind him. Just before he retired in 1945, and when his successor, John Sloan Dickey, was spending a few days at the Hopkins cottage in Manset, Maine, he gave him only one piece of advice: "Never have anything to do with murals."

José Clemente Orozco, the famous Mexican muralist, had come to Dartmouth in May 1932, at the invitation of the Art Department, to demonstrate to students the techniques of true fresco painting. Over a doorway in the corridor connecting Baker Library and the Carpenter Fine Arts Building he painted "Release," a fresco depicting man freeing himself from a junk heap of machinery and exalting his hands. In the library Orozco had noted the long stretches of bare wall, over 3,000 square feet of it, along the Reserve Room of the basement level. Here, the artist decided, was the place where he would like to carry out an ambitious mural project he had long had in mind: a portrayal of the epic of ancient and modern civilization on the American continent. Orozco's stay at Dartmouth had been a happy experience, his artistry had been respected and warmly appreciated, and he felt that an academic setting was preferable to a commercial building, such as Rivera had chosen, for what he hoped would be one of his greatest achievements.

Professor Artemas Packard, who had brought Orozco to Dartmouth, and the other members of the Art Department were enthusiastic about his idea, and President Hopkins gave his approval to the proposal that Orozco be made a Visiting Professor of Art and be allowed to go ahead with his mural epic. Work began in June 1932, and except for a trip to Europe that first summer, the artist painted steadily until he applied the final brush strokes and added his signature on February 13, 1934. Young assistants mixed the moist plaster and helped to transfer the cartoons to the wall, as Orozco, on his wooden scaffold, slowly worked his way down the long Reserve Room, leaving behind him in rich colors the story of the Aztec migration, the coming of Quetzalcoatl, the pre-Columbian golden age, the departure and prophecy of Quetzalcoatl, and then, at the eastern end of the room, the modern counterparts of these forceful panels.

Students picking up books at the reserve desk, working at the nearby study tables, or coming especially to watch formed a daily audience. Students in art courses at other colleges also came to watch, along with faculty members, the art cognoscenti from beyond Hanover, and the merely curious, who were not always aware that they were seeing the modern version of an art that had its glorious apogee in the Renaissance. All in all, it was a "course" in art such as no other college could match, and it was one of the great educational ventures of the Hopkins period, entirely aside from the art treasure the College was acquiring.

The controversy over the Orozco murals began with the very first announcement that they were to be painted. A year after the project was completed, Mr. Hopkins stated, "There is nothing of which I know in regard to College policies or College actions which has ever aroused the bitterness of controversy or made the College the recipient of vitriolic comment that these murals have." The "Release" panel had stirred up some alumni criticism, but the news that Orozco was to cover the larger and more public walls of Baker Library's Reserve Room aroused a storm of dissent. As is usual in such cases, the fervor of the opposition drowned out the approval of those who thought Dartmouth was to be congratulated. No one ever attempted a canvass of alumni opinion, but President Hopkins was convinced alumni sentiment in general was against him. In characteristic fashion, however, he stuck to his guns and, without making any claim to being an art critic, he defended Orozco as artist and man, protected his freedom to paint as he saw fit, and asserted the educational value of the mural project.

Opposition to the frescoes came primarily from the traditionalists and sentimentalists, and the crux of the matter, as President Hopkins saw it, was "the ultimate reputation which [the College] shall acquire in even greater degree of being a live institution, preserving the values of the past but constantly modifying these according to the new data and the new emotional and spiritual responses of a day which every morning becomes new." The four main bases for denouncing the Orozco murals were that the artist was a leftist, that he was Mexican and therefore un-American, that his art was grotesque modernism, and that his kind of painting had no place in a New England college or in a library so distinctly Georgian in its architecture. When Orozco got to the modern half of his frescoes, his devastating depictions of capitalists, militarists, and Anglo-American education gave the critics more reasons to howl. One of these panels, "His-pano-America," shows a Mexican peasant armed and rebellious against imperialist oppression. Asked what the whiteshirted Mexican represented, Orozco replied, "It is you! It is Artemas Packard! It is Mr. Hopkins! It is humanity!"

President Hopkins steered clear of the fight over traditional versus modernist art, other than to declare that he liked the murals more and more as he studied them, but on the other points of criticism he stoutly defended what the College had done. "I cannot imagine what all the shouting is about," he wrote, perhaps with just a touch of feigned innocence.

As for Orozco's leftist political views, Mr. Hopkins conceded that the artist was a pronounced socialist, "but with our muddled American incapacity to distinguish between disagreement with a man at one point and approval of his work at another," he added, "it seems to be the fact that consciously or unconsciously our reactionaries and conservatives are likewise the conventionalists in art." The sentiment of those approving the murals and those opposed, he figured out, was exactly parallel to their thinking on social and economic questions, which had nothing to do with the fundamental artistic and educational aims of the mural project.

That the painter of the Dartmouth murals was a Mexican and not a native of the United States was the basis for the xenophobic criticism. The National Commission to Advance American Art put Dartmouth on its "Regret List," and the D.A.R. of Colorado sent a protest because an American artist had not been put to work. The Art Digest also waved the flag by criticizing Dartmouth and praising the thirteen panels by William Yarrow on the walls of the Princeton gymnasium trophy room as "American murals by an American artist in a great American university." To complaints of this stripe Mr. Hopkins commented, "I had not supposed that art was restricted by race or time, and I do not think that it is."

He found the same lack of merit in the criticism that murals by Orozco, both in style and in subject matter, were out of place at Dartmouth, particularly in a Georgian Colonial building. In this connection he recalled the ridicule that Lord Dartmouth had for what he called the American period theory. The Earl had pointed out to Mr. Hopkins the great mixture of periods represented in the furnishings of Patshull House and wondered if he was shocked by it. His point of view broadened by the visit to Lord Dartmouth, Mr. Hopkins wrote to Mr. McDavitt, "I see no reason why because a library is built in the Georgian manner you should forgo the gift of a series of murals by a great Mexican painter," and since he was presiding over an educational institution and not a Colonial museum, he was sincere in expressing his "complete surprise at this particular agitation." By all odds the alumnus most outraged by the murals was one of Mr. Hopkins' closest Boston friends. He withdrew his son's application to Dartmouth and sent him to Williams instead.

If he felt inexpert as a judge of art, President Hopkins was on solid, familiar ground when it came to the matter of the educational value of Orozco's presence and accomplishment. His statements on this score were reminiscent of what he had said ten years before about his willingness to bring Lenin and Trotsky to the College. In a reply to Dr. George Van Ness Dearborn, 1890, he wrote: "My own sentiments in regard to the whole matter are that I would bring in anybody to espouse any project which would be as intellectually stimulating to the undergraduate body as these murals have proved to be. The very fact that opinion is so definitely divided among the students is in itself, I think, a far better effect than could be accomplished by something in which everyone was agreed."

In the same vein, he told another alumnus that it was his "very sincere conviction that as a stimulus to the thinking about art which is fundamental to education [the murals] are potent beyond anything else that we could have done. As such, I should have been willing to put them at any place in the whole college plant, and I would put anything anywhere that would through successive years cause as much discussion in any field of knowledge as these have caused among the undergraduates of succeeding classes."

His sense of humor was operative in almost any controversial situation in which Mr. Hopkins found himself, and the murals were no exception. In another of his frequent letters to Clarence McDavitt he wrote, "I bid fair, and I want you to be appreciative of this, to go down in history as one of the greatest patrons of art since the Middle Ages." This thought, he said, gave him fortitude in facing the opinion of a number of friends "who think that as a connoisseur of art I am a bum." The same light spirit was at play when Mr. Hopkins sent a memo to Treasurer Halsey Edgerton explaining the basis on which Orozco was joining the faculty. He exaggerated the fierce radicalism of the Mexican artist, reporting how Orozco thought that the faculty ought to be annihilated because they profiteered at the expense of the students ("a particularly interesting point of view at the present moment"). "This is really a letter of warning," Mr. Hopkins concluded. "Please do not oppose him at any point. I'd hate to lose a good treasurer and you represent all that he abhors."

One other incident of the Hopkins-Orozco relationship deserves to be told. When the artist came to the twelfth panel, "Gods of the Modern World," wherein he depicts skeletons in academic robes and protests against the worship of dead knowledge for its own sake, Orozco told President Hopkins that he was willing to alter this in order not to embarrass the College, for which he had developed great affection. It would have been surprising if Mr. Hopkins had made any answer other than the one he did. "I told him I would not do this," he wrote, "and that I would not allow it to be done in behalf of the College, for when we invited a man to the College, it was to represent himself and not to become a propaganda agency for some theory of our own." This was entirely in keeping with what he had said to Professor Packard: "In regard to the murals in general, I should like to have Mr. Orozco feel that he has the enthusiastic support of the College in the principles for which he stands and the ideas which he wishes to represent. I have been perfectly willing to uphold my official end of this controversy and to defend the privilege and right of Mr. Orozco in the whole matter."

If Mr. Hopkins had any decided dislike in the mural series, it was the Anglo-American panel showing the town meeting and the school teacher. The artist's idea was fine with him, but he didn't see why the school children couldn't look like New England children. "There never was a group of children in New England, either in Puritan times or since, that looked anything like this group of Scandinavian squareheads," he complained.

Three years after the Orozco murals were finished the College commissioned another set of murals of a quite different character. To decorate the Richard Hovey Grill in the new Thayer dining hall, which opened in September 1937, Walter Beach Humphrey, 1914, did a series of large oil paintings illustrating the song "Eleazar Wheelock." In the eyes of the Dartmouth traditionalists, the Humphrey murals were a rebuttal to the Orozco frescoes. Colorful and legendary, they included many clever touches, but when they were completed and put on public display in the spring of 1939 they shocked the prudish with their bevy of bare-breasted Indian maidens. Mr. Hopkins didn't see how he could get into another mural controversy with a subject as seemingly safe as "Eleazar Wheelock," but in a minor way he did. "How would you as President of Dartmouth College like to be shown years from now surrounded by a lot of naked Indian girls?" one upset alumnus asked him. Mr. Hopkins replied that he wouldn't mind at all, that he would in fact be quite pleased.

Dartmouth life in the early thirties was not all murals, although that controversy took up a deplorable amount of time. Simultaneously, in fact, President Hopkins had to give some of his attention to a lesser alumni rebellion against the head football coach, whose teams in 1932 and 1933 had mediocre records. The Depression had not gone away, and the financial problems grew bigger and more difficult to solve. Plant actions were taken: a squash-court wing was added to the gymnasium, Reed Hall was converted from a dormitory to a classroom and faculty office building, a new nine-hole golf course was built, and the plan to move the White Church from the northwest corner of the green to the Rollins Chapel site went up in smoke when the church, which dated from 1795, burned to the ground in May 1931. New policies were adopted: the financial aid program was revised so that scholarship awards would be made on the basis of need rather than scholastic standing; the Selective Process of Admission was further liberalized by abolishing any formal set of requirements and basing admission on the candidate's providing evidence that he was competent to carry on his course at Dartmouth; the philosophy of the Senior Fellowships was selectively extended to a small number of outstanding students in secondary schools by granting them early admission to college at the end of junior year; and the Committee on Educational Policy recommended changes in the requirements for the A.B. degree, making at least one year of language study in college compulsory for all students and requiring that two full-year courses in the sciences be elected. The alumni association in June of 1931 remembered the 15th anniversary of Mr. Hopkins' presidency and the 30th anniversary of his graduation by presenting him with a handsome silver service. And when the basketball season arrived, President Hopkins demonstrated his readiness to take action by concocting a scheme, with the connivance of the Dartmouth captain, to have the officials call technical fouls against the Dartmouth team when the home crowd engaged in unsportsmanlike conduct. This, plus the president's public apology for the way the Dartmouth students had treated the Columbia basketball team, was an unpopular action but it quickly restored reasonable behavior in Alumni Gymnasium. That figurative spanking accomplished, along with numerous campus and off-campus chores, Mr. Hopkins took off for Paris in May 1932 to spend ten days with Mr. Tuck.

For the opening of College that fall, President Hopkins prepared an address which has become as indelibly associated with his name as his "aristocracy of brains" address given ten years earlier. Its title was "Change Is Opportunity," a phrase that sticks in the memory. It is the fate of most college presidents to have none of their speeches remembered, but one does not think of Ernest Martin Hopkins without recalling "aristocracy of brains" and "change is opportunity." And to these two addresses should be added three others that were exceptional—the inaugural address "The College of the Future"; the sesquicentennial address "Dartmouth College: An Interpretation"; and the 1940 baccalaureate address "The Upright Man," about which more will be told later.

The 1932 opening address, which got the unusual tribute of a student ovation, was repeated in adapted form over the national radio network of the Columbia Broadcasting System. Delivered from the WNAC studios in Boston on October 1, the speech was part of the Columbia Public Affairs Institute series and was carried by more than one hundred stations coast to coast. The address was markedly different from anything President Hopkins had delivered to the students at previous Convocations. It was not educational philosophy or the liberal arts college that he chose to speak about, but "society's distress at the present time" and the shortcomings of American democracy that were an impediment to the nation's social and economic well-being. It was the start of a series of speeches given during the thirties, denouncing weakness, defeatism, and self-indulgence, and culminating in the attacks on those who preached isolationism and saw the war in Europe as of no concern to this country.

Conditions of hardship and struggle have their advantages, Mr. Hopkins told his student audience. For individuals and nations they can have the positive effect of developing strength and capability not gained in times of ease and plenty. Since this is not a point of view the general public will understand or act upon, "education must emphasize the fact that coopera-tive effort of the intellectually enlightened is necessary to overcome the inertia of mass indifference to lessons of the past or to possibilities of the future." Education must therefore insist that intelligence be supplemented by positiveness and forcefulness.

"If the processes of selection for admission to college could be more omnisciently accurate than they can be made," Mr. Hopkins declared, "I should urge that Dartmouth College in these critical days specify strength as its first requirement—strength of character, strength of mind, strength of conviction, strength of purpose. The weakling and the man who de-mands softness and self-indulgence from life are a greater menace to the world's recovery than are all the existent destructive forces."

With the concession that students had seen little in the outside world to encourage effort or to impose a sense of obligation, he moved into the main part of his address, which was a hard-hitting arraignment of the weak-nesses of American democracy. He was scornful of two prevailing attitudes —one the cynical and defeatist idea that nothing could be done to save society, and the other the head-in-sand failure to recognize that society was in danger and could be protected only by thoughtful, cooperative effort. As representative of the second attitude he cited the advocates of "ever-increasing gratuities to World War veterans." He compared the veterans to Rome's Praetorian Guard, whose acquisitiveness and demands for pref-erential treatment helped to destroy the empire. This comparison gave the newspapers their "lead" and earned for Mr. Hopkins the enmity of those promoting the veterans' bonus.

The essence of social and political democracy, he stated, is cooperation for the common good under intelligent leadership. Recalling his plea, of ten years earlier, for an aristocracy of brains, he said he was prepared to go much further and "to contend that the most serious danger threatening civilization today is the rapid development of a perverted sense of democ-racy, at home and abroad, which encourages public opinion not only to accept but to idealize mediocrity, and which allows public opinion to be ostentatiously arrogant in its indifference to intelligence and antagonistic toward any process of thought in its leaders which rises above its own average mental capacity. . . . Under the spurious standards of our present-day democracy, enthusiasm is reserved largely for the common man who remains common rather than for the common man who makes himself uncommon."

The spirit of democracy is not a natural instinct for mankind, he contended. It is an acquired characteristic for which individual and collective self-discipline is necessary. But discipline is abhorred; instead, "government by the people is being displaced by the militant insistence of organized minorities that their wills be made law, and government for the people is being set aside for the advantage of self-centered and remorselessly grasping blocs of special interest." The net result of the growing transformation of the republic into a "pure democracy" has been to produce "a public policy based on mass production of sentiment in the formation of which propaganda is more effective than reason and the demagogue is more influential than the philosopher."

President Hopkins concluded by saying, "I am fully aware that many of these assertions are more definitely in the controversial field than ordinarily is appropriate to an academic address, but I believe that circumstances of the time demand consideration of them. It is meet in behalf of those who idealize the theory of democracy, as well as in behalf of all others, that our practices of democracy be reexamined, reappraised, and re-formed, eliminating the grave hazards of weakness and developing the attributes of power."

The best in a democracy, so fervently desired by Mr. Hopkins, was not likely to come forth in a time of Depression. But one exemplification of the cooperation, discipline, and intelligent leadership he called for was to be found in the Dartmouth community. Although the College was financially pinched, like other privately endowed institutions at that time, it established its priorities and practiced frugality, and it was never in really serious trouble. The main job for President Hopkins and the trustees was to make ends meet, year by year, and although deficits were incurred for four years in a row, none ran above $43,205, the figure for 1932–33. Growth in the College's endowment and other assets, however, was far off its pace of the twenties. In the ten-year period from June 1930 to June 1940, total assets increased by only $3.8 million, most of which came in the form of bequests rather than gifts, which had dried up.

At the low point in April 1933, President Hopkins met with the faculty to inform them about College finances and to say that the prospect for the coming year was such that probably it would no longer be possible to hold to the existing salary scale. The 1932–33 deficit of $43,000, for example, had been kept that low only because of $20,000 Mr. Tuck had sent to help out and $48,000 that had been diverted from the faculty sabbatical reserve. Investment income was certain to shrink still further, and the Alumni Fund, which had produced $120,000 in 1930, had dropped to $66,000 for 1933. The faculty took this report in praiseworthy spirit and an impromptu group actually proposed that a 10 percent reduction in salary for faculty and staff be put into effect for 1933–34 if the trustees felt it necessary. This salary cut was adopted, resulting in savings of $139,000 for the year. Dormitory rents were reduced for 1933–34 to increase occupancy and therefore income. All freshman sports except football had been dropped in November 1932, and in December 1933 the Athletic Council cancelled varsity tennis, lacrosse, golf, and gymnastics as an additional economy. With these and other savings, the College wiped out the deficit which had been carried over, and it actually posted a $3,000 surplus for 1933–34. From that point on the financial situation gradually improved, with the books balanced in each of the next six years and $152,000 restored to the instructional budget. Throughout the whole Depression period Treasurer Halsey Edgerton did a remarkable job, and President Hopkins made it a point to give him a large share of the credit for the successful way in which Dartmouth weathered those difficult years.

One great advantage to the College was the stability in undergraduate enrollment, which not only held steady but increased by 235 men during the first half of the thirties. With a record freshman class of 707 men in the fall of 1934, enrollment exceeded 2,400 for the first time. An increase in the tuition fee, although badly needed, was put off by the trustees because of the financial struggle many students were already having and because of some fear that enrollment might suffer. An increase from $400 to $450 was eventually voted in 1936, but spread out over two years. This increase coincided with the adoption of a new health insurance plan, whereby the tuition fee covered the cost of all medical, surgical, and hospital care a student might receive while attending college. Part of the higher tuition income was also devoted to financial aid, which in the aggregate rose by 22 percent during the Depression years. Federally funded jobs, such as those under the National Youth Administration, were available to undergraduates, and the sight of students raking leaves on the campus was one reminder that the times were abnormal.

A blow to the College—bad enough financially but even worse sentimentally—was the gutting of Dartmouth Hall by fire on April 25, 1935. Rebuilding was begun almost immediately, and the opportunity was seized to do a complete remodeling and fireproofing of the interior, at a cost of $211,871. Only $86,727 of the cost was covered by insurance, but the Alumni Fund accepted the challenge of paying off the balance in addition to meeting the College's annual operating deficits, a goal which was achieved over the next six years. The Fund by this time was back in high gear, raising money in amounts comparable to the receipts for the years just before the Depression.

The rededication of Dartmouth Hall was held on February 14, 1936, and President Angell of Yale, alma mater of Eleazar Wheelock, came to participate in the ceremony and to receive Dartmouth's honorary Doctorate of Laws. That evening the annual Dartmouth Night was observed, with President Angell as one of the speakers. The occasion developed into one of the jolliest ever held in Webster Hall, and wit and good fellowship prevailed. When it came time to introduce President Angell, Mr. Hopkins mentioned their summer golf and said Yale's president was a delightful opponent but that he had the strange habit of bringing up weighty educational questions just as Mr. Hopkins was all set to putt. Angell's retort, when he arose to speak, was that after Dartmouth's president had taken four or five putts he felt obliged to ease the embarrassment by saying something.

IN THE SUMMER of 1933 President Hopkins decided upon a reorganization of his administrative staff, which had undergone no significant change since the establishment of the new positions of director of admissions and dean of freshmen in 1921. E. Gordon Bill, who had been named as the first incumbent of those two posts, was involved in the major change of 1933. He was elevated to the newly created deanship of the faculty, an office to which Mr. Hopkins assigned responsibility for oversight of the honors courses, supervision of majors, and coordination of the faculty departments "with the definite purpose in mind of a greater consolidation of the curriculum." As time went on, the dean of the faculty increasingly became the chief liaison officer between the faculty and the president, and the chief administrative officer having to do with faculty personnel.

To assume the positions of dean of freshmen and director of admissions, President Hopkins named Robert C. Strong, 1924, who had been his executive assistant since 1926. Albert I. Dickerson, 1930, assistant to the president for three years, was promoted to executive assistant; and the duties of director of the news service, which Mr. Dickerson had been handling, were assumed by Charles E. Widmayer, 1930, assistant in English and director of athletic publicity, who became the College's first full-time public relations officer. Sidney C. Hayward, 1926, who had become secretary of the College in 1930 after four years as a presidential assistant, continued in that office and held a major place in the group working in closest proximity to Mr. Hopkins.

With retirement approaching for Dean of the College Craven Laycock, the year 1933 also saw the appointment of Lloyd K. Neidlinger, 1923, as assistant dean for one year prior to assuming the deanship in 1934. In writing to Mr. Neidlinger to persuade him to accept this appointment, President Hopkins explained what he hoped the 1933 administrative reorganization would accomplish, and in the process he cast some interesting light on his philosophy of college administration.

After stating that he was completing his seventeenth year as Dartmouth's president and that he had no idea how long a man could retain his usefulness and effectiveness in such a position, he wrote: "The one great concern and the only great solicitude that I have at the present moment is to see this organization of the College set up and functioning in such a way that the actual presence and participation of the President in the affairs of the College at any particular moment is a very much less vital factor than it has been in the past. Obviously, in such a set-up as I have suggested relationships must be exceedingly close and understandings must be exceedingly hospitable between one man and another. The work of any one of us will be largely neutralized if anybody in the crowd is either unintelligent or uncooperative. The combined efforts of the group to make the work of Dartmouth College really great will be pretty largely contingent upon our ability to recognize and to hold our authority, without in any way giving our instruction corps the feeling that they are being subjected to the mechanical processes of a business office, largely unconscious of the fact that instructors are the agents through whom the purpose of the College is transmitted to the undergraduate."

In answering the question of how essential it was for a dean to have had organizational experience, President Hopkins dwelt at some length on his conviction that there must be a central authority resting in the president. In his letter he cited the cases of two fellow presidents, one incapable of delegating any authority to his associates and the other who had allowed the academic faculty to strip him of all power over the college within his university. "My own theory of administration," he wrote, "lies somewhere in between these two extremes. I believe that it is the function of the Board of Trustees to choose a President to run the College, and at the time of my taking office, I declined to accept any protection or immunities, which it was suggested at the time that I accept, because I believed, and believe now, that a president either makes good or he doesn't make good, in the former of which cases he should be supported by the governing board and in the latter of which contingencies he should be fired, *Spurlos versenkt*."

Like so many other administrative officers of that time, Dean Neidlinger considered that working with President Hopkins was part of the compensation for his job. Certainly the starting salary of $4,000 for an assistant dean was no great attraction. Mr. Hopkins quoted the Book of Proverbs to him: "Give me neither poverty nor riches." And to this he added, "I have always felt that in the large the man who was not making some sacrifice in financial prospects to serve a college ought not to be in college work. . . . No matter how much money became available, I should deplore in behalf of the College having positions here so lucrative that men were seeking them for financial rewards."

Shortly after he wrote that in June 1933, Mr. Hopkins became involved in the issue of what the financial reward ought to be for granite-industry workers in the Barre, Vermont, area. An earlier strike there had resulted in so much violence that martial law was declared. In the summer of 1933 the dispute over hourly wages was still unresolved and was placed in the hands of an arbitration board. The two representatives of labor and the two representatives of management chose President Hopkins as the fifth member of the board and elected him chairman. Meetings in July had to be recessed when the two sides could not agree on a statement of facts, but upon resumption in August an agreement was worked out and the board's binding decision on hourly wages was announced. No sooner had this been accomplished, however, than all the work of the arbitration board was wiped out by the issuance of new codes by the National Recovery Administration in Washington. This did nothing to sweeten Mr. Hopkins' already sour view of the federal bureaucracy.

A few months after this bit of public service Mr. Hopkins heeded the call of President Roosevelt and went to Puerto Rico for the announced purpose of making a survey of the island's educational system for the U. S. War Department. The real purpose was as much political as educational. Puerto Rico was in turmoil because of the actions of Governor Robert H. Gore, some of which affected the elementary schools as well as the university, where students and faculty had staged a strike and been fired upon by armed troops (fortunately supplied with blank bullets by a level-headed captain). *The New York Times* called the choice of President Hopkins a compliment to the people of Puerto Rico. He arrived there on December 11 and planned on a stay of two weeks, but President Roosevelt summoned him home on December 18 when an interim report to Washington stated Mr. Hopkins' opinion that the Governor was the prime trouble and ought to be replaced. Roosevelt, having appointed Gore, was not pleased with this recommendation.

The American authorities on the island were urging that English entirely replace Spanish in the elementary schools, and Mr. Hopkins thought this to be a tragic policy and pedagogically all wrong. In this view he was completely on the side of José Padín, Puerto Rico's commissioner of education, whom Gore wanted to fire. To underscore this support, Dartmouth later conferred an honorary Doctorate of Pedagogy upon Padín.

In a letter to Mr. Thayer in late December, President Hopkins wrote, "I reported successively to Secretary Dern and to President Roosevelt in effect that the country had a punk representative in the Governor's position in Puerto Rico and that it had a mighty good Commissioner of Education." He later recalled that when he saw President Roosevelt upon returning from Puerto Rico, the President put on a show of anger over the criticism of Governor Gore. "Why do you think I would appoint him if he wasn't a highly qualified man?" Roosevelt demanded. "I've been told that he was a big contributor to the Democratic Party," Mr. Hopkins answered. Roosevelt was about to become even angrier when Louis Howe, who was present at the meeting, said "Pipe down, Frank, pipe down; you know damn well it's true."

The upshot was that Major General Blanton Winship succeeded Gore as Governor in January (Mr. Hopkins was under the impression that he could have had the job had he wanted it), Padin was reappointed, and Spanish was retained as the language for elementary school studies, although English as a language course was compulsory in all eight grades. After this assignment in Puerto Rico it was not until World War II that Mr. Hopkins undertook any other government service. Roosevelt had relegated him to the category of former friend, anyway, after a Hopkins article in the *Atlantic Monthly* of October 1936 denounced the New Deal.

Upon returning to Hanover the latter part of December, without benefit of all the Puerto Rican sunshine he had counted on, President Hopkins was called upon to take a hand in signing up a new football coach for Dartmouth. To fill the vacancy left by the resignation of Jackson Cannell, 1920, at the close of the 1933 season, the Dartmouth Athletic Council had narrowed the field of more than one hundred candidates down to Dick Harlow, coach at Western Maryland, who later went to Harvard, and Earl Blaik, assistant coach at West Point. Asked for his opinion, Mr. Hopkins preferred Blaik and found himself with the job of persuading him to come to Dartmouth. The two men met at the Plaza Hotel in New York and spent the whole afternoon together. As had happened to so many others, Blaik was warmly attracted to this remarkable college president and decided that he would like to be football coach at a college that had such a leader.

Alumni pressure for a new coach had begun in the fall of 1932, when

Dartmouth failed to win a major game. The following season was somewhat better, with a victory over Pennsylvania and a tie with Harvard, but the alumni were still in full cry, led by Bill Cunningham, 1919, sports columnist for *The Boston Post*, whose frequent articles about the shortcomings of the Dartmouth football staff made inflammatory reading. Coach Cannell decided in November 1933 that he had had enough and announced he was resigning for the good of the College.

Some of President Hopkins' friends felt that he had been wrong in his adamant support of Cannell and in his failure to concede that all was not well with the Dartmouth football situation. In answering his alumni mail on the subject, Mr. Hopkins defended Cannell's approach to football and his understanding of its relationship to the educational purposes of the College. He wanted a coach, he said, who believed that "players are college men incidentally engaged in athletics rather than athletes incidentally enrolled in a college." As he saw the criticism of the coaching staff, it was basically that the staff didn't have the killer instinct. "I would rather lose every football game on the schedule," he wrote, "than have a coach that didn't deal with his men as self-respecting human beings or, again, have a coach who drove his team with vituperative abuse and invective." The alumni supported this philosophy, but they were agitating for a new regime that would uphold these principles and still produce winning football teams.

One inebriated alumnus telephoned President Hopkins after the Cornell game in November 1933 and told him that either the coach or the president would have to go. Mr. Hopkins replied that it would have to be the president because the coach's contract had one more year to run. He particularly resented the way in which some alumni had ruined team morale and dissipated undergraduate support during the 1933 season, and he was convinced that the season would otherwise have been more successful. His resentment was directed also toward those who argued that the College would suffer financially if it did not produce a winning football team. In a November 1933 letter to Alumni Councillor Ford Whelden, 1925, Mr. Hopkins wrote: "There is just one argument in the whole matter that makes me see red and that is the argument that men are not going to contribute to the Alumni Fund if we don't make provisions for having the kind of football team they want. If the privilege of association with the name of Dartmouth extends no further than the building up or the lack of building up of a football team, certainly the thought and self-sacrifice of the founders, to say nothing of hundreds who have given their fortunes or their careers to the College since, have been wasted effort."

Bill Cunningham, who knew that the official College deplored his newspaper attacks on Coach Cannell, sent the secretary of the College a long letter, which he intended to mail to *The Dartmouth*, resigning from the alumni body—"So strike my name off the list and turn my picture to the wall. Let's part as friends, but, if not, let's part anyhow." President Hopkins wrote to him at once, saying that, as a friend, he advised him to cancel the letter and not to indulge in a hasty and emotional action he would always regret. He also managed, without his usual diplomacy, to tell Cunningham what he considered fallacious in his barrage against the coaching staff. Two years later, when both men were speakers at a Dartmouth alumni dinner in Manchester, New Hampshire, Cunningham told the audience that they should never get into a correspondence argument with Mr. Hopkins. Dartmouth's president, he said, "had more polite ways of calling a man an S.O.B. than anyone I know."

The arrival of Earl Blaik in Hanover in January of 1934 marked the beginning of one of the most notable chapters in Dartmouth's football history. In the next seven seasons, 1934 through 1940, his teams won forty-five games, tied four, and lost fifteen. The "Yale jinx" was laid to rest when Dartmouth, in 1935, defeated Yale for the first time ever, and another highlight was the undefeated season of 1937.

Blaik and his hand-picked staff—Harry Ellinger of Army, line coach; Andy Gustafson of Pittsburgh, backfield coach; and Joe Donchess of Pittsburgh, end coach—arrived in style, in the private car of Edward S. French, 1906, president of the Boston and Maine Railroad and an ardent football fan. The four men were house guests of President and Mrs. Hopkins on their first day in town. That night, in the third-floor quarters above the Hopkinses' own bedroom, they began to devise the offensive system they were going to use. Enthusiastically jumping about to demonstrate the blocking and running routes they were charting, they lost all sense of time and all awareness of the rumpus they were creating. Finally, at three a.m., Mrs. Hopkins demanded of her husband, "Do you plan to have all the season's major games played upstairs?"

Mr. Hopkins became the good friend of each of the new coaches, but especially of Blaik and Ellinger, who golfed and fished with him and who had an annual date to spend some time at Manset, Maine, with him and Mr. French. Mr. Hopkins was a fairly regular spectator at football practice, and sometimes after the daily workout he would relax with the coaches in their Davis Field House quarters. They had fun designating him a member of the varsity football coaching staff, but on leave of absence.

In the book he wrote with Tim Cohane, *You Have to Pay the Price* (1960), Earl Blaik expressed his admiration for President Hopkins. With regard to the official and alumni control many head coaches have to contend with, he wrote, "The best a man can possibly hope for is to report directly to a college president, who has not only the authority but the character to support him as long as he justifies it. Where was I to find such a president? I have always considered myself extremely fortunate that I did find one in Ernest Martin Hopkins. . . . A man of great warmth and charm, with an insatiable intellectual curiosity, completely at home with prince or third-stringer, President Hopkins was an inspiring college leader, who is revered and held in highest affection by all Dartmouth men." In his account of his years at Dartmouth, Earl Blaik included the story of how President Hopkins had promised to use Crosby Hall, an old frame dormitory, as a bonfire if Dartmouth beat Yale. After the 14–6 victory of 1935, Blaik asked Mr. Hopkins when he was going to set the fire. Mr. Hopkins wriggled out of it by saying that he had decided that beating Yale had given the alumni enough of a shock and that they were not yet ready for another one.

The fortunate and happy events of early 1934 were swept out of mind on February 25 by the greatest human tragedy in Dartmouth's history. In the early morning hours of that wintry Sunday, nine undergraduates, members of Theta Chi fraternity, died in their sleep of carbon monoxide fumes from an improperly banked furnace. The tragic accident was not discovered until afternoon. President Hopkins, who was hosting a faculty gathering at the President's House, left to take personal charge of the many things that had to be done. It was he who assumed the heartbreaking task of telephoning the parents of the students who had died. In keeping with his belief that bad news should be disclosed as fully and promptly as possible, he gave instructions that news of the tragedy should be released to the press just as soon as the facts could be ascertained. A "flash" by Walter Winchell during his Sunday evening radio broadcast stated nothing more than that nine Dartmouth students had died in a fraternity house. Immediately the long-distance lines were jammed with incoming calls. Mr. Hopkins quickly persuaded the telephone company to clear their lines for emergency use, and by supplying the operators with the facts and the names of the students who had died, worried parents and others were given reassurance as expeditiously as possible. On March 1 the entire College attended a memorial service for the Theta Chi victims, and President Hopkins delivered the valediction.

Within two weeks the campus suffered another blow, in the death of Robert H. Michelet, 1934, the most respected and honored member of the student body. Pneumonia took the life of this remarkable senior who was class president, Phi Beta Kappa student, Senior Fellow, football star and track captain, Palaeopitus president, and Rhodes Scholar designate. It is doubtful if Dartmouth had ever had to go through a sadder period, and the arrival of spring recess was a relief to everyone. No one took these tragic losses more to heart than President Hopkins.

Student life at that time was concentrated in the College itself. Hanover's isolation was one of the conditions giving rise to a growing criticism of social life for Dartmouth undergraduates. Mr. Hopkins had hoped to improve matters with a student social center, and a planning committee had been put to work, but the Depression forced the abandonment of the project. The burden of social life rested mainly upon the twenty-six fraternities, but they too were increasingly criticized for the shallow, irresponsible way in which they met that role. In December of 1934, Palaeopitus declared that the fraternities were in "an unwholesome, unhealthy, and unnatural condition" and petitioned President Hopkins to authorize a study to determine whether the fraternities were impeding or contributing to the fulfillment of the College's purpose. He readily agreed but decided that the study should be broader than that proposed by Palaeopitus and should examine all aspects of undergraduate social life. He named a fourteen-man committee, made up of two faculty members, two deans, six undergraduates, and four alumni, and he designated Russell R. Larmon, Professor of Administration, to be its chairman. The committee worked for more than a year and submitted its report in the spring of 1936.

Shortly after the appointment of the Larmon committee, President and Mrs. Hopkins left for Europe aboard the *Conte di Savoia*, to begin a two-months leave of absence. Before they sailed home on February 18, they visited with their daughter Ann, who was studying in Italy; saw Mr. Tuck at Monte Carlo; and in the company of Mr. Thayer, who joined them in Naples, spent a few weeks in Sicily and Egypt. The greater part of their time abroad was spent in Italy, where Mr. Hopkins had a chance to observe the effects of the fascist government of Mussolini.

When the liner *Rex*, from Naples, docked in New York in February, Mr. Hopkins was met by reporters who wanted to know what impressions of Europe he had brought home. What had struck him most forcibly, he told the newsmen, was the danger that fascism posed for the democracies, unless they could somehow find ways to match the dedication, discipline, and sense of national purpose being inculcated in the citizens of fascist countries abroad. He abhorred the regimented thinking and the restriction of personal liberties imposed by these governments, he said, but nevertheless it would be a mistake to ignore what was being accomplished and he doubted that "a heterogeneous mass giving a thousand different kinds of loyalty to the democratic ideal can compete with the collective force of a people giving a single type of loyalty to a specific ideal." Rugged individualism was being overdone in this country, he added, and "the great danger to America lay in loyalty to an ideal of liberty that resented all discipline." There was danger of war because of this disparity in philosophies, he warned. Part of what he told the reporters was an echo of the criticism of American democracy he had voiced in his Convocation address of 1932. The trip to Europe had given him a basis for underscoring his point.

These Hopkins views received the usual generous press coverage, and one newspaper, the Baltimore *Sun*, editorialized that they represented "shoddy thinking." Mr. Hopkins did not deviate from the conviction that fascism was a grave threat to the western democracies and for some months after his return from Europe he continued to speak on this theme, with the added idea that the nature of the modern totalitarian regimes needed to be studied in U. S. colleges. The fullest statement of these convictions was made at the annual dinner of the Dartmouth Alumni Association of Boston on March 7. At that dinner he said:

I acknowledge that I do not come by natural inclination to a willingness to extend the privilege of freedom to the proponents of systems which stand for suppression of all freedom except for themselves. Nevertheless, even in the cases of these, I believe the principle to be more important than the cost. Moreover, I believe that the fallacies of such systems will reveal themselves more evidently in the light of open discussion than in the obscurity of whispered argument. . . .

Educational experience, educational method, and educational skill are being organized and mobilized with high effectiveness in country after country in Europe for regimenting thought and action in support of the respective philosophies and governmental policies of the different states. Among these peoples the human mind is being molded in the youngest children, while most pliable, to acceptance of all opinion prescribed by the state and denial of all opinion apart from this. As for the adults, they are held subject by espionage, secret police, and ruthless retribution for the slightest lack of enthusiastic support. . . .

Nevertheless, it likewise appears from consideration of conditions in these different countries that the constructive effects of consolidation and of a dominant will to do specific things have created a new strength, a new enthusiasm, and a new self-confidence among these peoples. These qualities are based upon conditions which have made the peoples willing to undergo self-discipline for the development of fortitude, to commit themselves in loyalty to a common cause, and to undertake cooperative efforts in their behalves. Unless we are willing in some like degree to commit ourselves to self-discipline and are willing to seek fortitude and moral stamina, we must inevitably suffer in comparison with peoples who, whether mistakenly or not, are working together in a great unifying effort toward specific ends.

So far as I am personally concerned, it is inconceivable to me that any intelligent man should be willing to exchange his status as an American citizen for the intellectual and spiritual stultifications which prevail among these peoples who have delegated either voluntarily or under coercion their lives, liberties, and possibilities of happiness to the state. There are among us grievous fallacies in the generally accepted social theories of what constitutes democracy, and there are vital defects in our practice of government. The correction of these, however, is in the development of processes which will enlarge intelligence and develop understanding not

only of what is, but of what might be. Salvation does not lie in exchange of
our liberties for political, intellectual, or spiritual serfdom. It lies in acceptance of a conception which asserts that liberty under law is the most
enviable possession to which man may aspire, but that the amount of
liberty to which an individual or a group is entitled is measured by the
extent to which responsibility will be accepted to hold its liberty as a trust.

In his address opening the college year in September 1935, the last formally prepared Convocation address he was to deliver, President Hopkins
continued to express some of the pessimism of the remarks he made immediately after his return from Europe. The United States, relatively un-
touched by World War I and expected to develop its intellectual, moral,
and spiritual faculties, had retrogressed rather than advanced during the
two decades since the war, he said. High idealism had yielded to expediency, responsibility to self-pity, and courage and the taking of risks to
cynicism. "As a people we have been afraid to grow up, and we have played
with our principles, with our emotions, and our responsibilities." This,
however, formed but a minor part of his address, entitled "Fragments of
Truth" and dealing with the synthesis of knowledge as the essence of
liberal education. The New Hampshire Anti-Saloon League, still smolder-
ing from Mr. Hopkins' advocacy of the repeal of Prohibition, declared that
he had no right to denounce the self-indulgence and retrogression of the
nation, after giving his active assistance to the government's encouragement of the liquor habit.

In his address at the Boston alumni dinner President Hopkins had
spoken not only of totalitarianism versus democracy but also of a curriculum change he believed to be urgently needed. He declared that "prompt
and radical modification of the curriculum must be made to adapt this to the
magnitude, the complexity, and the tempo of modern life. . . . I would have
the College recognize more definitely than any college has yet done the
overwhelming need of a knowledge of contemporary problems before attention is given to anything else. Specifically, I would argue that the curricula of our colleges should be rebuilt around the social sciences and that
undergraduates should be required to learn the fundamental principles of
government, economics, and social relations, with the historical data illus-
trative of these."

One of Mr. Hopkins' favorite photographs, taken in Virginia in the spring of 1939.

Mr. Hopkins and John D. Rockefeller Jr. at New York dinner.

Grandson "Rusty" Potter, ten months old, pays a visit to the president's office in 1941.

President Hopkins on the steps of the Administration Building with (l to r) Dean of the Faculty E. Gordon Bill, Dean of the College Lloyd K. Neidlinger, and Dean of Freshmen Robert Strong.

Mr. Hopkins with a student group in the early '40s. With him are Prof. Russell R. Larmon (l), who was his chief assistant from 1919 to 1926, and Robert O. Conant, Registrar of the College.

On his 25th anniversary as president, in 1941, Mr. Hopkins cuts a "birthday" cake at the dinner given for him by the faculty.

A conference about the College's defense courses, held in 1941 with Prof. Andrew J. Scarlett (l), educational policy chairman, and Prof. Wm. Stuart Messer, vice-chairman of defense instruction.

President Hopkins delivering valedictory to Class of 1942 at accelerated graduation in May.

President Hopkins and Captain Henry M. Briggs, commanding officer, reviewing trainees of the Naval Indoctrination School, which began at Dartmouth in July of 1942.

Mr. Hopkins with Captain Damon E. Cummings, who commanded the Navy V-12 Unit at Dartmouth from 1943 to 1945.

President Hopkins and President-Elect John Sloan Dickey at Manset in September 1945.

Mr. Hopkins with Prof. L. B. Richardson
ne year after his retirement.

Mr. Hopkins escorts President Eisenhower
in Commencement procession in 1953.

President Dickey, Sherman Adams, and Nelson Rockefeller with Mr. Hopkins at the mammoth 80th birthday party given for him in New York City in 1958.

President-Emeritus Hopkins at the dedication of Hopkins Center in November 1962. Also shown are Dartmouth Trustee Dudley Orr (c) and Governor John Volpe of Massachusetts, whose construction company built the Center.

This idea of more emphasis on the social sciences had been put before the Committee on Educational Policy the previous year, and the C.E.P., in turn, had requested the Division of the Social Sciences to devise a two-year program to be required of all freshmen and sophomores. Mr. Hopkins was in favor of a two-year interdepartmental course similar to the general courses then being given at Columbia and Chicago. The division was willing to go along with this idea for the freshman year but thought departmental courses should be retained as an optional part of the sophomore-year requirement. Mr. Hopkins believed this fell short of the breadth and inter-relatedness of knowledge that were urgently needed in undergraduate education, and he did not conceal his disappointment when he met with the study committee at a dinner at the President's House. At the same time, he recognized that curriculum revision was within the domain of the faculty, and he reluctantly accepted their judgment as to how far a new program could go with any prospect of success.

The division's report was accepted by the Committee on Educational Policy and then by the full faculty in December 1935. The new program abolished the required freshman courses in Evolution and Problems of Industrial Society (originally Citizenship) which had been in effect since 1919. Instead, all freshmen had to take Social Science 1–2, a course taught by an interdepartmental staff and largely historical in content. For the second year, sophomores were required to elect either Social Science 3–4, as a continuation of the first-year course, or two of three one-semester courses in economics, political science, and sociology. It was expected that students intending to major in one of the social sciences would elect the departmental courses. Along with these changes, joint majors within the Social Science Division were replaced by new topical majors in International Relations; Democratic Institutions; National Problems, Economic and Sociological; and Local Institutions and Problems.

Although the new degree requirements went a considerable way toward giving Dartmouth's curriculum the social science emphasis President Hopkins wanted, he was sorry the social science faculty had balked at taking the full plunge into a two-year integrated course, without the intrusion of departmental courses in sophomore year. His regret was keen enough to induce him to infer that departmental thinking and faculty self-interest had unduly influenced the formulation of the new program at the expense of the student's education. His position was simple: the primacy of undergraduate education at Dartmouth was well known, and in becoming a member of the faculty of the College a man accepted the responsibility of teaching within that framework, even if unconventional academic procedures were asked of him.

He did not remain silent at his dinner meeting with the social science planning committee, and in enlarging upon some of the points he had made at that gathering he wrote to Professor Howard A. Meneeley: "It is an involved subject and would require long discussion, without, probably, any eventual agreement as to the extent to which the point of view of professionalized scholarship is applicable to a policy of educating American youth or contributing to the values which American youth can contribute to the country as 'doers.' Personally, I believe that the effectiveness of the American undergraduate college as an agency of public good has been more vitally impaired by the domination of the ideals of professionalized scholarship in faculty groups than by any other single factor, and the tragedy of the whole thing from my own point of view is that in general the best minds and the men of greatest sensitiveness fall most easily subject to the lure of this ideal."

In further correspondence with Professor Meneeley, he added, "Some of the comments of men for whom I have great affection and respect at other points do not impress me at all when they get to discussing their own province in the faculty. I do not believe that any good teacher restricts himself completely to his own field, and I see no reason why he shouldn't make more frequent sorties out of it than in general he considers good form in the interest of connecting up with the work of associate teachers in other departments."

Professor Hugh Elsbree, who attended the dinner meeting, was also the recipient of an elaboration of Hopkins views. To him he wrote that "Nero fiddling while Rome burned was an entirely insignificant example of the spirit which dominates the vast structure of American education at the present time and which is most oblivious to its opportunity in the American undergraduate colleges." The main quarrel he had with conditions as they then existed, he wrote, was "the superimposition of university ideals on the American undergraduate college and acceptance of the point of view that necessarily the student's welfare is best conserved by the maintenance of conditions most comfortable to faculty convenience and desires. Personally, it seems to me that the fact that an individual instructor finds it pleasanter and more satisfactory to delve deeply in a single field, or that an administrative corps can feel a comfortable sense of superiority in gathering 'eminent scholars' about it, or that the graduate schools can more definitely define their distinction by the number of research students and production experts that they turn out and wish off on undergraduate colleges for subsidization—it seems to me that these things have but little to do with the obligation which the American undergraduate college ought to accept to be itself and to give the maximum education possible to its men."

Such open disagreement with the faculty on academic matters was unusual for President Hopkins. He had by-passed the faculty on the Selective Process of Admission and the Senior Fellowships, to avoid having these innovations diluted, and he had made some faculty appointments on his own responsibility when he felt there would be departmental rejection for insignificant reasons, but by and large Mr. Hopkins and the faculty had worked together cooperatively and with mutual respect. He was glad of any opportunity to praise Dartmouth's faculty for its high quality and its dedication to undergraduate teaching. In the case of the new social science requirements, however, he had experienced a dashing of his hopes that Dartmouth would show the way to other liberal colleges in the country. In his view, the two-year program in its finally accepted form was not much of an improvement over what was already being offered. His discouragement was a passing phase, but there was a residue of disillusionment regarding the social science faculty, which came out again, in the late thirties, at the time of the debate over World War II.

When the social science program was inaugurated in the fall of 1936, President Hopkins seemed pleased enough, describing it as "designed to make it impossible for any Dartmouth man to graduate from college in complete ignorance in regard to the theory and practice of government and the sources from which this had sprung." Three years later, however, he was confessing to Dean Bill that his enthusiasm for the required social science courses had cooled, as the result of his feeling that it was impossible to find men to teach them as they ought to be taught. "The instruction staff," he said, "is much longer on haywire philosophy than it is on practical knowledge."

Not long after the social science changes were announced, President Hopkins made public in April of 1936 the fraternity portion of the report of the Committee for the Survey of Social Life, which had begun its work under Professor Larmon sixteen months previously. This was the most ambitious survey undertaken by the College since the curriculum study of 1924. It also was the most important of a whole cluster of studies made in the mid-thirties for the purpose of improving student life, which had been criticized as the least satisfactory part of the Dartmouth educational experience. The study leading to the new student health service was conducted simultaneously with the social life survey, and its report was released within a week of the fraternity report. The previous fall, the Dartmouth Outing Club had been reorganized and broadened in its program, with a board of governors and a graduate director. About to happen was a one-year survey of all non-athletic activities other than publications and the Outing Club, which resulted in a reorganized Council on Student Organizations and added to its jurisdiction a new College Lecture Committee, under which was consolidated all public lecture programs. Student publications were later examined in a separate study, which produced recommendations not to the liking of *The Dartmouth* but finally settled by an arbitration committee. Indeed, hardly any phase of student extracurricular life escaped scrutiny during this period of surveys, reorganization, and consolidation. In total, some decided advances were made, but most significantly this attention represented a greater concern for a side of the College toward which a laissez-faire attitude had long prevailed. Some of the new vitality could be attributed to the new dean of the College, Lloyd K. Neidlinger, who took office at an opportune time.

The social life survey devoted most attention to the fraternities at Dartmouth, and such was the general interest in this portion of the committee's report that it was published separately. The majority report, supported by twelve of the fourteen committee members (two of the four alumni members dissented), was something of a bombshell with its recommendation that all national fraternity affiliations be severed on a common date. The committee charged that the national organizations provided little or no constructive stimulus toward either academic accomplishment or social responsibility and that an undesirable degree of control over the Dartmouth chapters was being exercised from beyond the campus. Special exception was taken to imposed restrictions on who could be pledged, and the committee questioned the value received from the financial payments regularly made to the national organizations.

The Larmon committee, although opposed to national affiliation, strongly backed a fraternity or club system as essential to student social life at Dartmouth. It therefore made the further recommendation that the College appoint an adviser to fraternities, to establish certain uniform policies and goals and to provide full-time direction to the revitalizing of fraternity life. It suggested that the College, before making any move to force the breaking of national ties, solicit the opinion of undergraduates and also the opinion of the alumni through the Alumni Council.

The committee's two dissenting members saw the severing of national ties as an action that would raise complex financial problems, since the houses in nearly every case were owned by alumni corporations. Adoption of the majority report, they warned, would split the Dartmouth alumni body wide open—a view which the other committee members did not share. They also pointed out that the undergraduates had voted against going local, even though an informal canvass had disclosed only a mild interest bordering on apathy toward the rituals and creeds of the national organizations.

After releasing the report on fraternities, President Hopkins made it clear that the official College would take no precipitate action, but would allow sufficient time for review and for undergraduate and alumni sentiment to clarify itself. This statement was made as part of his remarks at the College's opening exercises in September 1936. For that Convocation he abandoned the custom of preparing a formal address—"ceremonial hokum" he called it—and chose instead to speak informally from notes. The change was so well received that Mr. Hopkins thereafter spoke extemporaneously at the opening exercises throughout the remainder of his presidency.

To the student body, gathered in Webster Hall, President Hopkins said that he wished to talk about "our life together" because the new year offered many problems, many changes, and many opportunities. Although the fraternity situation was the major topic for discussion, he referred also to the new social science requirements being inaugurated with that year's freshman class, and to the new student health service which had just been put into effect under the supervision of a Council on Student Health. The Convocation was made the occasion for announcing the complete renovation of Freshman Commons over the preceding summer, the installation of a new organization skilled in serving meals to students, and the June action of the trustees authorizing the construction of a new upperclass dining hall to be ready for the following fall. These steps taken to improve meals and dining facilities for both freshmen and upperclassmen were some of the more concrete results growing out of the social life survey.

Regarding fraternities, President Hopkins made it clear he had no animus against the national organizations and that he would prefer to maintain the existing system if the fraternities could be made to function in consonance with the ideals of the College. "If, on the other hand," he said, "it should prove so difficult for the organizations of the national fraternities to consider Dartmouth as an individual institution with its own individual needs and its own individual opportunities, rather than just simply as another one of several hundreds of colleges and universities, and if the undergraduate chapters should show the presence of the national fraternities within the College to be incapable of being helpful in the realization of Dartmouth ideals, then the decision would have to be that an incompatability existed so great as to make a divorce preferable to a continuance of existing conditions.

"That in brief, gentlemen, is the situation in regard to this discussion now going on among the national fraternities in regard to the College, that they shall understand the individuality of Dartmouth, that they shall have some comprehension of what are its particular needs and its opportunities, and that they shall aid the College administration and the College supporters in enlargement of its purposes and advancement of its standards, rather than saying that conditions here are as good as at some other place and that therefore we ought to be satisfied with them."

The National Interfraternity Conference had been in touch with President Hopkins, through its executive officer, Alvan E. Duerr, and had indicated its understanding of Dartmouth's concern and its willingness to work with the College to bring about more satisfactory conditions. An Interfraternity Dartmouth Committee, made up of representatives of the national fraternities at the College, had in fact been formed soon after the survey of social life began. After the fraternity report appeared, the committee switched its efforts from providing information to working with the chapters to bring about improvement. It was recognized that the results of the Dartmouth survey and the College's subsequent action could influence the policies of other institutions throughout the country. President Hopkins agreed to a three-year trial period during which every effort would be made to revitalize fraternity life, and in January 1937 he designated a College officer to assist in this effort, naming Davis Jackson, 1936, a member of Sigma Chi, to be College adviser to fraternities.

President Hopkins took part in what amounted to Operation Uplift by speaking to all the fraternities in three groups on three successive Sunday evenings in March of 1937. His chief aim was to promote a spirit of responsibility and to clear up any questions that fraternity men might have about administration policy. The trial period had successful results, and at the annual banquet of the Dartmouth Interfraternity Council in May 1939 Mr. Hopkins praised fraternity life as greatly improved and as making unnecessary the proposal that national affiliations be abolished. In June of 1939 the Dartmouth trustees voted to table the survey committee's recommendation "in view of the gratifying changes in the status of fraternities in Dartmouth College in the past three years."

The fraternity portion of the Larmon committee report received all the publicity, but numerous other aspects of student social life were considered in the survey. Among them, in addition to dining facilities already mentioned, were dormitory life, the problems of freshman year, the lack of a social center, cars and weekending, house parties, drinking, community entertainment, and agencies for student counseling. The creation of general social rooms in the dormitories was recommended, to go along with an earlier action establishing dormitory committees which would give students greater responsibility for life in the residence halls.

The fraternity survey and the other studies of extracurricular affairs brought President Hopkins into direct touch with a larger number of undergraduates than he had met with for some years. *The Dartmouth* editorialized that the students wished closer and more frequent contacts with him and regretted that alumni tours and other outside activities took him away from the campus so often. Mr. Hopkins shared that regret. To Felix Frankfurter he wrote in March 1935: "I now find myself with hardly a moment free to remain at home and associate with our undergraduate body, with whom on the whole I prefer companionship in comparison with any other group in the world." He told Frankfurter of the continuous procession of promising young men passing through Dartmouth, "many of them sons of immigrants, some of them sons of homes of great wealth, that makes life so tremendously interesting to me. The existence of men of this type in ever-increasing numbers, and the privilege of watching their development as undergraduates and their achievements thereafter, are the reasons why I have never been willing to consider anything as an alternative to the job in the possession of which I have been blessed."

The same sentiment was expressed to Trustee John R. McLane. "It makes me regretful," Mr. Hopkins wrote, "that the President must necessarily give so much time to contacts outside, valuable both in arousing interest in the College and in giving the President better understanding of what is going on in the nation and the world. Sometime, however, I should like to take a year and spend it with the fellows here, and particularly with the undergraduates."

Prelude to War

IN the thirties, the world beyond the campus continued to absorb a considerable share of President Hopkins' time and interest. Before the end of the decade, this involvement was to be intensified by Hitler's aggression in Europe, which brought to the fore, for this nation, the question of isolationism versus an active, militant role in the defense of democratic freedom. Mr. Hopkins became an ardent and vocal advocate of the latter point of view, which had little support among the students at first. Before that trying period arrived, however, he had many non-controversial activities to which to give his attention.

Although Mr. Hopkins was trying to cut back on outside engagements, he was in great demand and still took on as many of these appearances as his diminished energy would permit, in the conviction that the welfare of Dartmouth College required it of him. Public speaking, however, was becoming more and more exhausting to him. To his friend "Hap" Hinman he confessed, "The one thing that I do not get used to and that becomes harder, if anything, year by year is public speaking. Even a short speech among indulgent friends produces a certain amount of nervous strain and exhaustion." This comment accompanied the news that he was currently carrying a fuller program of speaking than for a long time.

The arbitration of the Barre granite strike and the trip to Puerto Rico to survey the island's educational system have been mentioned as two outside assignments President Hopkins accepted in the early thirties. In October of 1935, President Roosevelt also named him to the Foreign Bondholders Protective Council and he served as vice-chairman of this group, which had Newton D. Baker, Philip LaFollette, and Charles Francis Adams among its members. The State of New Hampshire continued to call upon his services. Governor Tobey appointed him to the New Hampshire Unemployment Commission in December 1930, and later in the decade, in

May 1937, Governor Murphy named him a member of the State Commission for the Promotion of Wealth and Income of the People of New Hampshire. He also became, in September of 1932, chairman of the New Hampshire chapter of the National Economy League, an organization headed by Admiral Byrd and dedicated to economy in government. One of the League's specific campaigns was against the veterans' bonus.

Unfortunately, most outside activities involved the making of speeches, and anniversaries and inaugurations of college presidents seemed to predominate. In June of 1931, Mr. Hopkins gave the principal address at the celebration of the 150th anniversary of the founding of Phillips Exeter Academy. The next year he spoke at the centennial of Wabash College and at the centennial of the Perkins Institution for the Blind. The Harvard Business School in 1933 celebrated the twenty-fifth anniversary of its founding and Mr. Hopkins was a guest speaker. Harvard men continued to look upon President Hopkins as a special friend, and two other groups he addressed were the Association of Harvard College Class Secretaries and the class agents of the Harvard Fund. The Princeton Graduate Council also invited him to share his alumni wisdom with them.

Five college presidents whom Mr. Hopkins helped to install in the thirties were Stanley King of Amherst College, Douglas H. Gordon of St. John's College, William A. Eddy of Hobart and William Smith Colleges, Edmund E. Day of Cornell University, and William H. Cowley of Hamilton College. Day and Cowley were Dartmouth graduates and Eddy went from the Dartmouth English Department to the Hobart presidency. Walter Lippmann also spoke at the Amherst inauguration, which was something of a reunion for the principals, since he, Stanley King, and Mr. Hopkins had all served together in Washington during World War I.

After twenty years in the Dartmouth presidency, Mr. Hopkins' outside ties were largely related to education and only slightly to industry, although he continued to be a director of the Boston and Maine Railroad and in 1932 he was elected a director of the National Life Insurance Company of Vermont. He became a member of the reorganization committee for the bankrupt Brown Brothers Corporation of Berlin, New Hampshire, in 1935 —an appointment having some special logic since Dartmouth owned $225,000 of the company's bonds. Mr. Hopkins was proposed for head of the New York Stock Exchange in 1938, and one could characterize as semi-industrial his participation in a General Motors symposium, on opportunities for youth, at the New York World's Fair.

But President Hopkins had by now become one of the senior educators of the country, and the invitations that flooded in upon him came mainly from the academic world. He much preferred to devote his speaking energies to that field. He gave the principal address at a Boston dinner sponsored by Fisk University, for the promotion of Negro education, also the Founder's Day addresses at Western Reserve University and the University of Virginia. Mr. Hopkins recalled that on his 1933 visit to Virginia no one had bothered to inform him in advance that he was to speak at the grave of Thomas Jefferson before the main Founder's Day address. Fortunately he had done some reading about Jefferson before going to Charlottesville, and he was able to extemporize and bring off the graveside tribute without disgrace. He also remembered another occasion when he was not properly forewarned as to what was expected of him. It happened in Los Angeles where he was to make a short address and then present the Irving Thalberg Award to David Selznick, producer of *Gone with the Wind*, at the annual dinner of the Motion Picture Academy of Arts and Sciences. He had prepared an address on education and the arts and went through with it; but he found himself sandwiched in between two comedians on the program, and he considered his part in the proceedings a fiasco.

Two of President Hopkins' keenest outside interests were the Rockefeller Foundation and the General Education Board. In April 1939, after serving as a member for ten years, he was elected chairman of the General Education Board, succeeding John D. Rockefeller Jr. The year before this election, he was appointed to the Board of Visitors for the United States Naval Academy, which involved inspecting and evaluating the training program at Annapolis. Among the other organizations with which he had a long association was the Birth Control Federation of America, in which his friend, Margaret Sanger, had originally enlisted his interest. This led him to accept, late in the thirties, election as vice president of the National Committee for Planned Parenthood, representing the New England states. At about the same time, he accepted membership on the board of directors of the National Committee for Mental Hygiene. While he was doing personnel work in the business world and while he was serving with the War Department in World War I he had become convinced of the value of mental hygiene programs, and early in his presidency Dartmouth became one of the pioneer colleges in providing psychiatric counseling for undergraduates.

Four more doctoral degrees were added during the thirties to the honors bestowed upon Mr. Hopkins. He received the Doctorate of Laws from St. John's, Wabash, and William and Mary, and the Doctorate of Humane Letters from Hobart. In the Hobart citation, President Eddy, who had been on the Dartmouth faculty for eight years, said: "An administrator who relies on comradeship instead of bureaucracy, you have eliminated from your college family of over 2600 men all pedantry, pettiness, and persecution. You have used your office and your influence to advance others and to efface yourself, and have been content to practice modestly the charity which others preach. If you can be persuaded someday, in a national emergency, to leave the Dartmouth you love and accept the call to public office you have repeatedly refused, you will find the eager support of a grateful nation."

The reference to public office came from President Eddy's knowledge of the Cabinet positions which had been offered to Mr. Hopkins and of the efforts that friends and admirers had made to persuade him to run for the United States Senate, not to mention the newspaper editorials and political talk that dwelt on his qualifications for the United States Presidency. To all such talk Mr. Hopkins gave a consistent response: "I have no desire or aspirations beyond rendering the best service possible to Dartmouth and making its influence as potent as may be for producing intelligent leaders and discriminating followers. This effort I think to be as important as any I could render in any other field." As for becoming a public office-holder, he added, "I feel much as Gelett Burgess did in his poem on the purple cow— 'I'd rather see than be one.' "

There is little doubt that President Hopkins could have been the Republican nominee for Senator from New Hampshire had he wished to be, and *The Boston Traveler* in 1935 put forward a plan to make Mr. Hopkins Governor of New Hampshire and then to move him on to the Presidency. The paper said he was New England incarnate and described him as "this remarkable man, able, versatile, and whose record thus far plainly marks him as a competent leader of men." Had Mr. Hopkins sought public office, Republicans of New England would doubtless have given him strong backing, but despite his national prestige and wide circle of influential friends, there is considerable question as to how he would have fared at the national level. After Franklin D. Roosevelt had overwhelmingly been elected to a second term, the Republicans formed a policy committee to reshape the party, and Mr. Hopkins was among those proposed to be its chairman. His Republicanism, however, probably would have been much too liberal and idealistic for the party regulars.

In the 1932 campaign Mr. Hopkins refused to sign a statement that the country would be in grave danger if it elected Roosevelt, for whom he actually voted in his one desertion of the G.O.P. "I am a Republican," he answered, "but I take exception in maximum degree to the tactics of those who are undertaking to win the election by picturing all of the wisdom and all of the patriotism as monopolized by the Republican party. I think that on the whole there is more wisdom and more genius and more experience perhaps among the Republicans than elsewhere at the present time, but I consider it fundamentally disloyal to the country, to say nothing of its being highly impolitic from the point of view of expediency, to urge the campaign that the Republicans have been urging and that you ask me to endorse in a statement that the country is in real danger from a change in administration. I do not believe that it is."

In November 1935, Mr. Hopkins decided to file as a delegate to the 1936 Republican national convention, but when the convention dates conflicted with Dartmouth's Commencement, he gave up the idea. The month before, he had written, "The Republicans can be counted on to be safe and sane and uninteresting and to give all due indications that they will protect the Constitution but likewise Wall Street, the capitalistic system, and 100% Americanism. That does not afford an awful lot of nourishment for a successful campaign." When Landon was nominated Mr. Hopkins supported him, but he was not able to work up any real enthusiasm for a Republican candidate until Wendell Willkie arrived.

In the 1932 election President Hopkins voted for Roosevelt, and for the first two years of the New Deal he approved of the majority of the measures it sponsored. He came to feel, however, that the New Deal's personnel were second-rate and too much given to hasty and theoretical experimentation. The administration's talk of economic royalists and the fomenting of class antagonisms seemed to him to be folly, when what the nation clearly needed was unity and a spirit of cooperation. The slide toward a welfare state also worried him, and the Wagner Act of 1935 especially aroused his disagreement. In an exchange of views with Clarence McDavitt, he wrote that the legislation encouraged labor unions to take the position that work itself is a curse and that it promoted the theory that employer and employee have opposing interests and must be in a perpetual state of war. From his own experience in industrial personnel work he knew this to be a fictitious and damaging idea. In his opinion, President Roosevelt was resorting to demagoguery and for political reasons was setting up a new privileged class to whom was allowed the acquisitiveness that was being condemned in others. "Under the guise of humanitarianism," Mr. Hopkins wrote, "the New Deal has advanced the most exclusively materialistic policy of which I have known under any administration."

All his disillusion and philosophic disagreement with the New Deal was set forth in an article, "Thoughts Current," which he wrote for the October 1936 issue of the *Atlantic Monthly*. Like so many other things he had done before, it was forthright and the cause of both condemnation and praise. Aside from the specifics it dealt with, the article is a most enlightening exposition of the Puritan ethic of hard work, self-reliance, self-discipline, and personal subordination to a higher cause by which Mr. Hopkins lived and wanted the nation to live. Its content and tone can best be summarized by quoting a few of its key passages:

Here in America it is doubtless true that the aftermath of war and the natural forces of 1920–1930 have helped to weaken the American spirit, but it appalled me to see the artificial political forces of the Roosevelt regime devoted to breaking down and making soft the whole structure of life among us, not only in its physical but in its mental and spiritual aspects. It seemed to me that all the forces of democracy dedicated from the foundation of the Republic to hardening the self-reliance and personal responsibility of every citizen were now being utilized to belittle and undermine the very qualities of individualism which made this country strong and through which its future lay. It seemed to me that a premium was being put upon class warfare rather than upon cooperation. . . .

Materially, we are better off than we were four years ago. That I grant. I do not grant that this improvement is greater than it would have been without the ministrations of infinite government bureaus. But, absolutely regardless of this, it still remains a fact that the gain has been secured at a costly price. It has been purchased by the sacrifice of moral and spiritual values, for it has engendered a well-nigh universal spirit of covetousness. . . .

I do not doubt the idealism or the worthy purpose that has actuated the Administration in much that it has undertaken. Some positive performance was imperative. But I do believe that a plethora of unrelated measures hazily conceived, inadequately organized, and hastily put into effect *without any competent personnel to develop them*, is working to the detriment of the very purposes for fulfillment of which they have presumably been undertaken. . . .

What, meanwhile, of the organization of society in the promised land, if it be reached? It is to be unlike anything our people have ever known or desired. I question if they wish it now. Initiative, courage, hardihood, frugality, and aspiration for self-betterment are to be penalized, and the fruits of these are to be taken from those who have undergone self-sacrifice to attain them and bestowed upon those who have never developed the qualities to possess themselves of rewards. Humanitarianism is to be reduced to the economic code of a managed society. The necessity for struggle, by which men have developed strength, and the discipline of hardship, through which they have achieved greatness of mind and heart and soul, are to be replaced by a specious security. . . .

I would not be understood as arguing that society must not assume responsibility for its natural dependents or that concern should not be felt for and necessary help offered to its underprivileged members. . . . What I would assert is that, under the New Deal, dependency is being encouraged to the point where it is rapidly and needlessly increasing, that the least desirable tendencies of a materialistic age are being accentuated rather than diminished, and that by the exclusiveness of solicitude for the incapable at the expense of the capable we are inducing a deterioration in our national character to a point little short of self-destruction.

Particularly, I resent the extent to which the New Deal has felt obliged to go in soliciting support for its programme by reiteration to the public, and particularly to youth, of the misfortunes to which they are pictured as being subject. We are being made a people sorrowing in self-pity for ourselves. . . .

It is the effect of the New Deal on the imagination and aspiration of youth that I most dread. I am desperately afraid of it because it teaches young men and women to unlearn the lessons of America which school and college have striven so earnestly to teach. It encourages weakness and penalizes strength. It diffuses throughout the masses of our people the spirit of acquisitiveness which it condemns in groups of them. It punishes accomplishment and persecutes individuals and industrial enterprises alike simply on the basis of the magnitude of their achievement without regard to the social value or the imaginative and creative talent which brought them into being. It thwarts mutual understanding and cooperation, and stimulates antagonism in our industrial life. It foments class hatreds and exploits them for its own political advantage. It is tragic for an educator to watch these lessons taught to young men.

The thinking of President Hopkins was attacked as reactionary, outdated and divorced from the economic and social realities of the thirties. Labor unions and proponents of federal welfare programs viewed him as callous to the needs of the working classes and as an advocate of the capitalistic status quo. In the many rebuttals that were made to his *Atlantic* article not much consideration was given, however, to the larger issues of national character and national unity which were his real concern.

In his book, *The Folklore of Capitalism*, published in 1937, Thurman Arnold of Yale stated that President Hopkins was ignoring the fact that modern times required everyone to be dependent upon large organizations, private or governmental. He thought he could, he declared, explain the motivation behind Mr. Hopkins' attack on the New Deal: "President Hopkins was worried by facts that were making current mythology less and less tenable. Hence he felt called upon, in his capacity as educator, to do what he could about dictating the social philosophy of the future by pointing out the danger of deserting the old-time religion." This had all the insubstantiality of academic theorizing. It did not take into account the fact that Mr. Hopkins had been a Roosevelt and New Deal supporter and then had broken away when he became convinced the New Deal was becoming a doctrinaire theory of government, one-directional in its concern for the public welfare, and not unmindful of the political advantage to be gained from the class divisions it was encouraging.

The *Atlantic* article had its impact. Thousands of reprints were run off by the magazine, and scores of editorials were written, with the political coloration of the newspapers determining in general whether the comment was pro or con. One person who was intensely displeased with the article was President Roosevelt, who decided he could henceforth dispense with

Mr. Hopkins as friend and adviser. (In this respect, Mr. Hopkins joined Raymond Moley and Lewis Douglas, and the three men called themselves "The Expatriates.") In a letter to New Hampshire's Senator Fred H. Brown in February 1937, President Hopkins wrote, "Despite the fact that I understand I no longer enjoy the President's friendship, I have great admiration for him and for his courage, and real affection for him." Long after Roosevelt's death, he said, "I don't think that Roosevelt was a great man, but I think history is going to record him as such." He disapproved of the cold way in which the President discarded men and conducted his office. In Mr. Hopkins' estimation, "He played it as a game."

In the same month that his magazine article appeared, President Hopkins suffered a great personal loss in the death of Mr. Thayer, who had served as a Dartmouth trustee for twenty-one years. The two men had taken their last trip together the year before, when they toured Sicily and Egypt. Mr. Thayer resigned from the board in June 1936, because of failing health and died three months later. Mr. Thayer after General Streeter's death became the board member with whom President Hopkins had the closest friendship and the most effective working relationship. There was to be no one leading member of the board to team up with Mr. Hopkins after Mr. Thayer died. Thereafter the life trustees as a group took over the role individuals had played for the first twenty years of the Hopkins administration. John R. McLane, Edward S. French, and Victor M. Cutter were three trustees on whom President Hopkins relied perhaps more heavily than others. All three had been close friends of his for many years, but unquestionably Mr. French was the closest. The two men had an almost boyish friendship and went off on fishing trips together every year. They had the Boston and Maine Railroad as a common interest, and it would be hard to say which was the more ardent Dartmouth football fan. They usually had seats together at the Harvard game, and among Mr. French's frequent visits to the Hopkins cottage in Manset was the annual stag get-together for the football coaches.

Mr. Thayer showed his deep regard for Mr. Hopkins by leaving a $50,000 endowment to be known as the Hopkins Fund, its income to be used at the sole discretion of the president of the College. When the new dining hall for upperclassmen was opened in September 1937, it bore the name of

Henry B. Thayer, who had done so much to bring into being so many other buildings on the Dartmouth campus.

Thayer Hall was the major addition to the Dartmouth College plant during the thirties, which saw a great reduction in the building activity that had made the twenties such an exceptional period. With new construction stymied by the Depression, plant improvement was confined mainly to reconstruction and remodeling. The rebuilding of Dartmouth Hall had been necessitated by the fire of 1935. The interior of Reed Hall was completely remodeled, to provide classroom and office space; the Freshman Commons was done over, to make eating there more pleasant; social rooms were approved for three dormitories and those in three other dormitories were reconditioned, in accordance with the recommendations of the social survey report; the Hanover Inn, which kept its place on campus after talk of moving it, was extensively refurbished in 1937; and a new College-owned business block on Main Street, adjoining the Inn, was erected in 1937 to replace the buildings destroyed by fire that March. An addition to the College's athletic facilities was accomplished early in the decade, with the building of a new gymnasium wing to house squash courts. Late in the decade, the trustees voted to go ahead with the building of a new engineering school near the Tuck School, using funds bequeathed to the College by the widow of Horace S. Cummings, 1862. This was ready in September of 1939, and in that same month work began on a new dormitory, named Butterfield Hall in memory of Ralph Butterfield, 1839, whose name had been borne by the museum that was razed when Baker Library was built.

The more interesting part of the plant story in the thirties involves what did not happen. President Hopkins had intended to demolish Rollins Chapel and move the Old White Church to that site, but the complete destruction of the church by fire in May 1931 wiped out this project. The month after the fire, he jokingly wrote that he had counted on the demolition of Rollins Chapel as the high point of his administration. In exchange for the church site at the northwest corner of the College Green the trustees agreed to provide a site for a new church on College Street and to contribute some of the funds needed for its construction. The new Church of Christ, no longer officially connected with the College, was designed by the noted church architect, Hobart Upjohn, and was dedicated in November 1935.

The second major project that did not happen was a large student union, or social center, occupying the whole southern end of the campus. To make room for it Bissell Hall was to be razed and the Hanover Inn was to be moved to an outlying location. It was Mr. Hopkins' idea that the social center and new dining halls would complete in one college-wide unit what Harvard and Yale were trying to achieve in their house plans. A committee headed by Robert C. Strong began making plans for the student center in 1929. The trustees had every intention of building the center in the early thirties, but the Depression intervened. As blueprinted in the committee's 1931 report, Dartmouth House, as it was tentatively called, contained an auditorium seating 2500, a theater for 500, a freshman lounge and game room adjoining Freshman Commons, a cafeteria and grill, nine private dining rooms, a soda bar, a billiard room and card room, four basement bowling alleys, a second-floor music room, offices for student organizations, a Graduate Club for the Faculty, and living quarters for bachelors on the second and third floors. It would have been a huge structure, costing $4-million and balancing Baker Library at the opposite end of the campus.

In December 1937, when the financial picture was brighter, President Hopkins named a new planning committee, this time headed by Sidney C. Hayward, secretary of the College. Since Thayer Hall had been built, the assignment was to draw up plans for a smaller building that would meet the College's urgent need for an auditorium and a theater. The committee's first idea was to erect a new Webster Hall on the Bissell Hall site, to cost one million dollars and to provide an auditorium-theater seating 2,700, a Little Theater seating 420, music and drama rooms, and offices for student organizations. Revised plans dropped the Webster name as well as the exterior look of the old Webster Hall. An exciting new element was added in September 1938 with the announcement that the Dramatists Guild of New York had agreed to use the new theater plant for a summer drama festival. The trustees had by this time made the decision to build the auditorium-theater, plans were in near-final form, and a campaign to raise the necessary two million dollars, half for construction and half for upkeep, was soon to be launched under the chairmanship of Basil O'Connor, 1912, who had been Franklin D. Roosevelt's law partner (President Hopkins had brought the two men together). There was much talk of making Hanover the summer drama center of the nation. A World Drama Festival was pro-jected for the summer of 1941, and *Variety* became enthusiastic enough to predict that Hanover was destined to be "the Salzburg of the North." Alas, what the Depression did to the student social center the outbreak of World War II did to the auditorium-theater project.

President Hopkins, earlier in the thirties, had stated that the spirit of the liberal arts college was going to be most adequately expressed in the social sciences. To the General Education Board in November 1938 he ad-mitted that he was changing his mind in favor of aesthetics—art, drama, and music. He gave his full backing to the auditorium-theater plans and sometimes slipped into calling the projected building "our new symphony hall." Something of his old enthusiasm for plant development returned, and in June 1938 he was encouraging the trustees to think about a new physics building ($500,000), a new modern language building ($500,000), an addition to the observatory ($60,000), and a new engineering school ($200,000). The engineering school, thanks to the Cummings money, was the only one to be realized.

After the social life survey, which was responsible for some of the plant developments, the trustees, two years later, authorized a study of student publications. President Hopkins in September 1937 appointed a nine-man committee headed by Francis H. Horan, 1922, and made up mainly of former editors and business managers of the publications. Their report was made public eight months later, in May 1938.

Although all student publications were surveyed, the committee centered its attention on *The Dartmouth* and gave more than half of its time to it. Complaints about the shortcomings of the student daily, the way it mis-represented the views of both official College and undergraduates, and its lack of any sense of responsibility to the institution had been heard on campus and among the alumni for many years. These were supplemented by charges, probably from the less affluent publications, that members of *The Dartmouth* directorate were making inordinate amounts of money from a monopoly handed to them by the College. The latter half of the thirties was an especially controversial time in the life of the student daily. Under the editorship of Budd Schulberg, 1936, who later became a noted Ameri-can author, *The Dartmouth* of 1935–36 went far afield as a protagonist of radical social change and as an active supporter, over a prolonged period, of the workmen who were on strike at the Proctor quarries in Proctor, Vermont. The editorial directorates through 1939 raised the temperatures of College officials and frequently were at odds with the rest of the campus.

In its May 1938 report the Committee on Student Publications recommended that President Hopkins appoint an alumnus, more than five years graduated, to be called Alumni Trustee of *The Dartmouth*. The Alumni Trustee should serve as guide and counselor to the editors and have oversight of the business affairs of the paper, with authority to approve salaries and the distribution of profits. He should hold all or a controlling part of the corporate stock of the paper in trust for the trustees of the College, and should have the right at any time, for reasons that seemed good to him, to remove any member of the editorial or business boards. A similar proposal was made for *Jack-o-Lantern* and *The Pictorial* combined.

The idea of an Alumni Trustee and especially the powers assigned to him aroused a storm of campus protest—led, naturally enough, by *The Dartmouth* itself. The paper quickly organized a five-man consulting council and offered counter-proposals. The trustees at their June meeting decided to postpone action until the fall. In October they turned the decision over to a three-man arbitration committee, which consisted, when organized, of Dean Strong, editor O'Brien Boldt, 1939, and as chairman Maurice S. Sherman, 1894, editor of *The Hartford Courant*. The arbitration committee recommended, in February 1939, that there be a Board of Proprietors of eleven members, seven of whom were to be undergraduates from the editorial and business boards and four of whom were to represent Palaeopitus, the faculty, the administration, and the Alumni Council. A similar board of six members, four of them undergraduates, was recommended for *Jack-o-Lantern*. These forms of control were approved by the trustess and remain in effect today.

President Hopkins consistently defended the freedom of the student press, but there were times when adherence to this principle required heroic self-restraint. Although he would not countenance censorship, he was not reluctant to let *The Dartmouth* editors know about his irritations or his disagreements with them. His correspondence in the middle and late thirties included a good many letters of this sort. The peak period of annoyance, if one goes by the volume of correspondence, seems to have been 1937–38, not "the Schulberg era." But the involvement of *The Dartmouth* in the Proctor granite quarry strike was an especially trying episode for Mr. Hopkins. In a letter to Mr. French, in December of 1935, he wrote, "I am irritated beyond measure at the whole Schulberg campaign, but I do not see anything to do about it. . . . All in all, there is less detriment to the College in letting its publications entirely alone and allowing them to go their individual ways than there is in any attempted censorship. This is not a matter of theory, but it is plain practice and has been proved out time and time again in one college and another all over this broad land. . . . In other words, trying to stimulate thought in the undergraduate mind and to express the attitude of the liberal arts college that all matters of life ought to be subject to thinking, we cannot tell the undergraduate to hang his clothes on a hickory limb but not to go near the water."

Professor Stearns Morse recalled that he was in President Hopkins' office one morning when *The Dartmouth* was filled with the Proctor strike. Mr. Hopkins picked up the paper and commented that the College would have to say good-bye to a substantial gift that it had been hoping to receive from the Proctors. He recounted other instances of the paper's throwing a wrench in the works. "But we've lived with it," he said, "and shall keep on living with it." Interference with the editorial freedom of the paper was out of the question.

When reminiscing after retirement, Mr. Hopkins claimed that only once during his presidency had he insisted that *The Dartmouth* not print an editorial. Calvin Coolidge, while Vice-President, had come to Dartmouth as a guest speaker. His performance was disappointing and the editor of the student paper had written an abusive editorial to appear the following morning. Some staff members who had failed to dissuade the editor felt strongly enough about it to inform President Hopkins of what was going to happen. Mr. Hopkins went to the editor's office and insisted that the editorial be killed. Coolidge had come to the College as an invited guest and at some inconvenience, he said, and the editor, whatever his individual reaction to the speech, had no right to indulge in personal abuse or to ignore his responsibility to the whole College community. The editorial as written was not printed.

In that instance it was a matter of decency rather than opinion. Where opinion alone was concerned, the student press could not have had a stronger advocate than Mr. Hopkins. In response to alumni criticism of *Dartmouth* views considered socialistic he had written, "I did not feel, and do not feel, that it is right in principle or wise in policy for the administration to interfere in matters of this sort or to lay the hand of authority upon men for expressions of opinion of this kind, for there is nothing more detrimental to the atmosphere of an educational institution than anything approximating censorship, repression or control."

The freedom Mr. Hopkins was willing to give student editors was not based on any confidence in their ability to make mature use of it. His expectation was the opposite, but this did not move him away from his policy of no censorship. One of his sharpest characterizations of the student press was made in his 1928 Convocation address, where he was criticizing intellectual poseurs and cynics. "I have allowed myself these animadversions," he said, "not because I believe them to apply largely to the college youth of today but because they apply in some degree. Furthermore, at the most disadvantageous point they apply in major degree to the columns of the press of the American college. There, in comparison with one understanding utterance based on intelligent interest as to how education might be made more profitable to the individual, we find hundreds of cleverly written editorials and articles subversive of all conventions, of all standards, and of all ideals, if these interfere with individual desire, individual caprice, or individual self-indulgence. There, in place of any frequent discussion of what undergraduates might do to help their respective colleges we find the tiresome reiteration of what the colleges ought further to do for the undergraduate."

To John M. Clark, 1932, a former editor of *The Dartmouth*, Mr. Hopkins had more to say in a letter: "I will express my increasing doubt in regard to the policy of conferring the preferred position on undergraduate dailies that is conferred upon them, for they are given rights and privileges entirely out of proportion to any sense of responsibility that can be expected in those who are annually made responsible for them. To the College there is not even the safeguard of an education which comes by experience, and each year the College is in the position of being subject to the hazard of irresponsible injury from an institution the beneficiaries of which may find either temporary glory or financial gain in biting the College hand which affords practically all of the nourishment to the undergraduate institution."

More than thirty years had passed since Mr. Hopkins himself had been editor of *The Dartmouth*. He never lost his special interest in all kinds of publications, and at one point, as he neared retirement, he played with the idea of acquiring a weekly newspaper. His sixtieth birthday, on November 6, 1937, found him at Princeton, where he spoke at the annual banquet of *The Daily Princetonian* and was the house guest of President Harold Dodds, with whom he had developed a warm friendship. At sixty, Mr. Hopkins was still leading a very active life, but his health was a problem. The bronchial ailments to which he had been susceptible for some years were becoming more severe, and the trustees were insisting that he take a prolonged leave of absence, long enough at least to avoid another winter in Hanover. He finally agreed that he would take leave for the greater part of the 1938–39 academic year.

North country winters, which he loved and extolled, did not agree with Mr. Hopkins from the late 1920's on. Bronchial colds and asthma took turns in bothering him year after year, and in January and February of 1936 he was laid up with a particularly severe case of laryngitis. He and Mrs. Hopkins went to Florida for a short time to speed recovery, and for two weeks in March he continued his recuperation in Chandler, Arizona, with Mr. French and Nelson Perkins of the Harvard Corporation as companions.

In May 1938, Mr. French and Mr. Cutter on behalf of the Dartmouth trustees talked with President Hopkins and urged him to plan on a leave of absence of five or six months. This led to newspaper stories that President Hopkins was seriously ill and that the trustees were searching for a replacement. In writing to Mr. Cutter about this, he recalled the ages of Presidents Eleazar Wheelock and William Jewett Tucker and commented, "I think that I might count on being conscious and able to navigate and free from evidences of advanced senility for at least another half decade or even for a decade as each of those men did, God and the Board of Trustees (in inverse order) being willing."

After getting the College officially opened in September, President Hopkins went to Canada for some fishing and then to Manset until it was time for the annual fall meeting of the trustees in late October. He and Mrs. Hopkins left December 10 to spend four months in the South. After visiting Pinehurst and spending Christmas with friends in Virginia, they settled in at Palm Beach, where they rented a house for the winter season. Photographs of Mr. Hopkins on the golf course and with a seven-foot sailfish that he caught off Palm Beach indicated to friends back in Hanover that he was having an enjoyable time.

President and Mrs. Hopkins returned home on April 22, but as soon as they were back Mr. Hopkins' asthma flared up. Doctors decided that surgery would give him relief, and in July he underwent two sinus operations, which confined him to Dick's House for several weeks. He did not greet the freshmen at matriculation in September, and the next month he again went South, this time to Miami Beach, where he remained until early December.

Some months before he began his long stay in Palm Beach, Mr. Hopkins lost his great and good friend Edward Tuck, who died April 30, 1938 at the age of ninety-five. Except for Lewis Parkhurst, who had come to the board of trustees in 1908, the links with the Tucker years were all disappearing. It was Dartmouth's extreme good fortune to have had such a benefactor as Mr. Tuck, as it was Mr. Hopkins' to have had such a friend and supporter. At the time of his death, Mr. Tuck's various benefactions were carried on the College books at more than $4.5 million. During his lifetime he had given away the bulk of his fortune, to Dartmouth, to France, and to numerous other worthy causes. In 1921 he said, "I cannot for the life of me understand why the great majority of rich men desire to die with their safe deposit key in hand, instead of largely distributing the contents of the box while they are alive and can themselves participate in the enjoyment of the feast." As for his unparalleled support of the College, at times when it was most urgently needed, he said, "No investment I ever made has paid me so much in dividends of satisfaction and happiness as has what I have done for Old Dartmouth." The relatively modest remains of his fortune were set up as a trust fund, with Dartmouth as the residual beneficiary. As a final token of his affection for Mr. Hopkins, he left him $10,000. Mr. Hopkins, some years later, said that he was glad that Mr.

Tuck died before Hitler's occupation of France, because that turn of events would have broken his heart.

The years in which Hitler established his power and launched his aggressions in Europe were years in which America became deeply divided, the pacifists and isolationists in one camp, the advocates of preparedness and intervention in the other. The Dartmouth campus reflected this national division, with the anti-war forces considerably more numerous and more vocal. President Hopkins was unequivocally in favor of aid to Hitler's foes and of gearing up the country for the full involvement he foresaw as inevitable. His sharp disagreement, in this respect, with the thinking of the students and a large segment of the faculty produced the unhappiest period of his presidency and, as he said, "the hardest days of my administration." The final years of the thirties saw him at odds with the students and berating them for their cynical detachment and for running away from hard choices "like a crowd of sheep."

Instigated on a national scale by the American Student Union, the anti-war movement on American campuses began in 1933–34. The Dartmouth Peace Committee staged its third annual anti-war protest in April 1936 and for the first time brought the war issue into sharp focus at the College. In parody and ridicule of World War I, a chapter of "Unknown Soldiers of Future Wars" was formed and a bonus voted for Veterans of Future Wars. Although less than a majority of the students participated in a poll, the vote was 534 to 72 not to take up arms unless the United States was invaded, 587 to 28 in favor of the Nye-Clark-Maverick Neutrality Act, and 535 to 135 in favor of the Nye-Kvale Bill to abolish compulsory ROTC. The Dartmouth Peace Committee continued its crusade during the next two years with an anti-war symposium, another poll which showed students favoring neutrality and progressive disarmament, and a National Peace Week demonstration in April of 1938. This last event attracted only four hundred participants, indicating that the sentiments expressed in polls did not lead to active crusading. *The Dartmouth* recognized that the student peace movement had not been taken up as actively at Dartmouth as elsewhere, and explained it by saying that Dartmouth men were too individualistic and self-reliant. This, if true, was something to lighten the gloom with which President Hopkins viewed these campus events.

In a letter to Mr. French in February 1938, Mr. Hopkins was pessimistically predicting that pacifism was going to make inevitable a war that could have been avoided "if we hadn't been so determined to holler from the housetops to every international gangster in the world that they could go as far as they liked and we wouldn't do anything about it." He commented on Hitler and his bluffs and wrote, ". . . by the time that America gets around to realizing that isolationism means only eventually a greater crisis, France will be under a dictatorship, England will have compromised in her international relations to an extent that cheapens her, and the dictators won't have anything to be apprehensive about in three futile and paralyzed democracies." The following month Germany, in the name of Anschluss, took over Austria.

In his informal talks to the undergraduates at the opening of college in this period, President Hopkins did not speak specifically of the impending war. In 1937 he chose to speak again of changes in student social life and of the fruits of liberal education, among which he counted loyalty to the principles of freedom in the Anglo-Saxon countries. The 1938 Convocation was cancelled because of the hurricane that tore through New England the night before, but at a gathering of the freshman class one week later Mr. Hopkins referred to the ideologies engulfing youth in the totalitarian states, and he declared it was the purpose of the liberal arts college to enable youth in this country to escape such mental enslavement. In 1939 he told the students that cynical interpretations of the motives for World War I bore little semblance of truth and that criticism was a virtue only if based on fact. As for the "iniquities" of the Versailles Treaty, they could be judged fairly only if one took into account the known conditions Germany was ready to impose on the rest of Europe had she been victorious.

The valedictories to graduating classes of that time took a stronger line. They did not, however, deal with the war issue head-on, and it was not until 1940 that President Hopkins reached the boiling point and told departing seniors, in effect, to get up off their knees and stand on their feet. To the Class of 1937 he quoted the Biblical promise that the rewards of life will go "to him that overcometh." "It is difficult," he said, "to follow the arguments of those who, whether from conviction or for purposes of propaganda, would have us believe that your generation is subject to unprecedented misfortune in the difficulties before it to be overcome or that it is justified in the enervating indulgence of self-pity. Such a contention cannot convincingly be defended unless we are to concede that our civilization has become so soft that you, its youth, are incapable of developing those qualities of spiritual stamina, moral courage, and intellectual hardihood which generations before you have had in abundance and have demonstrated repeatedly.

"No real friend of yours could wish that you should never face misfortune, that you should never undergo hardship, that you should never be beset by difficulties. It is not so that vigor of mind or strength of character is developed."

In bidding farewell to the Class of 1938, he deplored the prevailing vogue of skepticism and defeatism and the eagerness to seek out the weakness rather than the strength in every social institution. This tendency is understandable in the incompetent and the ignorant, he said, but when college men fall subject to the contagion it is a hazard to the nation. Once again he asserted that the satisfactions of life are to be found in struggle, and his parting hope was that the graduating seniors would not slip into passiveness or lose the zest for battle.

When Hitler, after his moves against Austria and Czechoslovakia, invaded Poland on September 1, 1939 and provoked declarations of war by England and France, the possibility of U. S. involvement became real and the division sharper between isolationists and those ready to give aid to the Allies. Another Dartmouth poll in October showed that the outbreak of war had caused little change in campus sentiment. Although the students voted 840 to 505 in favor of amending the Arms Embargo Act to a cash-and-carry plan, 56 percent favored permanent neutrality and this view was shared by 42 percent of the faculty. Sentiment for the Allies, however, was overwhelming, 1,411 to 30.

Mr. Hopkins meanwhile was publicly supporting President Roosevelt's effort to get the Neutrality Law revised. In this campaign he was allied with William Allen White, Alfred E. Smith, James Shotwell, and others. This country's neutrality could only work to the advantage of Hitlerism, he declared, and in a wire to the Non-Partisan Neutrality Committee of New England he added that he was in favor of aiding England and France and against giving "preferential treatment to systems of government which maintain themselves internally by assassination and establishment of medieval serfdom and externally by terrorism and war." Offering immediate and unrestricted aid to England and France was, he believed, the only chance the United States had of avoiding direct involvement in the war.

In the spring of 1940 isolationism on the Dartmouth campus took several forms that angered President Hopkins. *The Dartmouth* in its editorials urged the United States to steer clear of the war and opposed extension of any aid to the Allied powers beyond what was permitted by existing cash-and-carry legislation. In May, one thousand students signed a letter to President Roosevelt stating that American intervention would in no way aid Western democracy and urging him to follow a policy that would preserve peace and democracy at home regardless of what happened in Europe. Most upsetting of all to Mr. Hopkins was the May 22 lecture given by Professor Lewis D. Stilwell of the History Department and wildly applauded by an overflow student audience. Professor Stilwell predicted that Great Britain and France would sue for peace in short order and that the peace imposed by Hitler would be less oppressive than supposed. In any event, it couldn't be any worse than that imposed on Germany by the Versailles Treaty. The effect of a Nazi victory on the United States would be negligible, he said, and a quick peace would allow Europe to settle down. In his opinion, Hitler, far from being insane, was showing that he had shrewd insight.

President Hopkins was disgusted with such a point of view, and with the sympathetic hearing given to it. The day after the lecture he wrote to Roy B. Chamberlin, the College Chaplain, "The thing that is on trial at the present time is the whole conception of liberalism and the liberal college, and in my estimation what is happening in the liberal colleges in the attitudes of men expressed by the undergraduate editors and members of the faculty like Lew Stilwell is not only a degradation of the liberal dogma but is suicide." Several days later he stated that he was not willing to have a college building used for a peace rally on Memorial Day, because he feared that the occasion would be used for isolationist propaganda and for derision of the country's war dead.

That same month, President Hopkins became a member of the Committee to Defend America by Aiding the Allies, headed by William Allen White. He also was a member of the so-called Century Group, a group of leading citizens who met at the Century Association in New York for the purpose of encouraging President Roosevelt to give ships and submarines to England. Among the members of this group were Henry Luce, Walter Lippmann, Lewis Douglas, and Admiral Stanley. Mr. Hopkins was also importuned by others to lend his voice to the Allied cause. Philip Cabot of the Harvard Business School wanted him to take the lead in telling the American public that the real nature of the crisis was tyranny versus freedom; and Robert D. Brewer, Boston bank president, wanted him to speak out on the food problem of war-torn Europe.

The depth of President Hopkins' discouragement in the spring of 1940 is all too evident in some of his correspondence. In a June 6 letter to Sumner Emerson, 1917, he wrote, "Something rather terrible has happened to this generation. . . . I never expected to reach the stage of distrust of everything which we had tried to do and of every ideal which I had ever held for the liberal college to the present time. . . . I have wanted to think that our men were at least sincere, even if mistaken, but in talking with them and with people who know the sentiment of other eastern colleges, I can't get any impression excepting that of a panic-stricken crowd of sheep, willing to run in any direction and to accept any refuge if only they don't have to do anything about it. That is the reason why for the first time in my life I hate my job."

The same pessimism cropped up in a memorandum to Dean Bill. Mr. Hopkins expressed concern about the cynicism of undergraduates and their lack of willingness to defend liberalism and democracy, and he wondered what was responsible—the curriculum, the faculty, or causes over which the College had no control. Maybe a new administration would produce a new confidence in the College, he said, but that would be too nearly a quitter's action. "This attitude isn't dictated by any desire to hang on to my job," he wrote, "because for the first time in my life I dislike it exceedingly and should be glad to get rid of it."

It was in this frame of mind, and against the background of the spring's events, that President Hopkins prepared the baccalaureate address he delivered to the Class of 1940 on June 16. For his theme he chose the story of

Ezekiel and his vision, wherein God spoke to him and said, "Son of man, stand upon thy feet and I will speak unto thee." Throughout literature, Mr. Hopkins pointed out, the upright man, standing upon his feet, had been synonymous with self-respect. Conditions of modern life, providing youth with ease and material comforts without any real effort on their part, had resulted in a lack of experience with life's essentials. Yet the inexperienced college man, perhaps brilliant in mind and persuasive with words, considered it to be his right to assert what should be the circumstances of life around him. "Whether consciously or unconsciously," Mr. Hopkins said, "many of those who have assumed the role of spokesmen of undergraduate bodies in America today have given the impression of the undergraduate as one wholly unwilling to stand upon his feet or to listen to any voice except the echo of his own desires."

Connecting his theme of the upright man to the issue of the war then raging in Europe, Mr. Hopkins left no doubt in the minds of the graduating seniors that he had a poor opinion of their isolationist attitudes of the spring. Without any side-stepping, he said: "No man who thinks responsibly of education can speak in such a time as this without thought of the lowering threat in the world to all that has made life worth living and that has made the past high accomplishments of education possible. And never before have the inadequacies of present-day education to be helpful to all been as definitely exemplified as by many of those who purport to speak for the student population of institutions of higher learning in America today. There is abundant reason for regret concerning the unconscious self-delusion of the man who escapes self-judgment for avoiding obligation by claiming major importance for some plausible and otherwise desirable objective. There is even greater reason for concern in regard to the influence of the colleges in the apprehensions among some student groups lest some word or deed offend the protagonists of force and brutality, race extinction, and mass murder. There is at least some basis for inquiry as to the extent to which the college breeds discriminating intelligence when hundreds of men sign petitions to the President protesting that they see nothing of the struggle against the forces of evil in the present exigency. There is concern about the relationship of intellectual development and common sense when undergraduates argue against a preparedness to meet double-dealing and treachery to which other peoples have been subjected and against which we are not defended. There is widespread bewilderment as to how the intelligent man can so ignore precedent as to believe that we can have anything more than a temporary immunity from the attacks of a group that has defined its antagonisms to everything which our race has sought to establish for centuries past and for which it stands today. The conclusion alike of the man on the street and of those in high position in regard to undergraduates of today are likely to be that they are a softened generation which capitulates easily to what it deems to be self-interest."

The fact that these attitudes represented a minority opinion among the undergraduates did not excuse the College from indictment, Mr. Hopkins asserted. The ultimate in these attitudes, he added, "is the hard materialism and cynical indifference of some few in every college group who admit that not only would they have a free people abase itself but would, if practicable, compromise with the murderous sponsors of indecency for such respite as might in return be granted to us. Neither the word of the Lord not the understanding of man can be invoked for these until they stand upon their feet."

Recalling this baccalaureate some years later, President Hopkins said he had been determined that the 1940 graduates "should not go out from the College feeling that there was any sympathy with them at all here." The atmosphere was definitely strained as he spoke. "The antagonism was so great in the audience that I could feel the thing," he recalled. "I mean, they just didn't like it, and I was very glad when that period got by."

President Hopkins' pessimism was too uncharacteristic to last for long. At the same time he was unburdening himself of his feelings about the anti-war events at Dartmouth he was stating his belief that the students would eventually come to the right assessment of the world crisis. In May of 1940 he wrote, "As a matter of fact, I have the greatest confidence in the capacity and the will of the undergraduates eventually to think this through and come out with an understanding that all of their generalizations lead to ends contrary to anything for which liberalism has ever stood. They will understand eventually, and I hope before it is too late."

This fundamental faith in the intelligence and good will of the Dartmouth student body, in every generation, was adhered to throughout the

Hopkins presidency, despite his temporary exasperation over their thinking and conduct. The times he scolded undergraduates for irresponsibility,
lack of self-discipline, and failure to appreciate the privilege of being in
college were invariably followed by happier states of mind and by expressions of satisfaction in their fine qualities and their promise as citizens who
would contribute to the public good. The students, in turn, took their
scoldings without antagonism toward President Hopkins. Although the
vast majority of undergraduates never had the opportunity to be in personal touch with him, they had great respect for him personally and for his
candor, his idealism, and his liberal spirit. And there was pride in the distinguished place that he held in American education and in the life of the
nation. Had he been more of a homebody, with regular and widespread
contacts with the undergraduates, it is likely that their respect for him
would have been accompanied by the same sort of affection the alumni had
for him.

Writing to Mr. Cutter in the fall of 1940, Mr. Hopkins explained, "I
have had my own reservations and criticisms to express in regard to [the
undergraduates] but these have been due to influences upon them rather
than due to any of their own native qualities."

A few years later, in a letter to Tom Braden, 1940, a former editor of *The
Dartmouth* who later became a Dartmouth trustee, Mr. Hopkins mentioned
a published biographical sketch of himself which dwelt on his annoyance
with college students in the years before the war. "I hope that sometime
somebody will correct this particular thing," he wrote, "if it becomes incorporated in the newspaper morgues and appears in post-mortem notices."
His real exasperation, he went on, was directed at "the complete lack of
realism with which our teachers, our churchmen, and our politicians treated
the affairs of the world. I still think that the best aphorism I know is that . . .
one of the most tragic things in the world is the amount of time and effort
it takes on the part of the wise to correct the mistakes of the merely good."
Foremost among the teachings that angered him were the claims that World
War I had been a sordid affair, fought for economic gain and fomented by
the munitions-makers for their own profit.

Mr. Hopkins, in looking back over the whole of his administration, said
that the pre-war years in the late thirties were the only time when he felt

the students were against him, just as the episode of the Orozco murals earlier in that decade was the only time when he felt the alumni were against him. Whatever the temper of the resident College in those "hardest days" when U. S. involvement in the war was being debated, the spirit and performance of Dartmouth men, once this country declared war, gave Mr. Hopkins the proudest years of his presidency, and made the late thirties but an aberration in the steady progression of his leadership and influence.

President Hopkins in the summer of 1940 became more active than ever in the effort to have war supplies sent to England. He was involved in the pressure upon the U. S. government to provide the fifty destroyers that finally were given, and he also urged that Flying Fortresses be released to the Allies. Some of the mail coming into Hanover accused him of being a warmonger, and while this was untrue in any jingoistic sense, he had already declared in a letter, "I wish that our Congress could be persuaded to make a formal declaration of war and thus release us from all the red tape which precludes us at the present time from doing a lot of the things that England so badly needs to have us do—to be of maximum help in keeping Hitlerism in Europe. Especially I wish that our harbors and repair shops could be opened for English shipping and the repair of naval vessels."

On June 28, 1940, President Hopkins addressed the New England Council in Boston. He used the occasion for the fullest and strongest statement he had yet made about the nature of the world crisis and about the urgency of having this country wake up to the fact that it had a vital stake in the outcome of the war against Hitlerism. He asserted that America was listening to what it wanted to hear and not to the wisdom of those who rightly saw the future of American freedom and democracy endangered if the forces of totalitarianism were not destroyed. "Let's not get mixed up in the tyranny of words, by the use of the word *war*," he said. "Let's not think that we are dealing with a war like anything else which ever happened in history, even the World War. We are not dealing with a war between England and France on the one side and Germany on the other. We are dealing with a vicious form of world revolution which started in Germany and is sweeping Europe and is going to sweep the world unless something is done about it."

Mr. Hopkins referred to a letter he had received criticizing his stand on

U. S. involvement and asking what was going to happen to the College if he had his way. "Well, I can answer for Dartmouth College," he said, "and I think I can answer for every school and college in the country. Whatever is needful to be done, the schools and colleges stand ready to do. And speaking personally, and officially for those interests which I represent, if there is anything at the present time that I can do, if there is anything that Dartmouth can do that will be helpful, in use of her plant or her organization or her funds or anything else, they are available to do it. Culture and civilization must be preserved, yes, and the ideas of freedom and liberty must be preserved, yes, but the time comes every once in a while when those who most value freedom and liberty recognize that these may have to be laid on the shelf for a while, properly tagged of course, in order that they may be available again in more auspicious times."

This declaration proved to be an accurate forecast of what was to happen for Mr. Hopkins personally and for the College during the remaining five years of his administration.

The Alumni Movement

MORE than once, when he was in the mood to pass judgment on his own administration, President Hopkins stated that he considered his greatest contribution to the College to be his work with the alumni. It is debatable whether this actually was a greater contribution than his success as interpreter and advocate of the liberal college, but certainly the development of the Dartmouth alumni movement under his leadership was of a special magnitude and established one of the great strengths that Dartmouth continues to enjoy today.

Dartmouth's reputation for eminence in alumni relations was firmly settled in the Hopkins years. The loyalty of Dartmouth men took on legendary proportions, and the ardor of it sometimes led the incredulous alumni of other colleges to gibe at it as a kind of madness. The members of the College called it the Dartmouth Spirit, capitalized, and Mr. Hopkins sometimes defined it as a religion. The latter concept may have had its origin in the deathbed statement of General Streeter, who said that Dartmouth had been religion enough for him. Whatever the form or degree of Dartmouth alumni loyalty, it had its basis in the belief, stated by President Hopkins, that no college could be truly great or of maximum influence without the understanding support of its alumni. That stood as one of the fundamental tenets of his administration.

As was the case with some other developments of the Hopkins presidency, the basic philosophy of the alumni movement had been established by Dr. Tucker. At a time when college trustees and administrators were inclined to look upon the alumni as a nuisance, except when they gave money, he saw the institutional strength to be derived from organized alumni support. Before he retired in 1909 the first steps had been taken to realize that potential. Mr. Hopkins, as assistant to Dr. Tucker, had played a major part in the early organizational effort, and as president from 1916 on he had the opportunity to implement the Tucker philosophy, to enlarge upon it, and to bring it to fruition.

The first formal organization of Dartmouth alumni took place in 1854, but the association then established was a vague body without any real influence. For the next thirty-five years the story of alumni relations was one of constant battle with the trustees over giving the alumni a greater say in the government of the College through recognized representation on the board of trustees. In the eyes of the trustees—then a board of cautious, self-perpetuating life members—this had the danger of opening the door to all sorts of change and new policies. In 1876 the trustees finally agreed to let the alumni submit four names for each of the next three vacancies on the board, but this still left them considerable latitude in making their own choices, and the three trustees thus elected became life trustees, putting things back where they were before. Discontent with the closed form of College control became more intense if anything, reaching a peak in 1881, when the New York alumni brought charges of maladministration against President Samuel Colcord Bartlett and actually staged a formal trial in Hanover. Alumni exasperation was at the boiling point again in 1890, when the trustees rejected General Streeter, the nominee of the alumni, and elected to the board a man of their own choice.

At this point, it became clear, even to the trustees themselves, that the existing state of alumni relations could not go on and that some way of meeting alumni wishes had to be devised. Dr. Tucker, who had been one of the three trustees elected under the 1876 agreement, was a strong influence for compromise. The resulting offer made by the trustees went considerably beyond the expectations of the alumni. The board agreed to make five vacancies available and to fill them with the nominees of the alumni for staggered terms, so that in due course there would be an annual vacancy to which, by gentlemen's agreement, a nominee of the alumni would be elected. This meant that, exclusive of the president and the governor, the five "alumni trustees" would comprise half of the membership of the board. Three trustees were thus elected in 1891 and two more in 1892. The development of the Dartmouth alumni movement to its high estate began at that point. And it began opportunely on the eve of the presidency of William Jewett Tucker, who got the movement off to the best possible start by enunciating a philosophy of the place the alumni should have, and responsibly fulfill, in the life of the College.

By the time the Hopkins presidency began, a little more than twenty years later, such effective organizations as the Dartmouth Secretaries Association and the Dartmouth Alumni Council had been created, and an alumni magazine established. Major credit for the founding of the Council in 1913 belonged to Mr. Hopkins, its first president. The Council took over responsibility for the annual Alumni Fund, and in its second year it became the agency for choosing the annual alumni nominee for trustee. The growth of Dartmouth alumni clubs, which was to have such acceleration under President Hopkins, also was well under way by 1916. Of the thirty-eight clubs existing in that year, fourteen had been established under President Tucker and thirteen others under President Nichols.

President Hopkins devoted a considerable portion of his inaugural address to alumni relations. It is not likely that any college president taking office previously had given so much attention to this phase of college activity. "There will be few such possibilities of added vigor to the college as in the development of what has come to be known as the alumni movement," Mr. Hopkins said. But this strength will be gained, he warned, only if the college accepted its responsibility to develop it and if the alumni directed their interest and their solicitude, beyond their financial support, to the true educational purposes of the college. At the very beginning of his administration he thus sounded the note he was to repeat innumerable times: the alumnus has little to contribute to his college if his relationship is merely a nostalgic and sentimental one, but he has much to contribute if he will strive to understand the changing function of the college and the educational effort to fulfill that function.

The alumni section of the inaugural address had special significance not only because it was a forecast of what was to become one of the really striking characteristics of the Hopkins presidency, but also because it was not surpassed thereafter as a succinct and balanced statement of President Hopkins' own philosophy concerning alumni relations. There followed, over the years, many talks to the students and to the alumni themselves in which he expounded his ideas about the place of the alumni in the life of the College. These discourses were always pitched to the ideals of the lib-

eral college and of Dartmouth College in particular. One Hopkins address
that had the alumni as its specific subject was the address he delivered at
the national conference of the American Alumni Council at Amherst College in May 1930. It was entitled "The College and the Alumni" and in it
Mr. Hopkins, in rather informal fashion, shared with the alumni officers of
other colleges the thoughts that Dartmouth men had heard him express
many times.

"The objective of the American college, it seems to me apparent," he
told the Amherst gathering, "is to prepare men to enter the society of our
time and enhance its intellectual and its moral standards. If that be so, I
think that we may reasonably assume that the purpose of the American
college is to produce alumni. And if the purpose of the American college is
to produce alumni, it is no less the purpose of the American college to retain the interest and the intelligent support of alumni that they may remain
a vital factor in the constituency of the college. . . . All in all, I have seen no
definition of what the alumni relationship with the college should be, but
I have known of no statement that seems to me more eloquent or more informing than that made in 1855, at one of the early meetings of the Dartmouth Alumni Association, when President Lord said: 'You ask me to show
cause why Dartmouth should continue to have the favor of her sons? My
answer is a short one—because Dartmouth is in her sons. There is no
Dartmouth without her sons. They have made her what she is, and they
constitute good and sufficient reasons why she should be sustained.'

"So far as I know, every administration at Dartmouth from that time until the present has accepted that concept as a working hypothesis. And the
fact is that a college cannot be of maximum influence except with the support of its alumni, and consequently that a college must have the support of
its alumni if it is to be truly great.

"That is the sum and substance of all I have to say this morning, and
that is to be considered in spite of the generalizations which are made from
time to time as to pestiferous alumni, troublesome alumni, and all the rest
of it. If alumni are pestiferous, and if alumni are troublesome, it is because
they are not given sufficient knowledge of what the college is about for
their interest and solicitude to be attracted to its present needs."

One of President Hopkins' strongest beliefs about alumni was that their interest in the college was basically serious and that if it was allowed to become superficial, it was mainly the fault of the college. "My permanent conviction," he told the American Alumni Council gathering, "is that the alumnus of the American college is vitally interested in education, and that if you give the individual alumnus the same opportunity to know about the educational policy, the educational theory, and the development of courses that you give him to know about the football games and the development of teams, he will respond with just as much interest and with just as much support."

The core elements of Mr. Hopkins' philosophy of alumni relations were: 1) the alumni are an integral part of the college constituency—indeed are essential to the full realization of the college's educational purpose; 2) they have the right to be fully represented in the governance of the college; 3) alumni interest can be taken to be quite the opposite of superficial and to have its most genuine expression in relationship to the educational work of the college; 4) alumni, in return for the influential role accorded them, have an obligation to seek understanding of the educational function and programs of the college; 5) the college has a corresponding responsibility to provide the full information necessary for intelligent alumni participation and support; and 6) the intellectual ties between the college and its alumni do not cease with graduation but ideally should continue for the rest of the graduate's life. President Hopkins probably never ticked off these elements in such fashion, but in his years of involvement in Dartmouth alumni affairs and in his steady commitment to the fullest possible alumni collaboration he meshed all these elements into a single rounded conviction which provided the underpinning for everything he did to give Dartmouth its unexcelled alumni program.

The organizational machinery for a nationwide alumni program, given its initial form by Mr. Hopkins when he was secretary of the College in the Tucker administration, was gradually developed into perhaps the most effective thing of its kind in the country. Recognition of this led to a steady stream of visits by alumni officers from other colleges seeking to find out how Dartmouth was doing it. The organization of classes and clubs, led by the Alumni Council and encouraged by a president and a board of trustees fully committed to the importance of the alumni, resulted in support of all kinds which was hailed as Dartmouth's "living endowment" and which made up for the College's lesser ranking among sister institutions when it came to financial resources.

As necessary and effective as the organizational machinery was, it was President Hopkins personally who was at the center of the developing alumni program and who provided its main impetus. Nothing he did in this field was more important than the tremendous effort he put into visiting Dartmouth alumni groups all over the country to tell them about the educational work and goals of the College. His annual alumni tours went on for the full twenty-nine years of the Hopkins administration, with the few exceptions when war or illness halted them. There were two pervasive results from the frequent contacts President Hopkins had with the alumni in their home communities: the maintenance of Dartmouth's excellence as an educational institution did become the foremost concern of the alumni, and the alumni did accept a sense of responsibility for the welfare of the College. A third result was alumni devotion to Mr. Hopkins personally, which grew stronger and stronger as his administration progressed.

Mr. Hopkins confessed he could never understand the attitude of his presidential colleagues who visited their alumni only reluctantly and re-garded doing so as a burdensome official chore. He genuinely enjoyed get-ting out among the graduates of the College, and this came partly from his innate liking for people. "I always had a great joy in meeting the alumni," he said. "I mean the thing just fascinated me—the difference between the groups." Mr. Hopkins had, of course, a wide acquaintance among the alumni, going back to his days in Dr. Tucker's office, and extended in the period from 1910 to 1916 when, outside of Hanover, he was one of the leaders in organizing the alumni. His associates in the president's office who occasionally made alumni trips with him were much younger than he, but they invariably became exhausted long before he did. After a formal dinner President Hopkins was willing to sit up until the small hours of the morning, talking with alumni friends who gathered around him in his hotel room. Then he would be up at 7 and off to the railroad station for the next leg of his tour.

The talks he gave before the alumni groups were hardly ever written out. He preferred to speak from scribbled notes, choosing his topics to fit what he sensed to be the concerns of a particular group. He found it easier to establish a common ground that way, and conversation with members of the host club would often turn up a misconception or a special interest to which he could address himself. Mr. Hopkins always claimed he got as much from his regional visits as the alumni got from him. The transformation and growth of alumni interest in the College gave him a lift, as well as a renewed appreciation of the force of alumni support that was available to the College if intelligently directed. The varying characters of the different alumni clubs were relished by him. The Cleveland alumni, for example, were known as a rambunctious bunch, with a tradition of heckling the dinner speaker. Mr. Hopkins recalled that Dean Laycock had been reduced almost to tears in Cleveland, and that Dean Bill, exasperated, had said, "You are a bunch of muckers and I'm never coming back," to which there was a shouted chorus of "Good!" Mr. Hopkins always looked forward to Cleveland, but he, as Dartmouth's president, undoubtedly got more respectful treatment.

One thing President Hopkins did not do in his alumni talks was to appeal for money. This would have been out of character for him. He was content, rather, to bring an up-to-date report about the College, to reinforce belief in the ideals of the liberal college, and to stimulate pride in Dartmouth as an exemplar of those ideals. It was his conviction that financial support would come of the alumni's own free will, when there was understanding and pride.

Neither was it in character for Mr. Hopkins to try the emotional approach in speaking of the College. Dean Laycock was the star in that line. The Hopkins talks were straightforward and informative, but lifted out of the ordinary by the idealism and liberal spirit that were a natural part of his leadership. On occasion, however, he could break loose, and one notable instance is to be found in an April 1932 talk which the Chicago alumni liked so much they had it printed from a stenographic record. Mr. Hopkins concluded his remarks by telling how one iconoclast had stood out from a group of students with whom he had met at the Mel Adams Cabin. "When the evening was over," he said, "we came out and perhaps the man among the whole lot whose loyalty would be doubted most among his fellows in the undergraduate body, if the devotion of any could be doubted, stood behind. And as I lingered beside the cabin door I turned around, and there in the bright moonlight I saw him with tears in his eyes. Some of you know the scene from the Mel Adams Cabin, facing down towards the village. Up on the right was the glistening slope of frosted snow, gleaming in the moonlight; down on the left was the long, low line of dark, the evergreens; over beyond you could see the terraced hills of the White Mountains hazily outlined in the moonlight; and down in the valley were the twinkling lights on Hanover plain, and amid these the lights of the College. As I left the cabin door and turned to go, the fellow put his hand on my arm and he said, 'Can you beat it?' And the answer was 'No.' "

In the maintenance of lines of communication between the alumni and the College, President Hopkins put as much personal effort into correspondence as he did into his travels. He carried on a voluminous correspondence with Dartmouth men all over the country, and it was his settled policy to make reply personally to all the letters that came in addressed to him. When a man writes to the president of his college, Mr. Hopkins told his office associates, he deserves to hear from him and not from someone else. The letters he wrote were often devoted to an elucidation of College policy, and where he thought that an alumnus had misinterpreted things or was lacking the facts, he took pains to write to him at considerable length to explain the official College position and the reasons a certain action had been taken. These replies were never perfunctory, and the recipient, although he might not be completely mollified, was likely to be gratified by the fact that the president had given him so much of his time and attention, and equally pleased to be told that as an alumnus he had every right to be concerned and to raise questions. Conservative alumni were often alarmed by some "leftist" speaker visiting the campus or by some professor expressing unorthodox views. In these cases, President Hopkins could be courteously firm in reminding the alumnus what the liberal college was all about. But critical mail did not predominate; many letters were friendly and supportive, and in those instances Mr. Hopkins was at his best in showing his appreciation and in telling the alumnus how important his interest and support were to the College.

President Hopkins initiated a good deal of his correspondence with the alumni. Some of it was simply the correspondence which would be expected to take place between friends. He took special pleasure in dropping notes, usually in longhand, to Dartmouth men whose achievements he had learned about. He often wrote to alumni friends whose sons he had matriculated or called into his office for a visit. Upon returning to Hanover from an alumni swing, he wrote not only the usual thank-you letters to those who had managed the meetings or been his hosts, but he also remembered to provide by correspondence the answer to some question which could not be adequately discussed in a brief encounter at the dinner. All these epistolary bits and pieces were part of a conscious effort on his part not only to foster alumni understanding but to make alumni feel they had a part in the Dartmouth enterprise and that it mattered how they thought of the College.

Mr. Hopkins' concept of the relationship of the individual alumnus to what Dr. Tucker called "the corporate consciousness" of the College was the real foundation on which the success of the Dartmouth alumni movement rested. He told Dartmouth men their lives could become significant only if they made themselves part of something much bigger than themselves and in which they could unreservedly believe. He left no doubt that Dartmouth College qualified as that something bigger. And he carried the idea further and gave it a warm and appealing dimension by speaking repeatedly of the Dartmouth family and emphasizing that being a part of the College was like being a member of a family. He strongly encouraged a policy that there should be no distinction between the graduate and the non-graduate in the Dartmouth fellowship. In his talk at the Amherst conference he expressed the family idea in homely terms: "Certainly the conception we ought to accept is the old conception of the New England homestead, in which the fires were kept burning and the lights were kept bright, and as the family increased, ells were added, so that there was always hospitality for all."

In his farewell remarks, when he turned the presidency over to John Sloan Dickey in 1945, Mr. Hopkins returned to the family theme. On that occasion he said, "A friendly observer of the College said to me that nobody could understand Dartmouth who didn't recognize that it was not simply another educational institution but that it was likewise a religion. Personally I believe very strongly that a third aspect is important for us to recognize—that it is a family. Through two or three decades of administrative leadership in the College, in association with friends and colleagues like yourselves and in association with thousands of the alumni—yes, and even into the families of the alumni and undergraduates—I have become impressed more and more with the sweetness that attached to the relationship between one and another which constituted this great family which we call Dartmouth. Wheelock was a patriarch. He viewed himself as the head of his family. Wheelock visualized all who worked with him as associates and members of his family, and in some very definite relationship, I think, down through the years that has prevailed. And at times when it has been most evident, most existent, the College has fared best."

The family idea, the sense of belonging in an individual, identifiable way, had its most effective realization in the alumni classes. Although the primary loyalty was always to the College itself, the class groups with their class spirit became the key units in the Dartmouth alumni program. The central importance of class groups and the attention to the individual alumnus which the class plan made possible were developed with great success. "So far as Dartmouth is concerned," President Hopkins wrote to one of his administrative associates, "I think the classes are a very essential factor in keeping up the family attributes of the College, which atmosphere I consider absolutely indispensable to being the kind of college that Dartmouth is." Very early in his administration he had written to an alumnus who was engaged in strengthening the class organization: "For the success and strength of the College, that it may carry out the great purposes inherent in its life, I believe that the alumni body must be moulded and welded into such an effective unit as we have never known before. All sorts of influences can be made to work toward this end; alumni trustees, Alumni Council, and other organizations calculated to treat the alumni body as an entity. But these agencies cannot be effective, and the lump sum cannot be important, if we do not continually work from the individual alumnus; and here of course we get right back to the individual class secretary and the class secretaries as a group."

The organized classes, sixty or more in number, proved to be ideal agencies for carrying out a variety of alumni projects. This was especially true with regard to the annual Alumni Fund. Class spirit and a certain amount of good-natured braggadocio led to results which never could have been achieved on a general alumni basis. This competitive character of the annual fund campaign was built up during the Hopkins years, and another special characteristic was the stress placed on a high percentage of participation, quite aside from the total of dollars contributed. This emphasis arose from President Hopkins' belief that where a man gave his free-will financial support there his interest and solicitude were most likely to be given also. In percentage of alumni contributing to the annual fund, Dartmouth took a commanding lead over all other colleges and universities, achieving as high as 72 percent. In the first year of the Hopkins administration, the fund had 1,066 contributors; in the final year, the number had grown to 13,348. The amounts of money given may not seem large today, but they were substantial for the 1916–45 period. In President Hopkins' first year, the Alumni Fund raised $17,541. In the year of his retirement, it produced $337,367. The grand total of the twenty-nine Alumni Funds during his presidency was $3.38 million.

No large capital fund drive among the alumni was undertaken during the Hopkins administration, and perhaps the College held back too cautiously from making such an effort to enlarge its endowment. There was fear that the all-important Alumni Fund would suffer. In a letter in July of 1944, Mr. Hopkins stated that he had always been opposed to an endowment drive, preferring to have the capital remain in the pockets of the alumni and to derive the income from it in annual gifts. He repeated the idea that where one is induced to give his money regularly he gives his interest in larger degree. In a much earlier letter to Edwin Webster Sanborn, he wrote that if he had the choice between an endowment of many millions and an alumni body keenly interested in the significant phases of higher education, he would unhesitatingly choose the latter. Such alumni support would in the long run be incalculable and would bring the necessary financial support. Answering an alumnus who had written about a special class fund drive, he explained, "Some years ago the Trustees decided wisely, I believe, not to go into the business of endowment drives and not to undertake a major attack upon the pockets of the alumni for a single occasion, but to ask instead for a continuing support, year by year. Hence came the rapid development and increase in the Alumni Fund."

Although not having quite the weight of the classes in the overall Dartmouth alumni program, the alumni clubs had their own special importance in providing the regional approach that was needed for balance. In club activities Dartmouth men of all ages joined together and thus came closer to the unity that had been set as a goal in alumni relations. The growth in the number of clubs during the Hopkins presidency was substantial. Forty-two new clubs were established, notably in New England, the South, the Middle West, and the Southwest, bringing the total to eighty.

Under the general supervision of the Alumni Council, the clubs assumed an important new function with the adoption of the Selective Process of Admission in 1921. The interviewing and rating of applicants for admission was most easily handled by committees set up by the regional associations. The resulting enlargement of club activity, which previously had been mainly social, was a stimulus to the whole network of regional alumni centers. From this interviewing function developed an expanded role in the College's national enrollment program, and this in turn led to the assumption of responsibility for establishing and financing regional scholarships. The clubs, during the Hopkins years, also increased their direct involvement in the College's educational program, notably in securing the best possible student body. In his periodic visits President Hopkins gave the clubs a broad view of the educational effort to which their work was contributing and, as with the classes, he managed to keep them on the track of serious concerns while not diminishing the fellowship and social pleasures which were indispensable to club success.

Because he had more to do with the creation of the Dartmouth Alumni Council than of any other unit of the alumni organization, President Hopkins always had a special interest in it. How he felt was indicated in a comment to Victor Cutter in November 1932: "I am inclined to think that when the College history of more recent years comes to be written, my own most significant contribution to College welfare will not be anything I have done as President but it will really be the fact that I had some essential part in the formation of the Alumni Council." The Council turned out to be everything that Dr. Tucker and Mr. Hopkins hoped for at the heart of their grand design—an organization to give authority to the idea of the vital role of the alumni in Dartmouth's development.

As the "senate" of the Dartmouth alumni body, the Alumni Council has earned for itself the role of sponsor, director, and arbiter of every alumni project of significance. Where alumni opinion and support are operative in the life of the College, it has a power second only to that of the board of trustees. The Council was only three years old when President Hopkins took office in 1916, and though it has grown in size and influence and has taken on a number of new functions in recent times, the essential character of the Council and its authority were fixed during the Hopkins administration. Direction of the Alumni Fund and the choice of nominees for the alumni-trustee positions on the board were its earliest responsibilities. Something of its development can be seen in the creation of standing committees having to do with admissions and schools, class and club organization, alumni projects, and undergraduate affairs. During the Hopkins period, the Council's backing was given to the introduction in June 1937 of Hanover Holiday, a summer program of faculty lectures for the alumni. This project, filling a void that had existed since the Guernsey Center Moore lectures in the early twenties failed to catch on, was especially encouraged by President Hopkins and was the forerunner of today's Alumni College.

The organizational machinery of the Dartmouth alumni program today is essentially what it was in the Hopkins period. Some of it antedated that period, although Mr. Hopkins was the architect of nearly all of it. The machinery worked well under the competent direction of College officers such as Eugene Clark and Sidney Hayward. But it was not so much the effective machinery as it was the philosophy and spirit supplied by President Hopkins personally that gave the Dartmouth alumni movement its distinctive force and success at a time when it was shaping itself for the long pull. Some degree of success would have occurred under any leadership, but in the early, formative years of the movement the loyalty of the alumni, their sense of responsibility for the College's welfare, and their concern for the educational excellence of the College all took deeper root because feelings of trust and affection toward Mr. Hopkins were so inseparably a part of the general alumni attitude toward the College.

It was mainly among the alumni that "Hoppy" became the affectionate way of referring to the president. On the campus the term was used by a few intimate friends, but faculty and students did not use it ordinarily and to the administrative associates working with him most closely the president was always Mr. Hopkins. There was tremendous respect for President Hopkins in the resident College, but the affection for him as a person and as the epitome of Dartmouth had its widest play among the alumni. It is doubtful if any college president ever had closer rapport with alumni. Analyzing the relationship would be a pointless exercise. It simply existed as a natural, human force. Mr. Hopkins liked and trusted the alumni; they in turn liked and trusted him; in addition to which they had for him the feeling that one has for the revered head of the clan. The "Hoppy" phase of the relationship became more pronounced as his administration progressed, and it was even stronger after his retirement, when as president emeritus for nearly twenty years Mr. Hopkins became so venerable a figure.

In a study of Dartmouth alumni relations conducted in 1958 by a subcommittee of the Trustees Planning Committee, President Hopkins was described as "the man who mastered the alumni movement and made it a force of positive strength to the College." His wisdom and executive skill were important factors in that success, but no one can fully appreciate how the Dartmouth alumni movement got where it did without giving weight to the faith that President Hopkins had in the alumni and the alumni had in him. The full measure of himself that he poured into every facet of the alumni program was the all-important ingredient which produced such remarkable success.

The War Years

WHEN students and faculty assembled in the fall of 1940 for the new college year, there were signs that the tide of opinion at Dartmouth had begun to turn against isolation and non-intervention. The sweep of Nazi armies across the face of Europe produced a clearer sense of the danger to America that President Hopkins had foreseen and had done his utmost to call to the attention of the country at large. He had been convinced that once the true nature of the world crisis was understood, there would be a swing to the point of view he and a minority on campus had held for two years or more. In this expectation he proved to be just as prescient as he had been in sizing up the Nazi threat.

Without waiting for any changed attitude on campus, President Hopkins had acted during the summer of 1940 to offer Dartmouth's facilities to the Army and Navy for any use they might want to make of them in training young men for the defense of the nation. He expressed willingness to have this assistance take the form of an ROTC unit, should either service wish to establish one at Dartmouth. Another summer action was to cable the Preparatory Schools Association in London offering the College as a distributing center for the 1,700 boys, aged eight to thirteen, who were to be evacuated to American and Canadian schools. Dartmouth's offer was accepted and a task force in Hanover began to make plans for carrying out this project, but ultimately the evacuation idea was abandoned.

By the time the College opened in 1940 there existed an American Defense Dartmouth Group, which President Hopkins had appointed in the late summer. Its six faculty and administrative members, under the chairmanship of Professor Harold J. Tobin, author of *Mobilizing Civilian America*, were given responsibility for coordinating all the College's defense activities, including a speakers bureau, and of serving as an information center about defense opportunities, Selective Service, and military reserve programs. From the outset the American Defense Dartmouth Group also took on the role of propagandist for American aid to the Allies, and three months after its formation it enunciated its basic policy: "The U. S. should take whatever action is necessary to prevent the Axis powers from winning the war." Nothing could have been more pleasing to Mr. Hopkins, who continued to work with national groups advocating full aid to Great Britain. Before College opened that fall he had expressed his concern that Dartmouth was becoming known as a place where students and faculty were disloyal to the defense of democracy in America and the world, and he considered dropping some courses and substituting new ones in defense preparation.

"To ignore the fact that to be without force is to invite war is to ignore all of the lessons of history," he declared in his Convocation address that September. "And more fatal than lacking force is the lack of will to use it." The main theme of his address was a denunciation of "spurious liberalism," which held that because Great Britain was not always the practitioner of ideal democracy, she deserved no sympathy in her fight against Hitler. It was the same spurious liberalism that allowed young men to grow up without an understanding of the history of the times immediately preceding their own and thus bred a cynicism and irresponsibility toward the preservation of values they did not fully prize because they had never lacked them. "It is to patient men of clear vision and flexible minds that true liberalism must look for its protection and development," he said. And for the sake of preserving itself, "the liberal college must be willing to forgo the privileges of liberalism for a brief time that liberalism shall not be destroyed for a long time."

President Hopkins was gratified to sense a more receptive audience than the one he had faced during the previous college year. The change in campus thinking about this country's role in the war did not become pronounced until the spring and fall of 1941, but the passage of the Selective Service Act and the October 1940 registration of some 570 Dartmouth students over twenty-one brought about one sign of the way the tide was running. On registration day a protest meeting against the draft was called, but only fifty students showed up. Two weeks later a campus poll on United States war policy showed that seventy-five students favored an immediate declaration of war against Germany and that 157 more would declare war if England appeared to be near collapse. In a poll the previous fall, only nine students had voted for immediate entrance into the war, and eighteen had favored getting ready for this country's eventual involvement.

The alarming course of Nazi aggression was unquestionably the prime factor in bringing about a change in the thinking of college students throughout the land. In Dartmouth's case, another factor, of a special order, was the influence of President Hopkins, who stuck doggedly to the task of puncturing isolationist contentions and of urging all-out preparation for America's inevitable entry into the conflict. Essential to adequate preparation was a national program of military training, and Mr. Hopkins in the summer of 1940 had written to Secretary of War Henry L. Stimson expressing his view that college students should not be exempted from conscription. He was in favor of having the draft begin at age eighteen rather than twenty-one, so men would begin college with the benefit of one year of disciplinary training; but the Army General Staff thought boys of eighteen were not mature enough.

Aid to Britain was the focus of the actions and thinking of the advocates of American intervention, and during the first semester a group of undergraduates formed a Dartmouth chapter of Student Defenders of Democracy, with the main objective of backing President Roosevelt's efforts to increase such aid. While agreeing with this, President Hopkins had moved on to a position of urging immediate preparation for this country's military entry into the war as a full-fledged ally. He was still pushing for unlimited aid, delivered in American ships, and in *The Dartmouth* of December 19, 1940, he joined with a small group of faculty members and students in reprinting, as an advertisement, an editorial from the *Louisville Courier Journal* denouncing the hypocrisy of what was passing for "aid to England." America had opened her heart and her order books to England, the editorial declared. It was willing to sell things and make England come and get them, it traded some rotting destroyers for air and naval bases, and it was considering the sale of a few planes. "What an inspiration we are to the suffering humanity of older, more benighted lands," the editorial concluded. This was the kind of attack on half-hearted measures that President Hopkins was delivering himself, and he wanted to make sure that students and faculty saw the editorial just before they took off for Christmas vacation.

The chance to have an active and important role in this country's defense efforts was offered to Mr. Hopkins in December 1940 when he was asked to come to Washington as an executive in the priorities division of the Office of Production Management. In the same spirit in which he had answered the call to the War Department in 1918, he accepted as a dollar-a-year man and made arrangements to carry out his Washington assignment without taking formal leave from his duties at Dartmouth. The one condition of his acceptance was that President Roosevelt should give his approval to the appointment. In view of his status as "former friend," Mr. Hopkins was not at all sure the President would want him in a government position. However, Roosevelt surprised him by not only approving but doing so in a very complimentary way.

Mr. Hopkins left for Washington on January 13, 1941. He was initially head of the Iron and Steel Priorities Board, but shortly after he took up that responsibility the OPM expanded its operations and he was named executive officer of the Minerals and Metals Section of the OPM Division of Priorities. The head of the Division was Edward R. Stettinius Jr., who in turn served under William S. Knudsen, director general of the OPM. Minerals and Metals was one of five priority sections, the others being Chemicals, Commercial Aircraft, Tools and Equipment, and General Products. Mr. Hopkins' job was to decide what apportionment of available minerals and metals should be made to the U. S. defense effort, to non-military industry, and to England and Russia, which had enormous war needs. Aluminum, zinc, magnesium, tungsten, nickel, and lead were especially in demand by all these users, and Mr. Hopkins and his staff spent a good part of their time meeting with government and industry groups to thrash out the facts of their needs and to establish the priorities under which these needs could be fully or partially met. Soon after he was on the job he felt it necessary to turn down a Russian request for a large supply of scarce aluminum, whereupon he ran into the problem of being told that the White House wanted the Russians to get what they were asking for. Mr. Hopkins balked at full compliance but worked out a compromise, even though he was convinced Russia had no priority. If any Roosevelt thunderbolt had been expected, it did not materialize.

The all-out production of needed minerals and metals was of course a vital part of the OPM program, and Mr. Hopkins' section had a relationship to that side of the national defense effort. His essential job, however, was the allocation of what was available, and in executing this responsibility he came to be known as an official of great impartiality and fairness, willing to put in long hours with the government and industry committees which were wrestling with the problem. He worked with Mr. Stettinius as effectively as he had with Newton D. Baker in World War I, and the two men became close friends. His friendly character and natural ability as an administrator produced exceptional morale and loyalty in his particular section of the OPM, and the letters written to him when he left indicate how devoted to him his associates had become.

President Hopkins made frequent trips to Hanover (usually over the weekend) for concentrated periods of College work, and a certain amount of Dartmouth work was handled from Washington. This double duty made for a strenuous life, at the age of sixty-three, but he did not want to forgo his leadership of Dartmouth in a period so crucial to the College, nor did the trustees want him to turn over that leadership to anyone else. When the Office of Production Management was about to be reorganized in June of 1941, Mr. Hopkins was offered a position of even greater responsibility, which would have required his full time, but he felt it necessary to submit his resignation, to become effective on July 1. His successor was his chief assistant, Samuel S. Stratton, Dartmouth 1920, who later became president of Middlebury College. In a Hopkins scrapbook in Baker Library is an uncashed government check for forty-nine cents, his pay for not quite six months of service with the OPM.

President Hopkins had hardly begun his duties in Washington in January 1941 when he was called home by the death of his mother in Perkinsville, Vermont, at the age of eighty-seven. Of her three sons, he was the firstborn and was especially close to her, as he had been to his father. Mary Martin Hopkins was the daughter of Horace and Lucinda Martin of Perkinsville, and she returned to the family homestead there in 1906 when her husband became minister of the town's Baptist church. After her husband's death in 1924, she lived alone in Perkinsville and showed all the qualities of sturdy, independent New England stock.

Although President Hopkins was in Washington during the first six months of 1941, the College did not slacken its efforts to develop the defense courses and programs the world crisis required. In April announcement was made that the trustees had established a Committee on Defense Instruction with full authority, on behalf of the board, to relate the curricula of the College and associated schools to the defense emergency. President Hopkins was chairman and Professor William Stuart Messer vice chairman. As one of its first moves, the committee approved a course in meteorology for men going into the Naval Reserve or Air Corps. Before the semester ended the committee had approved a number of new courses and curriculum revisions to go into effect in September. Social Science 1–2 was dropped as a freshman-year requirement, in order to give men more freedom to elect defense courses, and upperclassmen were permitted to take a sixth (defense) course without charge. Seven new courses for the fall included mathematics for navigation and ballistics, electronic physics for those who might serve in the Signal Corps, map interpretation, tests and measurement for military personnel, modern war strategy and foreign policy taught by Bernard Brodie, power politics taught by John Pelenyi, who had been Hungarian Ambassador to the United States, and components of democratic thought, taught by an interdepartmental faculty group. The committee also approved special summer versions of the defense engineering course and the civil pilot training course, which had already been taken by forty students during 1940–41. Ski instruction was expanded along military lines, and Piltti Heiskanen, a former Finnish army officer, was brought to Hanover to take charge.

In July 1941 there appeared the first issue of the *Dartmouth College Defense Bulletin* (later the *War Bulletin*) which summarized the entire defense program that would be in effect that fall and also outlined some service opportunities that would be open to students while they were still enrolled in college. In a statement he contributed to it, President Hopkins said: "As a general proposition, it is my strong belief that students will do well to await a call to service rather than to volunteer. The farther one has progressed in his education, the more valuable he will be to his country when the call comes." The second issue of the *Defense Bulletin*, distributed in September, made it clear that the College would adhere to its primary ideal of liberal education and would not try to copy the technological schools.

To finance the added cost of the enlarged defense program, President Hopkins announced that the College would use the $150,000 given by the Carnegie Foundation of New York in November of 1939 as a general development fund. The trustees agreed with him that, beyond this special fund, the College stood ready to spend whatever was necessary to prepare students for national service. Further help was available from the highly successful Alumni Fund of 1941, which covered the year's operating deficit and provided an additional $90,000 in reserve.

During Mr. Hopkins' absence in Washington, not only had the College's defense program moved ahead in a very substantial way, but the temper of the campus, which had shown a change in the fall, continued to swing decidedly toward this country's entrance into the war. A stirring expression of this sentiment appeared in *The Dartmouth* of April 24, 1941, when Senior Fellow Charles G. Bolté, 1941, wrote a front-page, open letter to President Roosevelt using the refrain, "Now we have waited long enough." He scorned the policy of "all aid short of war" and declared that the time had come to join the war against Germany as the only way to save America's freedom. The letter was picked up by the national press and overnight Dartmouth was viewed as leading the college student campaign for war against Hitler.

When College reconvened in September 1941, the American Defense Dartmouth Group joined the war advocates by issuing a new policy statement: "We believe that the United States should take vigorous action for the destruction of the Nazi tyranny. There can be no halfway measures, no compromises. If this means entering the war, then let us enter it."

Aid to Britain was a dead issue on campus. The Lend-Lease Act had been adopted and the Neutrality Act was about to be repealed, making it possible for armed American ships to carry cargoes into the war zone. Another campus poll in October showed how decidedly opinion continued to run toward this country's declaring war. Compared with the poll of one year before, the seventy-five students who had favored an immediate declaration of war had grown to 284, and the seventy-three who were against U. S. involvement in any circumstances had shrunk to twenty-one. The portion of students voting for war in the October 1941 poll was 32 percent, compared with a national student average of less than 20 percent and a Gallup Poll figure of 21 percent for the country at large. The press described Dartmouth as leading the nation's colleges in pro-war sentiment.

The existence of influences from beyond the College, as well as others within, make it impossible to say to what extent President Hopkins was personally responsible for the sharp reversal in war attitudes at Dartmouth. Certainly, he provided the most effective possible rallying point for those who shared his views, first on aid to Britain and then on the necessity of this country's joining the fight against Hitler's Germany. The important thing is that events proved the rightness of his thinking and gave Dartmouth men additional reason for respecting him and for admiring the courage with which he stuck to his convictions, even when there was, at first, very little support for his stand.

In December of 1942, one of *The Dartmouth*'s editors of the prewar period wrote to Mr. Hopkins: "I can't quite express the universal esteem the fellows in our class who know you have for you or for your fearless expression of your convictions at a time when student sentiment (and national sentiment) were hostile. The guts you displayed in holding up the other side has been an important part of the education of many of us, as have been your modesty, your humbleness, and your fairness."

The twenty-fifth anniversary of Mr. Hopkins' election to the Dartmouth presidency occurred on June 13, 1941. This provided opportunity for tributes to him for his educational leadership and public service over a quarter-century and also tributes for his defense role at the time. President Hopkins returned to Hanover from Washington to be honored at a dinner the Dartmouth faculty gave for him on Sunday evening, June 1. A birthday cake was wheeled in, and from the sentiments expressed by faculty spokesmen it was clear that the whole College felt safer and happier and surer of itself when he was in town and on the job. The hope that he would soon be back for good was realized sooner than anyone expected, for his OPM resignation was submitted shortly after the dinner. From that time on he remained steadily on the job in Hanover until his presidency ended in the fall of 1945.

The Dartmouth Alumni Fund for 1941 was conducted as the Ernest Martin Hopkins Twenty-Fifth Anniversary Fund, and the results were a record in both amount and in number of contributors. Part of the surplus, to be used as Mr. Hopkins wished, was devoted to bonus payments to the faculty, and the remainder went into the defense reserve fund. The 1941 Alumni Fund campaign was highlighted by a printed booklet of tributes to President Hopkins. Participants included President Roosevelt, Secretary of State Cordell Hull, Wendell Willkie, John D. Rockefeller Jr., Walter S. Gifford, Ray Lyman Wilbur, Kenneth Roberts, Lewis O. Douglas, Arthur Hays Sulzberger, Robert Sherwood, Claude Fuess, William S. Knudsen, President Angell of Yale, and President Dodds of Princeton. The Roosevelt statement was short and rather perfunctory, but the fact that it was made at all indicated that the 1936 episode of the *Atlantic* article apparently had been forgiven.

The anniversary gave rise to a spate of magazine and newspaper articles and interviews, notably in New York, Boston, and Washington. These afforded Mr. Hopkins a chance once again to espouse the cause of liberal education, even in a time of national emergency and technological need, and to state his views about America's inescapable responsibility to defend freedom at home and abroad. In an interview with Louis Lyons of the *Boston Sunday Globe*, he was critical of isolationist and obstructionist politicians in his own Republican Party. "As a lifelong Republican," he said, "I think a lot of our Republican leaders are doing a fine job of committing suicide for the party. I am in favor of giving the President all these emergency powers. It's the essence of democracy that at times like this you put a lot of your rights and privileges on the shelf for future use. You can't wage war on a totalitarian government by town meeting." President Roosevelt had declared a state of "unlimited national emergency" in May 1941, and it was in support of this action that Mr. Hopkins was speaking.

The twenty-fifth anniversary also occasioned a great many editorials of congratulation and praise. The New Hampshire press continued to be friendly to President Hopkins. The *Concord Monitor* hailed him as the first citizen of the state, an unofficial honor for which he seems to have had no rival since it was first accorded to him in the early twenties. "It has been the human side of Ernest Martin Hopkins which has won the respect of so many Americans, even more than his superior administrative abilities or his powers of advocacy and leadership," the *Monitor* editorialized. "Despite success, he remains a plain, genial citizen lacking in affectations. He has a faculty of enjoying the company of all men and of bringing out the best within them. He inspires others, but not in schoolmaster fashion."

Mr. Hopkins made another trip back to Hanover from Washington to preside over the June 1941 Commencement events, at which his anniversary was again celebrated with resolutions of admiration and loyalty by the General Alumni Association and the Dartmouth Alumni Council. In his valedictory to the graduating class, he seized a last chance to persuade the unconvinced that the United States must go the limit to defeat the Nazi tyranny. "It is your generation," he said, "that will determine, not in middle years but tomorrow, next year or at the latest within a few brief years, whether the preconceptions you impose upon facts, the faults you visualize in democracy, and the ruthlessness you ignore in totalitarianism shall paralyze your will to defend the one and to defeat the other or whether with eyes wide open to reality, you accept freedom as an obligation as well as a privilege and accept the role for yourself of defenders of the faith."

The opening of the new college year in September provided another opportunity to develop the war theme that so occupied his mind. "What we cannot defend by force we cannot keep," he asserted, and not only physical force was involved but force of mind and heart as well. Part of the blame for the national reluctance to recognize obligations he placed on sterile scholarship. "If we can genuinely argue that we have no responsibility to offer our powerful protection to brother human beings abroad against the brutalities imposed upon them by the arrogance and contempt of their conquerors, it will be a short step to like argument in regard to our brethren at home."

In October, only a few months after he had resigned his OPM job, Mr. Hopkins was named by President Roosevelt to be a public member of the National Defense Mediation Board. Through some slip-up, this was publicly announced before he had been informed or had accepted. He wrote to the President that the demands of the College, to which he had been unable to give full time during the first half of the year, made it impossible for him to accept the appointment. The Dartmouth trustees, concerned about the problems war would create for the College, were fully in accord with that decision. The board in that year was undergoing a greater than usual change in membership. Mr. Little died in September 1941 and at the

October meeting of the board Mr. Parkhurst, who was eighty-five and had been a member for thirty-three years, submitted his resignation. With the departure of Mr. Parkhurst, the last link with the Tucker and Nichols administrations ended, and the board for the first time became one elected entirely under President Hopkins. Mr. French and Mr. Grant were elevated to life trustees, filling the Little and Parkhurst vacancies, and early in 1942 Harvey P. Hood, 1918, of Boston and Dudley W. Orr, 1929, of Concord, New Hampshire, were elected alumni trustees. In June of that year, Nelson A. Rockefeller, 1930, was elected an alumni trustee to give the board its full complement of twelve members.

Dartmouth's fall enrollment of 2,348, including a record freshman class of 723, was only slightly less than in the previous year, but enrollment in liberal arts courses was down, as students in large numbers elected the defense courses. This situation of only minor change in the College's usual program ended abruptly on December 7, 1941, when Pearl Harbor was attacked. By December 11 the United States was at war with all the Axis powers. The entire College gathered for a special convocation on December 15, and there President Hopkins announced an accelerated academic schedule which the faculty had voted two days earlier. No college in the nation was better prepared psychologically for war. Dartmouth's speed-up was one of the very first to be adopted. In addition to the previous special arrangement of permitting a senior, if inducted into the armed services, to earn his degree at the end of seven semesters, the College shortened the remainder of the academic year by five weeks and advanced Commencement to May 10.

While the students were home for Christmas vacation, they received further word that the College was adopting a year-round, three-term schedule, with a summer term beginning May 25. Freshmen planning to enter in September would be given the option of enrolling early, in July, in a special eight-week summer term during which they could complete three-fifths of a semester's work. The accelerated three-term program would be optional, President Hopkins explained, and every effort would be made to preserve the traditional values of the liberal arts college, while at the same time providing emergency training and extending to those desiring it the privilege of completing the degree requirements in the shortest time consistent with the scholastic standards of the College.

At the December 15 convocation President Hopkins had spoken about Dartmouth's intention to maintain its liberal arts program, no matter how reduced its civilian enrollment might become in the midst of the war effort. He advised students to avoid impulsive action and to finish as much college education as possible, for its value both in military service and in resuming studies after the war. Germany was counting on American inertia and hysteria when war came, he said. "We have had the first, let's not indulge in the latter."

His whole manner in the convocation talk was calm and reassuring. The College had lived through crisis after crisis, he pointed out, and it would survive this one as well. "I don't lack the faith and I don't think any man in this room lacks the faith as to the outcome of the war," he told the gathering. "The outcome may be soon or it may be late; probably, as a matter of fact, it will be somewhere between the two extremes of thought—those who believe there will be a sudden collapse and those who believe that the war is going on for decades. But whatever be that result, the fact remains that the effects of the war are going to last through your generation and the generation of men who come after you. And the careful, scientific, efficient thinking of men who have laid a foundation of knowledge is going to be required if those postwar conditions are to be met, as their needs must be met if the welfare of the country is to be preserved." He closed the serious assembly by saying that there was no need to be tragic or to succumb to a spirit of melancholy. Americans were far better off than the people in the subjugated countries, and although hard days were ahead, it was going to be a challenging and stimulating time.

The Dartmouth trustees, meeting in January, devoted a good part of their time to discussing the financial difficulties the College might face during the war period. With one thousand students already registered for the draft, and another 650 scheduled to register in February, the extent to which enrollment would shrink was entirely unknown. President Hopkins advocated a courageous program, whatever the cost, so Dartmouth could emerge from the war years in a strong position. The maintenance of the faculty and a near-normal liberal arts curriculum was the key element in this stand. With the government's policy of permitting drafted students to finish out their current terms before being called to active duty, enrollment did not in fact take a sharp drop for 1941–42, and with the Alumni Fund again measuring up to the challenge, the College not only balanced its books for the year but added $23,000 to the War Emergency Reserve, the new name given to what had been the Defense Reserve Fund.

A crucial question for the College was the chance it had of being selected for some sort of military training unit. Nearly every other college in the country was also willing to be chosen, but men from Dartmouth had been outstanding in the Navy V-5 and V-7 programs, and their record in the Marine Corps Platoon Leader program at Quantico was best among all college groups, with respect to both the number and percentage of men commissioned. President Hopkins made no secret of the fact that he preferred a Navy unit at Dartmouth, if one could be obtained. In response to a government survey in February, preliminary to establishing training units at colleges and universities, Dartmouth offered its facilities to both the Army and Navy, with the explanation that its own educational program would have to continue along with any military program and, further, that it could not accommodate a unit of more than one thousand men at the start. Dartmouth made a specific bid for a Navy V-7 unit, and the College was inspected for that purpose; but since only one such unit was to be established, the Navy decided that a Midwestern location was preferable, and Notre Dame was chosen.

While these administrative activities were going on, President Hopkins undertook a certain amount of alumni and public speaking about the war. He addressed the New Hampshire Civic Forum in the State House at Concord on January 12, on the topic "Conditioning for War." The following month he spoke at the Taft School in Connecticut, but devoted most of his talk to postwar problems, rather than to the war. On the visit to Taft School, he later reminisced, his longtime friend Horace Taft, retired founder of the school, wanted Mr. Hopkins to be his overnight guest and made a point of asking the headmaster to be sure to deliver him at the house for tea after the evening lecture. In carrying out this assignment, the headmaster expressed the opinion that it was a strange invitation—tea at that hour—and he added that Mr. Taft, pointedly, had not invited anyone else. After he had welcomed Mr. Hopkins and seated him near the fire, Taft told his manservant that he could bring in the tea. The "tea" turned out to be bottles of bourbon and scotch. Mr. Hopkins made his customary choice of bourbon, and the drinks were prepared. Taft then raised his glass and said, "Here's to your health. And my apologies." This was his way of conceding he had been wrong in writing a critical letter, ten years before, when Mr. Hopkins had come out publicly against Prohibition. The gracious gesture made, the two settled down to their tea and had a renewal of enjoyable, wide-ranging conversations which had been interrupted for too many years.

In February, President Hopkins had a particularly severe attack of the lumbago which had plagued him for some years. The cause of this back trouble was diagnosed as a ruptured spinal disk and an operation was recommended. When the operation was performed in Hanover on March 13, doctors found that it was not a ruptured disk but an arthritic growth on the spinal column that was to blame. Mr. Hopkins remained in Dick's House for about a month, carrying on a limited amount of College business and also using the time to think about Dartmouth's postwar program, which was the subject of some of his memoranda as soon as he returned to his office on April 18. (During his recuperation he was amused to have one of his friends write that it was a poor time for the president of Dartmouth College to lose any of his backbone.) Reminiscing about this second bout of surgery, Mr. Hopkins recalled that Fred Harris, founder of the Dartmouth Outing Club, also had a back operation at about the same time, but had gone to Montreal for his. In comparing experiences, Harris learned that he had paid nearly four times as much as Mr. Hopkins had paid, and his operation was not so successful. "He could never get over it," Mr. Hopkins recalled. "He seemed to think that I owed him some money."

Once he was fully on the job, President Hopkins wrote to the chairman of the Committee on Educational Policy, suggesting the committee ought to begin to think about the kind of educational program Dartmouth should have after the war. In a follow-up memorandum he expressed his own view that more attention should be paid to geo-politics, more emphasis placed on Oriental languages and culture, more courses offered in physical geography to supplement what the College was doing in the field of economic geography, and more concern shown for the Pacific and the Far East. Geopolitics was studied in Germany to promote war, he wrote, and in this country it needed to be studied to prevent war. As for the social sciences, it was his very definite view that more reality needed to go into their teaching. They were too dominated by New Deal thinking and the theoretical exercise of remolding society. "I do not think that our colleges are yet in a position to accept it as the final revelation of truth," he wrote, "until the men preaching it have had some experience with reality and have come to learn something of the distinction between theory and practice."

President Hopkins knew Dartmouth's postwar program would be his successor's responsibility, not his, but with a characteristic propensity for looking ahead and being prepared, he thought it desirable for the Committee on Educational Policy to begin consideration of the educational moves the College should make after the war. He had earlier informed the Dartmouth trustees that he wanted to retire at the age of sixty-five, which he would reach in November of 1942, but the board looked upon him as indispensable during the war years and he agreed to remain on the job. As it turned out, he was president for three more years, relinquishing the office on November 1, 1945, just five days before his sixty-eighth birthday. By that time the College had come through the war period in remarkably good shape.

In the spring of 1942, the use that the government might make of Dartmouth's proffered facilities was still not known, but there was optimistic expectation something was about to be assigned to the College and that it would be by the Navy. Questions from Washington and visits by inspecting officers gave rise to such hope. President Hopkins later said that the trustees must have found it hard to keep up any faith that he knew what he was doing. Several possibilities of Army training units had been turned down because they would have made it practically impossible to maintain part of the College on a normal basis. Mr. Hopkins once again was playing the role of gambler, but not without odds that were in his favor. Finally, word came through, in June, that Dartmouth had been chosen as the site for a Naval Reserve Officers Indoctrination School and that one thousand commissioned officers would arrive on July 15 for the first eight-week course, to be taught by the Navy's own instructors.

The civilian College meanwhile held its first accelerated Commencement on May 10. Eighty-two percent of the 444 men in the graduating class were in service or about to be. Charles M. Pearson, the 1942 class valedictorian, who was to lose his life in action in the Pacific, said, "Do not feel sorry for us. We are not sorry for ourselves. Today we are happy. We have a duty to perform and we are proud to perform it."

President Hopkins, in his valedictory to the first war class, recalled his Convocation statement of ten years earlier: that for youth in a democracy change is enlarged opportunity. The dangers of war will be followed by bewildering problems, he said, and out of meeting them will grow fuller realization of human capability. He spoke of the Biblical reference to "the children of Issacher, who were men that had understanding of the times, to know what Israel ought to do," who joined David in time of crisis and waged war against the Kingdom of Saul. "If the men of this college should be able to earn the encomium that the sons of Dartmouth were men who had understanding of their times, to know what America should do, the fondest hopes in your behalf of us who with solicitude and affection have followed your careers would have been realized, and the name of the College would have been glorified for all time."

Shortly after this early graduation, the College opened its wartime summer term on May 25, with 1,100 students enrolled. On July 8 these men were joined by two hundred freshmen who had elected the special eight-week term, entering ahead of four hundred other members of their class who arrived in September. When the question of early admission of freshmen was first considered, Dartmouth decided it would adopt a schedule which would not interfere with the completion of secondary school work or with June graduation. In the fall of 1942 it announced that it would not admit freshmen who had completed only half of the senior year in secondary school—a policy that was praised by the schools, which were then being raided by colleges seeking to boost their own enrollments with students under draft age.

With the arrival of the Navy Indoctrination School the College underwent a great sea change. The town of Hanover, on the banks of the Connecticut River, took on the look and spirit of a naval base. Its streets were filled with men in uniform, marching or at liberty; five dormitories on the east side of campus became "ships," and sea chanteys rang out from Baker's bell tower. An atmosphere of serious purpose predominated, however, and more than before, the war became real for Dartmouth. Captain

Henry M. Briggs, USN, an Annapolis graduate and submarine commander in World War I, took command of the school. With him came a staff of forty officers of instruction and administration, to whom College Hall was turned over as a headquarters. President Hopkins spoke for the entire community in extending a warm welcome, and he and Captain Briggs found it easy to work together and to make harmonious the existence side by side of a Navy school and a civilian college. When free from their stiff daily regimen, the student officers took part in the life of the College, and a happy relationship existed from the start. To keep things going smoothly, Mr. Hopkins named Sidney C. Hayward, secretary of the College, to be the liaison man between the College administration and the Navy staff.

The Indoctrination School was in operation from July 15, 1942 to June 4, 1943, when it closed down to make room for the Navy V-12 Unit assigned to Dartmouth. A total of 5,400 newly commissioned officers passed through the training school in seven classes. The presence of the school was of considerable financial help to the College. Total government reimbursement for the fiscal year 1942–43 was $535,000. The College again balanced its books, despite a sizable drop in civilian enrollment. Only $38,000 of a record Alumni Fund of $245,000 had to be used to cover what would otherwise have been a deficit, and a large addition was made to the College's emergency reserve fund. The names given to this reserve provide a capsule history of the period. First it was the Defense Reserve Fund, then the War Emergency Reserve, and in 1943 it was called the Postwar Reconversion Reserve. Whatever its name, the reserve fund gave Dartmouth strong financial assurance as it went through the war years and looked ahead to the postwar period. It continued to grow during the next two years, and by June 1945 it stood at $778,000.

Although the College never came close to having a financial problem during the war years, its prospects were quite uncertain prior to the assignment of the Navy units. In June of 1942, before any official word had come through from Washington, President Hopkins had stated that Dartmouth was determined to maintain its regular curriculum and all of its faculty not called away for military or government service. Deficits could be absorbed for a few years and as he put it, "I'd rather go down with all flags flying than just ooze out." He voiced this attitude a number of times during the course of the war, and in one of the strongest expressions of it he declared Dartmouth would keep going if only a dozen students were enrolled.

When lowering the draft age to eighteen was first proposed, Mr. Hopkins did not join those college presidents who saw such an action as a catastrophe for their institutions. The lower draft age would create problems for colleges, he admitted, but he was sure they could somehow adjust. Service to the nation demanded it of them. He had for a long time been in favor of universal military training, he added, and eighteen might as well be the starting age. Men needed to grow up faster in a time of national emergency, and there was a bright side—after military training at eighteen or nineteen, young men would enter college as better and more mature persons.

If the College had been forced to rely only on its civilian enrollment, with the liberal arts program fully maintained, the financial problem would have been severe. Civilian enrollment went down gradually at first and then in a great rush. In the fall of 1942 it had declined to 1,984, from the previous year's 2,348, and when the winter term opened it was down to 1,259, including 760 men in the various reserves who were soon to be called. By the fall of 1943 the enrollment figure was down to 229 men and only Crosby, Wheeler and Richardson Halls were needed to house them. When the seventh war term opened in March 1944, the civilian enrollment was a mere 174, the smallest in 125 years. One had to go back to 1819, the year of the Dartmouth College Case, for a lower total.

By the time the college year opened in September 1942 the Navy at Dartmouth was well established. Students who had not attended the summer term found a whole new atmosphere awaiting them. President Hopkins in his Convocation address spoke of "unusualness" in the life of the College and recalled how the same condition had prevailed in World War I. This was not the only parallel with the earlier war period, he pointed out. It was again a time when Bagehot's prescription for acquiring wisdom—"much lying in the sun"—had to be put aside in deference to the applied arts. It was again a time of crisis from which the College would emerge stronger than before, with new vigor imparted to its purpose. As he had told the students of 1917 and 1918, those seeking enlargement of mind and spirit need feel no guilt in getting as much education as possible before being called into the armed services. But the war itself was not the same. This time, he said, history might record that it was a conflict that had saved civilization from extinction.

The fall term saw an increase in the number of war courses in the curriculum. They included nautical astronomy, map making, bacteriology for the hospital corps, graphics, inorganic chemistry, Russian civilization, and languages for war purposes, among them two courses in elementary Russian and elementary Chinese. A non-credit course, Introduction to Naval Training, was also offered, especially for men entering the V-7 Naval Reserve. It was announced that a new Department of Geography would be inaugurated in the next term. The Senior Fellowships were discontinued for the duration, and the local use of student cars was banned.

President Hopkins on November 16 gave the keynote address in New York at the opening session of the New York Herald Tribune Forum on "Our Fight for Survival in a Free World." The roster of distinguished citizens participating included President Roosevelt, Wendell Willkie, James F. Byrnes, Sumner Welles, Henry J. Kaiser, and Elmer Davis. In his address Mr. Hopkins declared that the young men of the nation had been let down by those who dogmatized about life but who had no real knowledge of it. America, critical and patronizing toward the rest of the world, had been living in isolation and unreality. The first requisite for survival in a free world was, he declared, "to open our minds, rechannel our thinking, and understand the world in which we live." Winning the war was of paramount importance at the moment, he said, but it was essential that thought be given also to the future. He foresaw the United States as the most powerful nation on earth, and if that power were intelligently developed and responsibly held, the people of America would have the greatest opportunity ever given to any people, to bring about "a brave, clean world wherein all men of whatever race or whatever color should be free to live their own lives, to think their own thoughts, and to dream their own dreams." Balanced education would be a prime requirement after peace had been restored. Especially, the liberal college must not lose its importance to the free world. "Neither efficiency nor professional scholarship by itself alone makes for a sufficient goal in life to make a fight for survival worth while."

The outside demands upon President Hopkins' time were lessened in

December 1942 when he resigned as chairman of the General Education Board, on which he had served since 1930, and as a member of the Rockefeller Foundation, to which he had been elected in 1928. Earlier in the year he had ended sixteen years of service as a trustee of The Phillips Academy at Andover. In December of 1942, since the assignment was of short duration, he agreed to serve as chairman of the board of military and civilian educators named to review West Point's wartime accelerated curriculum, which had been adopted in order to graduate officers in three years instead of four.

On December 17, 1942 the government announced that it planned to use three hundred colleges for military training units under the Army Specialized Training Program and the Navy College Training Program, both to go into operation in July. The Navy's plan, which came to be known as the V-12 program, had been carefully formulated over an extended period by both the Navy and a group of leading educators. Unlike the Army, the Navy decided that it would rely upon the colleges for all officer procurement, except aviation cadets, and would require its trainees to have a high school education or its equivalent. With this admission standard, the Navy sought "to give prospective naval officers the benefits of college education in those areas most needed by the Navy," and to do so within the normal pattern of college life and with instruction provided by the college faculties.

Two days after the government announcement, President Hopkins sent a memorandum to the Dartmouth trustees stating that the College stood ready to accept either an Army or Navy unit, but that it would much prefer a Navy unit, since relations were already established with that branch of the service and since the Navy curriculum was far less rigid and would enable the College to use more of its own faculty. He had never made any secret of his disapproval of the way the Army had handled its relations with colleges in World War I, and in writing to Earl Blaik at West Point he expressed the opinion that the Army was again being high-handed and one-sided, with none of the concern for the colleges that the Navy was showing. There was no comparison between the two training programs, he wrote, and Dartmouth was doing everything it could to keep its ties with the Navy.

In order to assure adequate teaching personnel in the subjects basic to military education, the Dartmouth faculty showed a remarkable resiliency by going back to the classroom to be instructed in subjects other than their own. During the 1942 Christmas recess, for example, a group of faculty volunteers went to class three hours every day, in order to be qualified to serve as laboratory assistants in physics. Similar groups became students again in mathematics and engineering drawing. By January more than fifty faculty members were being "retooled." It was hard work for men from the humanities and the social sciences to make themselves acceptably proficient in the sciences, but all these "associates" and more were needed later in the year. The early start made soon after the government's December 17 announcement was one more example of the foresight and energy with which Dartmouth went about the job of transforming itself into a wartime college.

President Hopkins sent another progress report to the trustees on February 2, telling them there was still no definite word regarding an undergraduate training unit at the College, but that he was pinning his hopes on the Navy. He would rather take no military unit at all than have Dartmouth's existence as a liberal college interrupted, he wrote. Whatever the circumstances in which it carried on its traditional work, the College was willing "to stand the financial gaff" of such a choice. Although this sounded like a one-man pronouncement, there had been several policy discussions at board meetings, and the trustees were in full agreement.

A short time after this second memorandum to the trustees, press stories from Washington listed Dartmouth among the colleges and universities chosen by the Navy for training units. No details were immediately forthcoming. The designation was first reported to be for basic engineering training, but this was changed to the regular V-12 program, plus small detachments for Navy medical and engineering training. The Tuck School was approved for courses preparing trainees for the Supply Corps. All this was officially confirmed two months later, on April 5.

While the form of Dartmouth's participation in Navy training was being clarified, President Hopkins began to assume a new role—that of advocate of some kind of postwar world organization to preserve the peace. On February 17 he addressed a joint session of the New Hampshire legislature on "Some Aspects of Planning for Postwar Peace." He called for a commonwealth of nations, served by an international police force. Prussianism must be crushed for good, he said. The peaceful nations must never again be the victims of attempted conquest by the Germans, who largely escaped paying any penalty for losing World War I, while propaganda painted them as cruelly treated by the Allies.

In a letter at the time, Mr. Hopkins wrote of the danger of leaving consideration of a world organization until the postwar period, when weariness and lassitude would prevail. There could be no effective approach to lasting peace except through some organization inclusive of all the peoples of the earth, he stated, and the planning for such an organization should begin at once. He conceived of the world organization as one that would define needful basic law, establish a judicial body to determine whether the law had been violated by an aggressor nation, and maintain a military force to enforce the law. He added that the United States must get over the idea that it is self-sufficient economically. That idea had been as completely blasted as the idea that isolationism could keep us out of war.

In March, Mr. Hopkins was named by the American Red Cross to be on the advisory committee for its 1943 War Fund Drive. He also took on an additional business connection by becoming a director of the Continental Can Company. He was at the time a director of the Boston and Maine Railroad and the National Life Insurance Company of Vermont, and a member of the advisory board of H. P. Hood and Sons of Boston. In the following year he was to be elected a director of the New England Telephone Company and Encyclopaedia Britannica Films. Of his Continental Can directorship Mr. Hopkins later said, "I appreciated the status of that appointment as much as anything. They sent a plane with two pilots and a stewardess for me for every meeting. I always felt very important."

The assignment of the Navy V-12 unit to Dartmouth became official on April 5, 1943. The size of the unit was first set at 1,300 trainees, but ten days later it was announced that Dartmouth would have two thousand V-12's, the largest unit in the country. The new program was to begin on July 1 and was to consist of three sixteen-week terms each year. In order to bring its civilian calendar into conformity with the Navy schedule, the College had already arranged to have a special seven-week intersession. To learn about the general nature of the Navy V-12 program, its requirements, and its relationship with the participating colleges, President Hopkins attended two days of meetings at Columbia University in May. Accompanying him were Treasurer Halsey C. Edgerton and Sidney C. Hayward, who was to continue as the College's chief liaison officer with the Navy staff in Hanover. The Navy officers in attendance at the conference were headed by Vice Admiral Randall Jacobs, chief of naval personnel, who summed up the spirit of the V-12 plan in the title of his address, "The V-12 Program—A Cooperative Venture in Education." From the point of view of the officials from 131 participating colleges, the V-12 program was superbly designed to meet the needs of the Navy, while concurrently using the educational experience and teaching skills of the colleges and causing as little disruption as possible in normal academic life. The Navy asked that regular academic credit be given for the courses it prescribed and that college faculties enforce all necessary regulations to keep academic standards high. "We desire our students to have the benefit of faculty counseling, of extracurricular activities," it said, "in short, the best undergraduate education the colleges can offer." The encouragement of extracurricular programs meant, in Dartmouth's case, the continuation of intercollegiate athletics, which the trustees had already approved. The Navy officers at the conference made it clear they had no wish to take over the colleges, and that they expected to compensate the colleges fairly for the services provided. All in all, the V-12 program was soundly and liberally conceived, and the colleges which had contracted to carry it out could hardly have been more pleased.

In a letter to John D. Rockefeller Jr., President Hopkins said of the V-12 program: "I am bound to say, as compared with conditions in the last war, that the Navy program is an intelligent one, of all possible breadth, and designed not only to make good Naval officers but to make them intelligent men. If war must be and colleges must bend to the necessities of war, as of course they must, I can imagine no more fortunate circumstance than that in which we are placed at the present time."

Before the V-12 Unit got under weigh in July, the College had to finish its winter term, the last one with any sizable civilian enrollment, and then hold the special intersession to get in step with the Navy calendar. On April 17 the College held a closing convocation, requested by Palaeopitus as a substitute baccalaureate exercise. President Hopkins, using his favorite theme, spoke of the adaptability of the liberal college in time of crisis and cited the defense preparations and war programs at Dartmouth as an example of this. He defended the liberal college against those who said that the success of technology in war argued for practical, accelerated education. He praised the role of technology but said that those who would make it the sum and substance of American education were advocating the Prussian theory of education that had brought on the world conflict. His prediction was that the liberal college would have greater not less usefulness in the postwar world. These views were set forth more fully in an article President Hopkins wrote for the Sunday magazine of *The New York Times* of August 15, 1943. He disapproved of acceleration and streamlining as a permanent thing, and he looked forward to the leisurely acquisition of learning after the war. Character and culture cannot be hurried, he wrote, nor can wisdom and understanding.

In June of 1943, President Hopkins came as close as he had ever come to being a candidate for the United States Senate. Liberal Republicans in New Hampshire, favorable to some form of world organization, were concerned about the isolationist views of conservative Senator Charles W. Tobey, and the *Concord Monitor* spoke for them in urging Mr. Hopkins to enter the Republican primary against Tobey. Mr. Hopkins told party leaders he was willing to run if they thought this was the only way to give citizens of New Hampshire assurance that the United States would assume its responsible role in the postwar world, but that otherwise he had no desire at all to be a candidate. Among those backing him against Tobey were Robert P. Bass, Huntley Spaulding, George Moses, and John R. McLane, all highly influential in the state's Republican party.

Congressman Foster Stearns of New Hampshire, who was an internationalist, was anxious to seek the Senate nomination. He met with Mr. Hopkins and told him he thought his Congressional experience gave him the right to run and that he thought he could make the better race against Tobey. An informal Gallup Poll in the state indicated Mr. Hopkins was first choice of Republican voters, with Stearns, Robert O. Blood, Tobey, and former Governor Francis P. Murphy in that order. A meeting of Republican state leaders was held at Manchester on July 9 to settle the question of who had the best chance of defeating Tobey in the primary, and Mr. Hopkins wrote that if it was decided he was the man, he would agree to be the candidate. Partly because Stearns had indicated that he would run anyway, the party leaders in a split vote backed him to oppose Tobey's renomination. The vote was ten to six for Stearns, but it was thirteen to three for Mr. Hopkins on the question of who was best qualified. On July 22, Mr. Hopkins announced that the circumstances that had led him to consider being a candidate no longer existed and that he now had no intention of entering the primary race.

Some years after his retirement, President Hopkins told an interviewer that he had never seriously entertained the idea of running for the United States Senate, but his correspondence with Robert Bass and others in June 1943 would persuade one that he had at that time been willing to put aside his personal disinclination and to be a candidate for the sake of assuring an international role for this country after the war. He considered Senator Tobey incapable of understanding the international situation or of being persuaded to a different point of view. "His assumption of divine guidance in all that he does," he wrote at the time, "is based on an egregious misconception of the extent to which the Lord is at all times in intimate contact with him." With a gift for that sort of barbed comment, it is to be regretted that he never took to the political stump. As things turned out, Tobey defeated Stearns in the Republican primary and was reelected to the Senate. There was some gain, however, in that the primary fight shook his isolationist point of view.

Mr. Hopkins was a political activist all his life, going back to the days when he was an ardent supporter of Teddy Roosevelt in the Bull Moose campaign. Aside from the near exception in 1943, however, he was an influence and a policy maker, rather than an aspirant to public office. The Republican whom he supported most enthusiastically was Wendell Willkie, in the 1940 presidential campaign. He had a hand in bringing about Willkie's nomination, against the opposition of the Old Guard, and the two men became the closest of friends. They had a great deal in common, in their thinking and in the warmth of their personalities. Both opposed the New Deal philosophy, both supported aid to Britain, selective service, and an international role for the United States. It was at the invitation of

Willkie that President Hopkins later, in July 1944, became a sponsor and then the national chairman of Americans United for World Organization. (After receiving a Dartmouth honorary degree in 1941, Willkie dropped in on President Hopkins while making a political swing through New England and said he was in Hanover as an alumnus, to check up on how the College was being administered. Mr. Hopkins quipped that he might be an alumnus, but that he certainly wasn't a contributor to the Alumni Fund. The next time he made a surprise visit, Willkie arrived at the President's House at breakfast time, stuck his head through the pantry door, and asked if a non-contributor to the Alumni Fund could have a cup of coffee and a doughnut.) Willkie was supported by Mr. Hopkins again in the 1944 presidential race, but his crushing defeat by Thomas E. Dewey in the Wisconsin primary that April killed his chances for the nomination. He had dinner with Mr. Hopkins in New York just before he entered the hospital for a check-up. His unexpected death in the hospital on October 8, 1944 was a stunning personal loss to Mr. Hopkins and to all those with whom the author of *One World* was working for an enlarged American role in the affairs of the world.

The importance which attached politically to a Hopkins public endorsement was illustrated by an episode in Dewey's 1944 campaign. The Republican nominee was speaking in Boston some days before the election, and he asked Sinclair Weeks to arrange for Mr. Hopkins to have dinner with him after the meeting. This took place in a private railroad car in the South Station, and there Dewey asked Mr. Hopkins why he hadn't made any statement supporting him. Mr. Hopkins replied that he had been unable to figure out just where Dewey stood on international relations. "John Foster Dulles represents my thinking on foreign affairs," Dewey told him, and since Mr. Hopkins had served on the Rockefeller Foundation board with Dulles and knew his views, he said this cleared up the doubts he had. Without losing his opportunity, Dewey at once called in the press and announced on the spot that President Hopkins had just given him his backing in the election.

The Navy V-12 Unit, which was the major development in the closing years of the Hopkins presidency, opened at Dartmouth on July 1, 1943. On that date, the influx of 2,042 Navy and Marine trainees gave the campus twice the military air it had taken on with the Indoctrination School one year earlier. The College again had a sense of the fullness of prewar days, but the 361 civilian students in residence were thoroughly overshadowed by the multitude in Navy white and Marine green. Hanover's color scheme even had a spot of khaki, provided by the small detachment of fifteen Army medical students. The dormitories were again alive, nine of them occupied by the Navy, three by the Marines, and one by the Army.

The V-12 curriculum prescribed for the first college year (first two terms) consisted of mathematics, English, physics, engineering drawing and descriptive geometry (graphics), the historical background of the war, and naval organization. A minimum class schedule of eighteen hours a week was prescribed, and all hands had drill and physical training as part of their daily routine. Dartmouth's liberal arts curriculum provided the core of the V-12 instruction given by the College's own faculty. Each V-12 course had a director, appointed by President Hopkins, its regular departmental faculty, and a number of "associates" enlisted from other departments. In all, nearly one hundred members of the faculty served as associate instructors in fields not their own, and the plan worked remarkably well. The naval organization and graphics courses had a thousand students each, and physics with 890 students in the first term, was another course in which the hard-working faculty went all out to fulfill Dartmouth's commitment to the Navy. In addition to the so-called V-12 courses, the College on its own offered a course in naval world geography, as well as sixteen other war courses. The arrival of Robert Frost to take up his post as Ticknor Fellow in the Humanities was a bright sign that the civilian College had not forgotten its pledge to maintain excellence in the liberal arts. In his "conversations" with students in Baker Library the poet was always surrounded by young men in uniform.

While the College had responsibility for instruction, housing, messing, and medical care, all other operations of the V-12 unit were under the control of the Navy. A staff of thirteen officers and fifty-four enlisted men was headed by Commander William F. Bullis, USNR, who came to Hanover from Smith College where he had been executive officer of the Naval Training School for WAVES. The Marine detachment was commanded by Major John Howland, USMCR, a veteran of Guadalcanal. At its maximum, in the third term, the Navy staff had thirteen officers and sixty-four enlisted personnel. Commanding officer of the Army medical unit at the start was Colonel William T. MacMillan.

When assignment of a Navy V-12 Unit to Dartmouth was first officially confirmed, the trustees voted that the unit would constitute an associated school of the College and that trainees sent to Hanover would not automatically be matriculated in the College proper. In December 1943, President Hopkins named an Advisory Committee on Postwar Enrollment, since it was expected that the normal number of applicants would be swollen by military returnees and by V-12 men without previous college connection who would want to come back to Dartmouth. He later told V-12 students who had not attended any other college that if they wished to apply for admission to Dartmouth after the war, probably with advanced standing, they would be given a priority second only to that accorded to Dartmouth undergraduates returning from military service.

In many respects there was little or no distinction between the civilians and V-12 students attending college together. They were in the same classes and they worked together in extracurricular activities, such as *The Log*, the weekly newspaper inaugurated by the College in July 1943 as a wartime replacement for *The Dartmouth*. The Dartmouth athletic teams were manned by the sailors and marines of the unit. Fraternities were closed for the duration, and in social life the unregimented civilians were warned by President Hopkins to conduct themselves with the maturity and self-discipline that was required of V-12 trainees.

The happy amalgamation of liberal college and Navy training school did not come about without some initial difficulty. Commander Bullis, having run a school for boys headed for the service academies, was inclined to command the V-12 unit with an authoritarian hand, and a stream of regulations and restrictions flowed from College Hall. The Navy's wish to maintain the normal pattern of college life, as expressed by Admiral Jacobs and others at the Columbia conference, got small fulfillment, and in the heralded "cooperative venture in education" Dartmouth found itself a subordinate partner. President Hopkins made known his disquiet to Commander Bullis. "I said to him that he was acting as though he was dealing with conquered territory, and he said he hadn't any reason to dispute that and he thought technically that was so."

Secretary of the Navy Frank Knox visited the Dartmouth V-12 Unit on

August 5, and Under Secretary James Forrestal came for an inspection on August 18. It was to Forrestal (who had attended Dartmouth for one year) that President Hopkins made known his objection to the way the commanding officer was running the Dartmouth unit. It did not take long for a change in command. On September 14, Commander Bullis was assigned to new duties with the Bureau of Naval Personnel in Washington. Major Howland, who was named acting commandant, promptly rescinded the more restrictive orders governing the college life of trainees. A new commanding officer, Captain Damon E. Cummings, USN, arrived in Hanover on October 4. A regular Navy man with a long and distinguished career of active service, including the command of ships at sea and two years as chief of staff of the Panama Canal Zone just before coming to Dartmouth, he quickly took hold with administrative skill and with understanding of the V-12 program's philosophy. His first unit order included a significant paragraph: "In the performance of their duties, officers shall cooperate closely with the appropriate College authorities, and shall be careful not to assume authority in matters which are the responsibility of the College." Captain Cummings, keenly interested in the whole educational program being offered the men under his command, introduced supplementary training in military character. Gradually, under his leadership, the Navy V-12 Unit at Dartmouth acquired the reputation of being not only the largest such unit in the country but also a model for all others.

The Navy V-12 Unit at Dartmouth was in operation for seven terms, and was a financial lifesaver for the College in the latter years of the war, just as the Indoctrination School had been in 1942–43. Navy and Army reimbursements to Dartmouth in fiscal 1943–44 totaled $1.145-million and covered a bit more than half of the year's operating expenses. Nearly all of the 1944 Alumni Fund of $284,000 could be added to the Postwar Reconversion Reserve. Dartmouth was said to have the best Navy contract of any college because Treasurer Halsey Edgerton had actual costs worked out with stunning exactitude. For the second V-12 year, Dartmouth's Navy and Army income was $981,000, with remuneration for instruction reduced to a flat rate per man. The 1944–45 books were balanced with the help of $108,000 from the Alumni Fund, and $210,000 more was added to the Postwar Reconversion Reserve, then in excess of three-quarters of a million dollars.

The financial well-being of the College was such that the trustees at their June 1944 meeting voted to enlarge the physics building as soon as war conditions would permit, and they also voted to go ahead with the new auditorium-theater on the same basis. At that time $1.3 million was the estimated cost of the Dartmouth Center, which never got built in the form given to it in the third round of everlasting planning but which grew finally into the vastly more ambitious Hopkins Center. The year after Mr. Hopkins' retirement in 1945, the Postwar Reconversion Reserve, amounting to $972,000, underwent still another change in name. It became the fund for the Hopkins War Memorial Program, embracing the Hopkins Scholarships for sons of Dartmouth's war dead, enlargement of the physics building, and the Hopkins Center.

Although the College enjoyed only modest growth in its assets during the war years, it was fortunate to be able to keep its invested funds intact. From 1941 to 1945 total assets increased by $3.4 million, of which $2.6 million was added to endowment. Three major bequests of the period were $1.2 million from Judge William N. Cohen, 1879, most of which went into scholarship endowment; $612,000 from Sherman B. Ward, 1913; and $500,000 from Emil Bommer, Brooklyn industrialist. Mr. Bommer first willed his money to Yale, but then switched to Dartmouth, renowned as a male college, when he learned that Yale had awarded degrees to female nurses. He stipulated that income from his fund was to be used for male students only, and that none was to be used to support the dead languages or competitive athletics.

Dartmouth men, spurred by President Hopkins' twenty-fifth anniversary and pleased by the College's all-out war effort, contributed generously to the Alumni Fund in the war years and provided most of the accumulated reserve that enabled Dartmouth to make its postwar plans with confidence. The Alumni Fund provided $126,000 in 1940, and five years later, in President Hopkins' final year, it had grown to $337,000, from which point it took off in its amazing climb to the $4-million level of today.

Although much attention had to be given to the Navy at Dartmouth, the College was not unmindful of some seven thousand of its sons who had gone off to war. President Hopkins sent a 1943 Christmas greeting by V-Mail to each Dartmouth man in service. "For myself, as well as in behalf of my associates of the resident College," he wrote, "I wish to send Christmas Greetings to each and every Dartmouth man in the armed services. To say that we at home have deep interest in you and in the records you are making is but faint suggestion of the concern we have for you and the affection with which we think of you. Because of you, among others, the world has possibility of being a far different place than otherwise it could have been. Not solely, however, with thought of the world's welfare, but very personally likewise and intimately in thought of the welfare of Dartmouth men in days to come, in many cases sons and successors of you Dartmouth men in service, we here in your College home breathe constantly and very reverently the prayer that God will watch over you, wherever you may be. This is the word I wish I might, with a clasp of the hand, say to each one of you face to face."

President Hopkins had been unsparing of his time in writing hundreds of letters of recommendation for Dartmouth men seeking commissions or other assignments in the national war effort. He made a special point of writing personally to the families of Dartmouth men killed in service. The replies to his 1943 Christmas letter came from all over the world in such volume that he could respond to only a part of them. In December of 1944 he sent another V-Mail message, this time a New Year's greeting to 8,500 undergraduates and alumni in the services. In this second letter, he wrote in part: "Amid all the matters of concern these days and amongst the scrambled emphases of mixed loyalties, one fact stands clear. There is always an existent bond, today closer than ever, between the College symbolized in 'Dartmouth Undying' and the individual Dartmouth man. Assurances of this come in constant flow from men of all ranks and from all areas of the earth's surface. It is in answer not only to the many letters whose receipt is so welcome but as much in response to the unuttered word or the only partially formulated thought of thousands of others that I want to send greetings in behalf of the College—and as much, too, I want to send them personally.

"To each one of you, wherever you are, who is a brother in this great fraternity which centers in Hanover, please understand that, however hackneyed the words which may be used, the impulse to utter them springs from a heartfelt desire that you shall understand the mingled feelings of

pride in you, anxiety about you, and affection for you that we here have
for you there."

While war was being waged, the matter of Dartmouth's postwar curriculum continued to be of concern to President Hopkins. In collaboration
with the Committee on Educational Policy, a special committee under his
chairmanship had been authorized by the trustees to make plans for the
postwar period. In the winter term of 1943–44 he put forward the idea of
establishing a new Department of Foreign Relations, to make sure that
adequate attention would be paid to this field of study after the war. He
was skeptical that his proposal would get over the hurdle of faculty approval, and he half-seriously played with the idea of a separate school of
foreign affairs. In the fall of 1944, a new divisional major in International
Relations was announced, along with a similar one in Public Administration.

In his thinking about postwar education, Mr. Hopkins still had his mis-
givings about the way the social sciences were being taught. Earlier he had
written to the chairman of the Committee on Educational Policy about
"the vague vaporizings of young social scientists who are intolerant of all
which had constituted scholarship before the war." He also wanted some
thought given to what the science departments could do to attract more
student interest. The answer, he suggested, might be to stop teaching the
sciences as vocational subjects with an instinctive leaning toward the standards of graduate schools.

Looking ahead to the postwar period in yet another way, President Hopkins got the trustees to authorize a Special Committee on Academic Adjust-
ments, to take up the cases of returning service men and to determine how
much academic credit should be given for various forms of war service. He
was anxious not to repeat the loose policy adopted by the College in World
War I, and he proposed that there be no mass or routine decisions and that
each case be handled individually, with justice but with no lowering of
standards. The committee's basic decision was that military service was
not to be confused with academic achievement, and that not even a war
hero could be awarded an unearned Dartmouth degree. The committee
was given wide latitude to grant academic credit for special military training, to decide who would be eligible to continue Dartmouth studies in

the cases of men never admitted under the Selective Process, to approve irregular study programs that would qualify veterans for the degree, and to recommend directly to the trustees for their degrees the men who had met the committee's stipulations.

In the spring of 1944, about a year and a half before he was succeeded in the presidency by John Sloan Dickey, Mr. Hopkins informed the trustees that chest pains from angina were making it doubtful he could much longer carry on with his job, and he asked the board to begin the process of finding his successor. He read a letter from Dr. Paul Dudley White, the Boston heart specialist, saying that the angina was not curable but that it could be arrested with a light schedule and careful living. (Mr. Hopkins lived for another twenty years.) "Mrs. Hopkins was anxious for me to retire," he recalled. "She always took my health more seriously than I did. Besides, I suddenly came to the realization that the world was changing faster than I could keep up with it." The trustees agreed, of course, to do what was best for Mr. Hopkins and to meet his wish that they begin the task of choosing a new president. The board decided to act as a whole, without a special search committee, and for more than a year its members singly or in small groups met with nominees, including five or six that President Hopkins himself had suggested at the board's request. The search was conducted quietly and without the help of anyone beyond the board of trustees, as Mr. Hopkins wished it to be done. He wanted no warring cliques to form, and he had always contended that, with full authority for electing a president vested in the board of trustees, the desirable procedure was to make simultaneous announcement of the retirement of the old president and the election of the new. This flew in the face of conventional academic procedure, but that was something President Hopkins had never hesitated to do if he thought his way was best for Dartmouth College. The trust in Mr. Hopkins' leadership and his dominance in Dartmouth affairs were so great that his procedure was accepted as wise rather than radical. Moreover, the absolute surprise of the joint announcement, when it was made, left little room for any other reaction.

Public speaking was the part of the president's job that involved the most stress and sometimes brought on his angina attacks. Even so, there were certain invitations Mr. Hopkins very much wanted to accept. One of these was to deliver the principal address at the sesquicentennial of Bowdoin College, whose president, Kenneth Sills, was one of his oldest friends. His June 24 address at Bowdoin, on "The Faith of the Historic College," was one of his notable interpretations of the liberal college. On that occasion he received his fifteenth honorary degree, a Doctorate of Laws. Two months later he was awarded the honorary Doctorate of Letters from Middlebury College, where the week before he was principal speaker at the twenty-fifth anniversary of the Bread Loaf School of English. Two other honors came to him that year. He was elected to the American Academy of Arts and Sciences and to the board of the newly founded Arctic Institute of North America, a joint American-Canadian enterprise.

By far the most important of the outside activities in which Mr. Hopkins engaged in that period was Americans United for World Organization. In mid-July of 1944 he accepted the invitation of Wendell Willkie to join him as a sponsor of this new national, non-partisan organization, formed by the consolidation of six existing organizations and the collaboration of eleven others to work for the establishment of a world agency with power to enforce peace. A second purpose was to support the Congressional candidates favoring such an agency, and a third was to make available to the public information by which they could identify and classify those individuals and organizations whose views and actions could lead to fascism.

President Hopkins became chairman of the national advisory council of Americans United on August 10, and three weeks later he was elected chairman of the board of directors, making him the national head of an organization which was steadily growing, with chapters from coast to coast. A major factor in his willingness to assume this responsibility, when the doctor had told him to slow down, was the chance to work with Willkie, who was deeply committed to Americans United but who felt that his identification with politics made it unwise for him to be its head. Willkie had promised to be in New York and to give his time to the organization— but one month later he was dead. In expressing his great confidence in Mr. Hopkins' leadership, he had written, "There is no item on the agenda of the American citizen today more important than the building of an agency of world cooperation against war—an agency that will draw the nations together in a moral sense and will at the same time carry sensible, practical arrangements for putting down aggression." Mr. Hopkins agreed completely with that assessment, and although he was denied the working partnership that had at the outset so attracted him, he carried on as national chairman until the United Nations was achieved. He worked mainly from Hanover, with frequent trips to New York headquarters, where Ulric Bell served as director and Hugh Moore was organizing chairman. Three months after he became chairman, Mr. Hopkins sent Mr. Hayward, secretary of the College, to New York to strengthen the work of getting chapters organized and functioning.

Perhaps the greatest chore for Mr. Hopkins as national chairman was to keep Americans United on the main track. This country's support for the United Nations was its clear and preeminent goal, but with so many strong-minded individuals at work there was constant temptation to weaken the effectiveness of Americans United by getting bogged down in side issues, such as trade treaties, amendment of the Bretton Woods monetary agreement, and the anti-bias principle in international relations. Mr. Hopkins could be strong-willed himself, insisting that no other cause be allowed to sidetrack support for the San Francisco Charter, and he threatened to resign as chairman unless this became a firm policy. His many connections with national leaders were a special asset to Americans United. He was able to arrange for Under Secretary of State Stettinius to meet, under the auspices of Americans United, with representatives of eighty national organizations, to explain the Dumbarton Oaks security proposals, which provided the basis for the United Nations Charter. His educational prestige was an advantage in getting many college chapters of Americans United formed. On October 25 he led a Vote for Freedom rally at Hunter College in New York City, and the crowd of four thousand was one of the largest Americans United drew anywhere.

When the United States Senate finally ratified the United Nations Charter in August of 1945, Mr. Hopkins resigned as chairman of Americans United for World Organization. There is no way of precisely measuring the influence that Americans United had on the outcome, but it was the largest, best organized, and best financed of the citizen groups working in support of the United Nations and it probably was the most effective. President Hopkins had a right to feel that he had rendered a service to the nation.

With this country's membership in the United Nations an accomplished fact, he believed that Americans United should disband and leave the field to such agencies as the United Nations Association. Some of his associates thought that a good organization should be used for other international causes, but the Hopkins view prevailed and Americans United went out of existence on a positive note.

Shortly before he was elected chairman of Americans United, President Hopkins had been asked by Herbert Lehman, Director-General of the United Nations Relief and Rehabilitation Administration (related to the Atlantic Charter), to be Deputy Director-General and to take charge of the office in London. He was eager to do it, but Dr. John F. Gile of Hanover, who as a trustee of the College was acquainted with his health problem, advised him that his angina and asthma made it too hazardous for him to take on such a demanding assignment abroad. This undoubtedly added to his receptivity when it was proposed that he be national chairman of Americans United.

On December 17, 1944, the inauguration of Harold W. Stoke as president of the University of New Hampshire was another occasion when President Hopkins had a special willingness to run the risk of public speaking. In extending the greetings of the educational world, he warned against the return of the national complacency that had prevailed before the war, and he repeated the idea that education's goal should be the development of an intelligent electorate, rather than masterminds. Hardly more than three years after Pearl Harbor had shocked the nation out of its apathy and irresponsibility, he said, "the complacent attitude is beginning to reappear and we are convincing ourselves that our recovery is clear evidence that socially, intellectually, and spiritually nothing has been wrong with us in the past." While dictatorship can be maintained by one man, he added, it takes a host of good people to maintain a democracy. "What is not quite so clearly understood is the greater need in a democracy of dependence upon the common sense of the people at large than upon the brilliancy of leadership. I have long believed it to be a valid assertion that political leadership would emerge more definitely from educational policies designed to cultivate more intelligent use of the suffrage than from processes primarily designed to produce masterminds. Educational effort should be directed toward equipping men for roles of influence rather than toward cultivating an appetite for mastery."

The continuation of universal military training after the war was an issue in which President Hopkins became involved early in 1945. A delay in proposed Congressional action was urged by a group of twelve college presidents, among them Conant of Harvard, Dodds of Princeton, Wriston of Brown, Day of Cornell, and Hutchins of Chicago. To counteract this public statement, a group of fourteen college presidents, including Mr. Hopkins, made public a letter to President Roosevelt supporting universal military training and urging that Congressional action not be delayed until after the war. In this view Mr. Hopkins had the company of Seymour of Yale, Compton of M.I.T., King of Amherst, and Gates of Pennsylvania. In the educational world, however, it seemed to be a minority view.

In a long letter printed in *The New York Times* of May 6, 1945, President Hopkins gave his reasons for supporting universal military training. This was picked up by the North American Newspaper Alliance and distributed to member papers in two installments. Universal training should be military training exclusively, Mr. Hopkins contended, and it should be "a proposition purely and simply to enhance the military security of our people." Without it a huge standing army would be necessary. The United States could not count on another time lag in the next war. Nor could it afford to repeat the mistake of allowing any aggressor to be uncertain about the disposition of the democracies to fight for their freedom. Even if the question of national security was not involved, universal military training was well worth trying. Home, church, and school were, under modern conditions, no longer capable of creating the old-time sense of responsibility for preserving freedom.

At the end of the winter term in 1945, the College held a more formal graduation ceremony than usual, with Captain D. L. Madeira, USN, director of training in the Bureau of Naval Personnel, present as guest speaker. He drew the rapt attention of his Dartmouth audience by discussing the recent Congressional approval of the Navy's plan to establish twenty-three new NROTC units in the colleges, bringing their number to fifty. The expanded Naval Reserve Officer Training Corps would supersede the Navy V-12 program, and some of the trainees in the audience, he tantalizingly added, might well have only one more term or so in V-12. "The fact that Dartmouth hasn't sent two senators and twenty-five representatives to see us about getting a unit can be attributed either to Dartmouth's commendable faith in the Bureau of Naval Personnel or, perhaps, to the fact that New Hampshire doesn't have twenty-five representatives," Captain Madeira said with a glance at President Hopkins. He knew that Dartmouth had had an application on file since before Pearl Harbor.

On May 3, 1945, word came from Admiral Jacobs that Dartmouth had, indeed, been chosen for one of the new NROTC units, to be activated on November 1. Once again the College had to take steps to bring itself into line with a new form of alliance with the Navy. The trustees established a Department of Naval Science and Tactics, to be staffed by naval officers with faculty rank. The department actually began with the July term, and eight officers were assigned to teach seamanship, navigation, and communication to the V-12 men eligible for transfer to NROTC in November. To ease the transition, the degree requirements were modified for some men, with major courses reduced from ten to eight, and a special degree, Bachelor of Naval Science, was authorized by the trustees. For the July term the Navy reduced Dartmouth's V-12 enrollment to just under eight hundred, and it announced that although NROTC was taking over in November, those V-12 men not being transferred to the new unit would be permitted to remain in college as trainees for an additional term.

Amidst all the activity of getting itself shipshape for a new chapter in its relationship with the Navy, the College began to show the first signs of gradual return to a predominantly civilian college. On May 2, with only thirty-nine seniors present, the first civilian Commencement since May of 1942 was held in the Faculty Room of Parkhurst Hall. V-E Day in May, with the ringing of bells, the dismissal of classes, and an impromptu parade around town, brought the prospect of veterans returning before long. A vanguard of forty veterans was back before the July term, which saw the revival of Freshman Rush and Wet Down. In November the College registered another 317 veterans, fifty of them accompanied by wives. The place that Navy trainees had made for themselves in Dartmouth's life was indicated by the fact that ninety-five of November's returning veterans had first come to the College as V-12 students. And for those Navy men not returning as civilian students, a continuing association with the College was made possible through the Dartmouth Navy Alumni Association, which both the Alumni Council and the student leaders of the V-12 unit had established in September 1944.

With his administration close to its end, President Hopkins still had time to get into one more controversy, and he also managed one more swipe at the faculty's love of departmentalization. In a letter to Professor Francis Lane Childs, chairman of the Committee on Faculty Reorganization, he stated his belief that a better college would result from "some system that removed the barriers between departments and gave men the opportunity to capitalize their breadth of learning as well as their specialized training. In other words, I have always believed, and still do, that the man is far more important than the subject and that it ought to be possible somehow for the undergraduate to do what in the great majority of cases he so greatly wants to do; namely, to elect men rather than departments." He confessed that he would like to go fascist for a brief time and "manhandle this situation with the authority of the Trustees behind me."

The public controversy in which President Hopkins became involved arose in August 1945 and was the result of a reply he had made to a telegram soliciting his support for the creation of a National Fair Education Practice Committee to eliminate quotas and other forms of racial and religious discrimination in the nation's colleges. The telegram, sent on February 10, was occasioned by the effort of the American Dental Association to get Columbia and New York University to set some limit on the number of Jewish students they would admit. In his telegraphed reply of the same date, Mr. Hopkins said, "Understand complexity of problem and am sympathetic with purpose you have in mind. Cannot join with you, however, if your protest is against proportionate selection, for I believe nothing would so increase intolerance and focus racial and religious prejudice as to allow any racial group to gain virtual monopoly of educational advantages offered by any institution of higher education."

It would have been easy for Mr. Hopkins to sidestep the request or to lend his name perfunctorily to what seemed to be a high-minded proposal. But once again his candor and his unwillingness to express anything but an honest opinion landed him in trouble. It was not until six months later that the New York tabloid press made a sensational story about the position he had taken about a selective and balanced student body. Herman Shumlin, New York theatrical producer, was responsible for giving the story to the press. He was connected with one of the organizations that had sent the telegram to college presidents, and some weeks after the exchange of telegrams he resigned from Americans United for World Organization and accused Mr. Hopkins, its chairman, of anti-semitic prejudice. Mr. Hopkins wrote to him on May 2, explaining his position at considerable length. Three months later, for some unaccountable reason, Shumlin gave the Hopkins letter to the *New York Post*, which telephoned Mr. Hopkins to verify his views. Then, on August 7, the paper printed a front-page story headed "Dartmouth Limits Jews to Stop Anti-Semitism, Says Its Prexy." The next day *PM* and *The Daily Worker*, not to be outdone, picked up the story with headlines and editorials charging Dartmouth and President Hopkins personally of anti-semitism.

In his letter to Shumlin, Mr. Hopkins explained the objectives of the Selective Process of Admission and wrote: "In the large our selection of students is based upon such specifications, and the system was never set up nor has it ever been operated, as some disappointed Jewish parents have argued, as a smoke screen to conceal racial prejudice. However, in the desire to be completely honest, I have never been willing to deny that in the interest of avoiding racial prejudice and in the desire to maintain the age-long compatability here at Dartmouth among boys of different races, I should not be willing to see the proportion of Jews in the College so greatly increased as to arouse widespread resentment and develop widespread prejudice in our own family.

"It was upon the basis of my own reasoning in regard to our conditions here and my certain knowledge of the original sparks that led to the later conflagration of anti-Jewish feeling in Germany that made me unwilling to sign the protest which was sent to me."

Elsewhere in the letter he stated: "I would not for anything forgo the representation of Jewish boys that enroll year by year at Dartmouth. Some of our outstanding alumni are Jews, as are some of the foremost benefactors of the College. They are exceedingly welcome in the Dartmouth family, whether as undergraduates or as alumni, and I personally number some of my most intimate friends among them. However, I know that this would all be changed overnight in Dartmouth, or in any other college, if Dartmouth were to disregard the fact that it would become an urban college, which it does not want to become, and would lose its racial tolerance, which it is desperately anxious not to lose, were we to accept unexamined the great blocks of Jewish applications which come in, for instance, from the New York high schools and other great metropolitan centers."

Had he confined himself to the Selective Process of Admission as Dartmouth policy and to the case for proportionate selection, President Hopkins doubtless would have been spared the charges that were heaped upon him, mainly by a few New York newspapers. The idea that Dartmouth's policy could be a way of combating anti-semitism was angrily denounced as either hypocrisy or blindness, and Mr. Hopkins' unfortunate use of the Stephen Roberts book, *The House That Hitler Built*, as a source of facts about the origins of anti-semitism in Germany led to the distorted comparison of his views with those of the Nazis. *PM* in one story ran his picture alongside that of Dr. Alfred Rosenberg, the Nazi ideologist.

The controversy ran its course in about a month, and was largely ignored by the national press, as it was by the major New York papers. *Time* and *Newsweek* carried objective stories in their issues of August 20 and made much of the fact that President Hopkins had not sidestepped an issue which sent other college presidents running for cover, and that he had been willing to bring it out into the open. The invitation to comment on President Hopkins' position was politely declined by officials at other institutions, although there was no hesitancy at Harvard, Princeton, and elsewhere to assert that there was no racial or religious discrimination whatsoever in their admissions policies.

President Hopkins experienced an influx of abusive mail as a result of these newspaper stories, but he had the satisfaction of hearing from many Jewish alumni who recalled their student days at Dartmouth and deplored the characterization of the College as anti-semitic. The only follow-up statement he made for publication was one he gave to the *Dartmouth Log*: "The letter to Mr. Shumlin speaks for itself. The telephone interview with the *New York Post*, made up of extracts of conversation and statements removed from their context, was wholly misrepresentative of anything I ever believed or said. The import of my statement made in reply to interrogation was that with our excess of applications for admission over any enrollment possible for us to accept, we have for many years selected a balanced student body to include varied geographical, economic, racial, public school, private school, and other groups; and that this policy was designed to preserve a balanced student body truly representative of our general population; and that thus we believed we could serve democracy best."

Public announcement of President Hopkins' retirement was made before the controversy had died down. This led to some editorial comment that it was too bad that just as Mr. Hopkins had brought the anti-semitic issue out from behind the vagueness and subterfuge with which it is usually treated in the academic world he was to leave the college scene. This would mean, it was feared, that the subject would again be buried before the discussion had been thoroughly pursued. In the opinion of the *Louisville Courier-Journal*, "He was the catalyst of the new ferment, the peg for the argument, and now that he has removed himself . . . the stir must subside and we are back where we started."

The irony of the attacks on Mr. Hopkins just as his presidency was ending was that he had been consistent throughout his long administration in denouncing anti-semitism and in being willing to discuss openly the question of the admission of Jewish students under the Selective Process. As early as 1921 he had been one of those making public protest against anti-semitic writings and propaganda in the United States. In April 1926 he had rebutted the charge of Adolph Lewisohn and Gustavus Rogers that the Selective Process was a form of discrimination against Jews. (This occurred at the time that Arthur Brisbane was making a similar charge against Harvard.) In a March 1930 memorandum to Dean Bill, President Hopkins stated that he was not disposed to sidestep the question of the number of Jewish students being admitted to Dartmouth and that he was thinking of seeking a conference with a selected group of alumni to discuss it. "The only matter about which I should be concerned," he wrote, "would be that we should do this with a frankness and a fairness which our own self-respect could defend and that would not cause needless offense or injury to the sensibilities of a lot of our very loyal alumni."

Writing in February of 1934 to Bill Cunningham, who had recommended two Jewish applicants, he said, "We haven't any barriers against the admission of Jews, and as a matter of fact I should not like to see the time come when we were not including Jews in our undergraduate body in reasonable proportion. It is true, however, that in recent years the applications have increased so overwhelmingly from boys of Jewish blood that we acknowledgedly take a smaller proportion of the Jewish applicants than of the Gentiles. . . . It is a problem full of difficulties, as far as being certain of our fairness is concerned, but after all it would be quixotic to allow ourselves to be overrun racially as it would be unfair to have a definite exclusion. Compromises are never wholly satisfactory, but we are doing the best we can."

The news that President Hopkins was retiring was released by the trustees on August 29, 1945. That and the simultaneous announcement that his successor would be John Sloan Dickey of the Class of 1929, Director of the Office of Public Affairs in the U. S. Department of State, took the Dartmouth family completely by surprise. For more than a year the trustees had done their work without the slightest breach in the strict confidence with which Mr. Hopkins had asked them to treat his request to be relieved of his duties. The surprise was least appreciated by the Dartmouth faculty. One professor indignantly told Mr. Hopkins, "I want you to understand that every member of the faculty recognizes it as a slap in the face." The choice of a president should be primarily a faculty function, he contended, and the faculty had been ignored. That they had been ignored was true, Mr. Hopkins admitted. "But I still think that's the way to do it," he said. He was a tenacious believer in the authority vested in the trustees by the Dartmouth College charter, and no responsibility of the board was more clearly defined than the choosing of the president. Mr. Hopkins was never persuaded that the faculty was capable of matching the broad, institutional concern with which the trustees acted, but more than anything else, in this case, he was determined that there was not to be any repetition of the unpleasant divisiveness that marked the period just before his own election as president.

President Dickey was inducted as twelfth president of Dartmouth College on November 1, 1945. The installation was a simple one, held in the Faculty Room of Parkhurst Hall in the presence of the trustees, faculty, administrative officers, and a few guests. The half-hour ceremony was more a special meeting of the faculty than a formal inauguration, and only the academic robes worn by the principals were a concession to academic custom. The trustees at their meeting the night before had elected Mr. Hopkins president emeritus, and it was in that role that he presented the historic and symbolic Wentworth Bowl to President Dickey, after Trustee John R. McLane had entrusted the Dartmouth College charter to the College's new head.

President Dickey spoke briefly in acceptance of the symbols of office, and then in the moment of silence that followed the audience's loud applause, Dean Bill stepped forward and announced that he had the rare honor and privilege of presenting a candidate for Dartmouth's honorary Doctorate of Laws—Ernest Martin Hopkins. President Dickey's first official act was the conferring of that degree, with this citation:

ERNEST MARTIN HOPKINS: New Hampshireman by birth and choice; graduate of Dartmouth College, Class of 1901; disciple and collaborator of Tucker; eleventh President of the College in the Wheelock Succession. The measure of your devotion and of your doing, like that of other true north-country men, will never be weighed in any man's scales. Your services, both in counsel and in administration, have been often sought in the nation's public and private affairs. You, regardless of the prizes proffered— and some men know how great they were—chose, when choice was necessary, to serve this College. In this thirtieth year of your leadership the College you and Mrs. Hopkins so lovingly served and you in all respects so largely built stands ready to carry forward, in the fore, today's great tasks of the historic college. That, sir, is your work and your reward. On behalf of the men of Dartmouth, by virtue of the authority vested in me by the Trustees and in grateful and affectionate testimonial of your place in the Dartmouth family as the most beloved of the College's sons I hereby confer upon you the degree of Doctor of Laws.

It was an emotional experience for everyone present. The applause that went on and on was a way of expressing thanks and love to this unassuming man who, with wisdom and grace and courage, had given the best of himself to Dartmouth College as president for twenty-nine years. Mr. Hopkins' voice came close to breaking as he said that he was going to depart from precedent and respond to this surprise honor. His sense of humor came to the rescue and he had everyone laughing when he admitted, "In years past I have been avaricious for this degree and wondered whether I was ever going to get it or not." He went on, "I wanted to say this final word under any circumstance. I can imagine no greater happiness that can come to a man than to feel absolutely confident that the work in which he perhaps has had a part is to be carried on in hands fully competent. And I want to say here and now what I think most of you know, that there is no confidence lacking and there is every belief that the administration which is to follow will be one of the great and one of the distinctive administrations which Dartmouth has had. . . . And I want to say a word of appreciation for the confidence and support that you have given me. I have often been conscious of the words of Stevenson, in *The Lantern Bearers*, that 'they who miss the joy miss all.' . . . It has been a joyful period and I have had a happy time. I have known that I have dwelt among friends, I have known that support and confidence were available when they were needed, and gentlemen, there is no belief I have in life stronger than the belief that it can be said of Dartmouth today, as Mallet said of Oxford, that 'Through all the changes, greater than the traditions gathered round her, wiser than the prejudices she has outgrown, saved by the new blood ever flowing through her as strongly as the waters underneath her walls, still young in heart and ineffaceable in beauty, the College lives, sharing her treasures ungrudgingly with those who seek them, her spirit with those who understand.' It is in my deep conviction that in the new leadership of the College you have one who understands the treasures to be shared and, from my point of view even more important, understands the spirit, that I have the happiness in this occasion and in the anticipation of years to come."

"They who miss the joy miss all." It was a sentiment Mr. Hopkins had expressed in his first Dartmouth Night talk to the undergraduates in October 1916. And it was fitting that he should return to it in his final valedictory, for there were very few times during the twenty-nine years of his presidency when he was not happy in his job. "I don't know that I could have asked for any better life than I had," he told an interviewer some years after his retirement. "It's wonderful to be working in a cause where you have so many collaborators."

It was characteristic of Mr. Hopkins, as he reached the end of his long administration, to spread the credit and to express appreciation for the help of others. If he had "so many collaborators," it was because he attracted them and made them happy to have the privilege of working with him and for Dartmouth. It was not uncommon for his co-workers to remark that they felt their own lives elevated by the association with him. The Hopkins story, with all its institutional and personal achievements, is at heart the story of a remarkable human being, whose personal qualities shaped the goals he set for Dartmouth and made doubly effective his leadership in reaching them. The Dartmouth of today cannot be understood without some knowledge of those contributions, both material and spiritual, made first by William Jewett Tucker and then, in an even more extensive way, by Ernest Martin Hopkins.

Epilogue

FOR their retirement home President and Mrs. Hopkins bought the former Sydney Junkins house at 29 Rope Ferry Road in Hanover. It had been their intention to winterize their cottage at Manset, Maine, and to spend at least half of the year there, but a break in Mrs. Hopkins' health not long after her husband's retirement did not encourage the carrying out of this plan. Although in Hanover most of the year, Mr. Hopkins made a special point of remaining in the wings and of being an infrequent participant in the official life of the College. "It wasn't exactly an agreement," he explained, "but I established an understanding between John Dickey and myself even before he took office that I wasn't going to have a hand in things and I didn't want to be consulted. And John has respected it very completely." The leadership of the College and the limelight belonged to the new president, and Mr. Hopkins was determined that he was not going to be like the president-emeritus of a sister institution who made conspicuous appearances at college events and constantly threw the planned programs off balance.

Late in 1945, President-Emeritus Hopkins was named honorary chairman of the World Trade Foundation of America and was elected a director of the Rumford Press in Concord, New Hampshire. His principal interest during the year immediately after retirement was the Cardigan Mountain School for boys in nearby Canaan, New Hampshire. In association with a number of his Dartmouth friends, he took a leading part in its founding and was a member of the first corporation of the school, which opened in September of 1946. Today one of the school buildings is named for him. The Dartmouth trustees, in June 1946, officially approved the recommendation of the Alumni Council that the College's projected new auditorium-theater be named the Hopkins Center. Before construction began about a dozen years later, this project was completely restudied and transformed into the multi-purpose center for the arts. It was dedicated in November 1962, and Mr. Hopkins was present to acknowledge it as a splendid eighty-fifth birthday tribute.

In January of 1947, Secretary of the Navy James Forrestal named Mr. Hopkins to head a three-man civilian committee to make a study of the Navy's administration of Guam and American Samoa. The committee's report three months later recommended U. S. citizenship for the natives of the two island territories, and this later was voted by Congress. Also in January 1947, Mr. Hopkins was elected to the board of directors of the Brown Company of Berlin, New Hampshire, while continuing to serve as a member of the Voting Trust.

President-Emeritus Hopkins had since 1935 been a director of the National Life Insurance Company of Vermont. On January 28, 1948, as a way of resolving a stalemate over who should be the new head of the company, the board elected him president with the understanding that he would fill the job only until matters were settled and a new executive organization had been effected. His experience in industry and education, and his uncommon grasp of administration, made him ideally qualified to tackle the company's problem objectively. One thing that led him to accept this post, he remarked, was that he did not have to do any public speaking. The board of directors gave him a relatively free hand, and one of his first moves was to request the resignations of two directors in order to clear away the adamant partisanship on the two sides. Mr. Hopkins served as president for a little more than two years. During that time he restored harmony within the executive ranks and effected the agreement whereby Deane Davis, the company counsel, was chosen president.

When Mr. Davis, who was later to become Governor of Vermont, took over as the president of National Life, he wanted Mr. Hopkins' help and advice available to him. The new position of chairman of the board was therefore created by the company, and Mr. Hopkins was elected to it in April 1950. He held it for the next fourteen years, up to the time of his death. As chairman, Mr. Hopkins served also as head of the committee dealing with plans for constructing the company's new home-office building, which had been decided upon during the short period he had been president. At first he had been in favor of moving the headquarters from

Montpelier to South Burlington, but the final decision was to erect a new building in Montpelier, but away from the central business district. He saw this project through to completion. The new site was on a hill, and he recalled with amusement how he had impressed the uncertain engineers by proposing a seven percent grade as ideal for the roadway. He had learned this from Mr. Rockefeller when they had discussed, years before, the problem of building a road up Mt. Cadillac on Mt. Desert Island in Maine.

Mr. and Mrs. Hopkins maintained legal residence in Montpelier during the period of the National Life presidency. After he became chairman Mr. Hopkins commuted from Hanover to Montpelier twice a week for the first two years, thereafter once a week. During these first years of the National Life job Mrs. Hopkins' heart condition steadily worsened, and after a series of attacks she died in Hanover on May 18, 1950. Her death was a grievous loss to Dartmouth's president-emeritus. Celia Stone Hopkins had been at his side during the years of his early business career and the long years of his Dartmouth presidency, and he had shared everything with her and had counted on her support. Their homes in Hanover and Manset now became places of loneliness for him. Mrs. Hopkins' widowed sister, Grace Stone Tibbets, who had been an intimate of the family in Hanover for three decades, became someone on whom Mr. Hopkins relied for help and companionship. They were married December 14, 1951, in Darien, Connecticut, at the home of Mr. Hopkins' daughter Ann, then the wife of John Rust Potter, 1938. The second Mrs. Hopkins died three and a half years later, on June 10, 1954, of an acute coronary attack. For the remaining ten years of his life Mr. Hopkins cherished more and more the family ties with his daughter and his four grandchildren, Amy, Jessie, "Rusty," and "Hop" Potter, whose graduation from Dartmouth in 1964 was the last College event President-Emeritus Hopkins attended.

At Commencement in June 1953 Mr. Hopkins made one of his rare appearances in an academic procession, when he escorted President Dwight Eisenhower to receive a Dartmouth honorary degree. In that same year, Governor Hugh Gregg of New Hampshire offered him an interim appointment to the United States Senate, to fill out the term of Senator Charles W. Tobey, who had died in office. Mr. Hopkins declined the honor, as he did again, some years later, when Governor Wesley Powell offered a similar appointment when Senator Styles Bridges died.

Mr. Hopkins in retirement never knew any period of inactivity. He accepted the honorary chairmanship of the Jackson Laboratory Association of Mt. Desert Island, and in 1954 he was elected chairman of the corporation of Hanover's Mary Hitchcock Memorial Hospital. His correspondence continued to be heavy, and much of it was with his Dartmouth alumni friends. He and President Dickey kept in regular touch and enjoyed a close personal relationship, but it was only when his advice was specifically sought on some major policy decision, or when clarification of some past action was needed, that he allowed himself to be at all directly involved in College affairs. He was happy with the progress of the College under President Dickey, whom he deeply admired.

As he advanced in years, President-Emeritus Hopkins more and more became "Hoppy" to Dartmouth men and enlarged his hold on their affection and esteem. The alumni sought opportunities to honor him. When the Dartmouth Alumni Council inaugurated its Dartmouth Alumni Award in 1954, he was its very first recipient. When the classes that were in college under him returned to Hanover for reunions, many of the graduates called on him; and had he been willing, he would have had an endless string of engagements as guest of honor at their reunion dinners. On February 2, 1958, more than two thousand alumni and friends filled the Grand Ballroom of the Waldorf-Astoria Hotel in New York City to pay tribute to him on his eightieth birthday, although the party took place three months after his actual birthday. Nelson Rockefeller, 1930, served as chairman of the event and presented "Hoppy" with a full-sized replica of the silver Wentworth Bowl. It was the largest Dartmouth gathering ever held outside of Hanover. Mr. Hopkins was honored again at the fiftieth anniversary dinner of the Dartmouth Alumni Council, which he had founded in 1913; and in January 1964 he was the guest of honor at the one hundredth anniversary dinner of the Dartmouth Alumni Association of Boston.

Dartmouth's most tangible tribute to Ernest Martin Hopkins, one that goes on unabated today, was the naming of the Hopkins Center for him. It was fortunate that this building, so important to the contemporary College, could be brought into being during his lifetime. The trustees in January 1956 gave their approval to a new concept for the center and voted to go ahead with planning and building it. They also authorized a capital fund drive of $17-million which had the Hopkins Center as its major component.

John D. Rockefeller Jr. gave one million dollars toward the center as his personal tribute to Mr. Hopkins.

President-Emeritus Hopkins took part in the ground-clearing program on October 24, 1958, and construction began the following spring. He was the central figure when the building was formally dedicated on November 8, 1962, two days after his eighty-fifth birthday. He spoke informally and perhaps the family warmth of the occasion enabled him to do it without the strain he had feared and with all the graciousness and modesty that had endeared him to Dartmouth audiences for nearly fifty years. He began by telling how much of a liar he had turned out to be by bringing Warner Bentley to Dartmouth as director of drama with the promise of a new theater. But he exulted in his failure to carry out those early plans, he added, because without the vision and larger plans of President Dickey and others there would have been no center of such scope and attractiveness.

"I am happy to see Dartmouth a pioneer in a project of this sort," he said. "If one believes, as I do, that education is not education if it is simply an education of the specialist; if one believes, as I do, that something more is necessary than to become technically expert in the sciences; if one believes that beauty and art and all that microcosm that we call culture are as essential to man as anything else, then the significance of this occasion begins to be apparent. This is something more than the addition to the campus of a structure of dignity and grandeur. It is something more than a meeting place for undergraduates. It is something more than an exhibit of what a college plant can be made. It will in the course of events, I am certain, become the heart and soul of Dartmouth. Man is something more than a chemical compound enclosed in a skin, the mind is something more than a computer, and the soul of man—nobody knows what it is, but it exists. And this Center stands for all those things.

"I have been associated with Dartmouth for sixty-five years—sixty-five years ago I entered here. . . . It has been a delightful experience entirely beyond its educational advantage to be associated with the College. And perhaps this is the capstone of it all."

It was the capstone, not of President Hopkins' career, but of Dartmouth's prolonged effort to let him know what high value it placed upon his contributions to the College. Not many more occasions to show that affection and esteem were left. Mr. Hopkins' infirmity was becoming more pronounced and the fainting spells brought on by his heart condition were a growing concern to his family and friends. Wearing his favorite McGill cap and using a cane, he took part in the 1964 Commencement at which his grandson, Martin Hopkins Potter, received his degree. Soon after that he went to Manset, where many of his happiest days had been spent. There in the early morning hours of August 13, 1964, in his eighty-seventh year, he died peacefully in his sleep.

Index

303

Composed and printed at The Stinehour Press, Lunenburg, Vermont